Counterproductive W

M000222678

There has been a growing interest among scholars in the fields of organizational behavior and industrial psychology in what can be termed "the dark side of organizations." A main concept in this regard is both important and relevant *counterproductive work behaviors* (CWBs), which can be defined as deliberate actions that harm the organization or its members. These behaviors include a variety of acts that can be directed toward organizations (CWB-O) or toward other people (CWB-P). Whereas destroying organizational property, purposely doing work incorrectly, and taking unauthorized work breaks are examples of CWB-O, hitting a coworker, insulting others, and shouting at someone are forms of CWB-P.

Despite the growing interest in CWBs as a research issue, not enough is known about the determinants of CWBs. Recent literature suggests that malevolent personality, such as the dark triad traits (psychopathy, narcissism and Machiavellianism), is one of the main causes for CWBs.

The goal of *Counterproductive Work Behaviors* therefore is to cover this stimulating, important, and innovative issue of dark triad personalities in the workplace. The book deals with important aspects of this issue, such as the characteristics of dark triad personalities, how they operate and damage organizations, what organizations are more vulnerable to them, ways to diagnose and detect them, and ways to handle dark triad personalities and prevent them from harming organizations and employees.

There is no doubt that the issues covered by *Counterproductive Work Behaviors* will continue to attract academic attention; therefore, the book is essential reading for researchers, academics, and business professionals alike in the fields of organizational studies and Behavior, organizational psychology, strategy, human resource management, leadership, and related disciplines.

Professor Aaron Cohen is currently at the Division of Public Administration, School of Political Sciences, University of Haifa, Israel. He received his D.Sc. in management at the Technion–Israel Institute of Technology. His current research interests include commitment in the workplace, organizational citizenship behavior, organizational fairness, and misbehavior in organizations. His work has been published in the *Academy of Management Journal, Journal of Vocational Behavior, Journal of Management, Journal of Organizational Behavior, Human Relations, Cross-cultural Psychology,* and *Applied Psychology: An International Review, and Human Resource Management Review.* He has authored two books, *Multiple commitments in the workplace: An integrative approach* published by Lawrence Erlbaum Associates in 2003 and *Fairness in the workplace: A global perspective* published by Palgrave McMillan in 2015.

Routledge Studies in Management, Organizations and Society

This series presents innovative work grounded in new realities, addressing issues crucial to an understanding of the contemporary world. This is the world of organized societies, where boundaries between formal and informal, public and private, local and global organizations have been displaced or have vanished, along with other nineteenth century dichotomies and oppositions. Management, apart from becoming a specialized profession for a growing number of people, is an everyday activity for most members of modern societies.

Similarly, at the level of enquiry, culture and technology, and literature and economics can no longer be conceived as isolated intellectual fields; conventional canons and established mainstreams are contested. **Management, Organizations and Society** addresses these contemporary dynamics of transformation in a manner that transcends disciplinary boundaries, with books that will appeal to researchers, students, and practitioners alike.

Recent Titles in This Series Include

Counterproductive Work Behaviors

Understanding the Dark Side of Personalities in Organizational Life

Aaron Cohen

Routledge
Taylor & Francis Group

NEW YORK AND LONDON

First published 2018
by Routledge
605 Third Avenue, New York, NY 10017

and by Routledge
2 Park Square, Milton Park, Abingdon, Oxon OX14 4RN

First issued in paperback 2020

Routledge is an imprint of the Taylor & Francis Group, an informa business

Library of Congress Cataloging-in-Publication Data
A catalog record for this book has been requested

ISBN 13: 978-0-367-73530-2 (pbk)
ISBN 13: 978-1-138-21065-3 (hbk)

Typeset in Sabon
by Apex CoVantage, LLC

To Ruti Zohar, my spouse, for her endless support and encouragement and to Vana for just being there for me.

Contents

Figures

1 Introduction

The Dark Side of the Workplace

One of the more notable examples of a dark triad personality in the business world is that of Bernard Madoff, the ex-chairman of Nasdaq, a competitor in the New York Stock Exchange, who has been called a sociopath and a psychopath (Boddy, 2016). Commentators have reported that Madoff shared many of the traits of a psychopath and was a genial, charismatic, greedy manipulator who did not care whom he hurt in the process of becoming extremely wealthy. His psychopathic traits helped him to climb the corporate ladder and inevitably brought about his downfall (Quow, 2013). Described as a terrific salesman and as a leading celebrity in financial circles, it was reported that Madoff showed no remorse or regret when confronted with his crimes. Madoff ran the largest Ponzi scheme in history and fraudulently took more than $60 billion from his investors. Madoff's use of a Ponzi scheme illustrates his lack of fear of getting caught for his actions. His desire to accumulate wealth, dominate others, and prove his intelligence allowed him to dupe investors and regulators for years. He cheated his investors out of their life savings with promises of substantial financial returns from the stock market. His former employees described Bernard Madoff as a ruthless, detached individual who showed little remorse for robbing his innocent victims of their life savings (Quow, 2013). He left investors emotionally traumatized, financially impoverished, depressed, and sometimes suicidal in the wake of his fraudulent scheme (Boddy, 2016).

Madoff is only one example of a malevolent personality in the business world, definitely a notable one. There are destructive personalities in almost every organization in every occupation and in every country. Although it does not reflect real life, the focus of researchers in the scientific field of organizational behavior and management has been too much on positive behavioral aspects, overlooking the disastrous effects of negative behaviors in the business world and the workplace (Schyns, 2015). The reason behind this is probably that most theories of organizational behavior are based on the "human relations" approach, emphasizing positive theories on management and employees (O'Boyle, Forsyth, Banks, & McDaniel, 2012; Fineman, 2006; Vardi & Weitz, 2004). Derived by the exchange theory (Blau, 1967), the assumption behind the "human relations" approach is that individuals will strive to contribute to the welfare and success of the organization as long as their needs are met by the organization. The "human relations" approach further contended that all organizations and their managements need to do is to provide the employees with the appropriate conditions, remuneration, extrinsic and intrinsic needs, and an appropriate work setting. The employees will respond with higher levels of performance and job satisfaction. Employees' negative personality and behavior was a concept that was practically excluded from the "human relations" approach. The mainstream research in management and organizational behavior ignored wherever possible the likelihood of employees performing activities to harm the organization and their colleagues. As a result, models "fail to account for the negative aspects of work behavior...." and "offer only partial explanations for the wide range of organizational behaviors in the 'real world'" (Vardi & Weitz, 2004, p. XVI).

In the past two or three decades, significant change has occurred, and there is now a growing interest among scholars in the fields of management and organizational behavior in what can be termed "the dark side of organizations." In the wake of public scandals during this century, such as the Bernard Madoff scandal, an increasing amount of attention has been paid to the negative aspects of organizational life (Spain, Harms, & Lebreton, 2014). The recent ethically questionable events that have occurred in organizations, in politics, and in the economy, as well as in other settings have caused researchers and practitioners to ask how and why these events occurred (Wu & Lebreton, 2011). Workplace negativity has emerged as a focal topic in the management and organizational behavior literature (Schilpzand, De Pater, & Erez, 2016). Indeed, it seems that in the past few years, there has been a growing recognition that to understand organizations better, we must not ignore their dark sides, namely, counterproductive work behaviors (CWBs) (O'Boyle et al., 2012) and their causes. As a result, there is a greater acceptance of this issue.

CWBs are deliberate actions that harm the organization or its members, and they constitute one concept that has been developed to capture the activities that represent unethical behaviors (O'Boyle, Forsyth, & O'Boyle, 2011). According to Wu and Lebreton (2011), CWBs represent extra-role behaviors designed to harm a person or an organization that are different from core task behaviors and organizational citizenship behaviors. O'Boyle et al. (2011) presented a dichotomized categorization of CWBs, according to which one group of such behaviors includes a variety of acts targeting organizations (CWB-O) and the second is directed toward other people (CWB-I). Whereas destroying organizational property, purposely doing work incorrectly, and taking unauthorized work breaks are examples of CWB-O, hitting a coworker, insulting others, incivility, and shouting at someone are forms of CWB-I.

A similar conceptualization was advanced by Berry, Ones, and Sackett (2007), who argued that a common distinction is that between interpersonal deviance, which encompasses deviant behaviors that target individuals (e.g., violence, gossip, and theft from coworkers), and organizational deviance, which encompasses deviant behaviors that target the organization (e.g., intentionally working slowly, damaging company property, and sharing confidential company information). The authors suggested treating these two types as separate behavioral families. According to them, a perspective that differentiates between interpersonal deviance and organizational deviance creates behavioral families larger than each specific behavior but smaller than an overall deviance construct. If interpersonal deviance and organizational deviance are related differently to different behaviors in organizations, they lend a sharper focus and specificity to the study and prediction of such behaviors beyond the overall construct approach.

A concept similar to CWBs is "bad behaviors" (Griffin & Lopez, 2005). This term is used to refer to any form of intentional (as opposed to accidental) behavior that is potentially injurious to the organization and to individuals within the organization. Examples of such behaviors range from physical violence to sabotage and theft, verbal abuse, and counterproductive political activity. Griffin and Lopez mentioned four central forms of bad behavior in organizations: deviance, aggression, antisocial behavior, and violence. According to them, these four areas have received a preponderance of the attention of organizational scholars. These behaviors are also susceptible to theoretical and operational confusion and ambiguity. Other related concepts, such as incivility, workplace abuse, destructive work behavior, noncompliant behavior, organizational misbehavior, and bullying, are found in the literature, but a substantial body of work regarding any of them does not yet exist (Griffin & Lopez, 2005). Wu and Lebreton mentioned Robinson and Bennett's (1995) framework that also organizes the myriad of CWBs into four major categories, differing in terms of severity and the target of the behavior. According to this framework, "production deviance" refers to minor offenses directed at the organization, "property deviance" refers to serious offenses directed at the organization, "political deviance" refers to interpersonal but minor offenses, and "personal aggression" refers to serious interpersonal offenses.

As a result of the different conceptualizations of CWBs, different measures of this behavior have been developed, having in common the notion that they are deliberate actions aimed to harm the organization or its members (O'Boyle et al., 2011). This book applies a general and broader definition of CWBs, relying on the general conceptualization of Griffin and Lopez (2005). Following their conceptualization, CWB is defined in this book as any behavior that is potentially injurious to the organization and to individuals within the organization.

In addition to their theoretical conceptual importance, CWBs are considered some of the costliest behaviors in terms of damage incurred by organizations. According to Moore et al. (2012), the Association of Certified Fraud Examiners recently estimated that global businesses suffer annual losses of

U$2.9 trillion as a result of fraudulent activity. This is an enormous amount, indicating that unethical behavior is far more widespread than suggested by the few high-profile scandals on which the news has focused. Linton and Power (2013) cited Lutgen-Sandvik, Tracy, and Alberts' (2007) data that the prevalence rates of at least once weekly workplace bullying are 46.8%, 24.1%, and 15.8% in American, Finnish, and Danish studies, respectively. Moreover, studies estimated that CWBs not only cost organizations billions of dollars annually but also have negative consequences for employees. For instance, being the target of these broad CWBs can lead to an employee's decreased job satisfaction and increased stress and intentions to quit, among other things (Berry, Carpenter, & Barratt, 2012). Furthermore, bullied employees are at an increased risk of physical and psychological problems, including depression, psychosomatic symptoms, post-traumatic stress, and coronary heart disease (Linton & Power, 2013). Clearly, CWBs should be a major concern for organizations worldwide (Fine, Horowitz, Weigler, & Basis, 2010).

The growing interest in the subject has led to a growing amount of studies on the causes of CWBs (Schilpzand et al., 2016). This is evidenced by several meta-analyses that quantitatively summarized research findings (Berry et al., 2012; Berry, Sackett, & Tobares, 2010; Salgado, 2002). However, despite the growing interest in CWBs as a research issue and the growing amount of research findings regarding this construct, not enough is known about the determinants of CWBs (Cohen, 2016). The meta-analyses conducted on the relationship between CWBs and possible correlates exemplify this contention. Salgado (2002) found a weak to moderate relationship between CWBs and the Five-Factor Model (FFM) personality dimensions. More specifically, Berry et al. (2007) and Berry et al. (2012) found that CWBs are related (negatively) to agreeableness, conscientiousness, and emotional stability. Weak to moderate relationships were found between CWBs and organizational justice, while the relationships between demographic variables and CWBs were negligible.

Hershcovis et al. (2007) found that of the personal variables, gender (male) and the trait of anger were moderately related to workplace aggression. Other researchers also found a strong effect of gender (male) (Baughman, Dearing, Giammarco, & Vernon, 2012; Bowling & Burns, 2015). The dimensions of organizational justice and poor leadership were also moderately related to workplace aggression (Hershcovis et al., 2007). Tests of integrity were found to be moderately related to CWBs in another in-depth meta-analysis (Van Iddekinge, Roth, Raymark, & Odle-Dusseau, 2012), as were aggression (Berry et al., 2010) and workplace harassment (Bowling & Beehr, 2006). Finally, Schyns and Schilling (2013), in their meta-analysis, found quite a strong relationship between CWBs and destructive leadership.

The modest relationships found in these studies imply that other explanations and directions must be sought to understand the causes of CWBs. It seems therefore that there is a strong need for expansive theory-building work that addresses the various antecedents of CWBs more comprehensively. This work will require a variety of perspectives, given that the antecedents involve micro-and macro-level elements. To the extent that personality disorders and pathological factors are seen as potential predictors, different kinds of expertise may also be needed to better understand CWBs (Griffin & Lopez, 2005). Indeed, one of the stimulating explanations of CWBs suggested in the recent literature, based on a clinical approach (MacLane & Walmsley, 2010), is that the dark triad personalities are a possible and important determinant of CWBs (Cohen, 2016; Michel & Bowling, 2013; Smith & Lilienfeld, 2013). The dark personality is often defined as a subclinical level of the personality characteristics of the dark triad: narcissism, Machiavellianism, and psychopathy (Paulhus & Williams, 2002). Not surprisingly, these traits have repeatedly been seen as part of the dark side of human nature (Jonason, Webster, Schmitt, Li, & Crysel, 2012a; Jonason, Slomski, & Partyka, 2012b).

The dark triad has only recently been studied in the literature on management, organizational behavior, and industrial psychology. In fact, it has been even less adequately researched than CWBs. As mentioned by Harms and Spain (2015), the study of the dark personality and its impact in the workplace is only now entering the mainstream of organizational research. Smith and Lilienfeld (2013) noted that compared with the high coverage of the concept by the media, only a few scholarly articles on the issue exist, citing fewer than 50 papers published from 1990 to October 2012. The divergence between popular coverage and scientific research on business psychopathy is both substantial and troubling. Thus, although the problems posed by psychopathy in the workplace have been discussed widely in popular publications, this theoretically and pragmatically important issue has been the subject of relatively little systematic research (Smith & Lilienfeld, 2013; Furtner, Maran, & Rauthmann, 2017). The outcome is that too little is known about the possible effect of personality disorders on CWBs.

The importance of the dark triad in reaching a better understanding of CWBs is highlighted by the distinction between the bright side and the dark side of personality (Smith, Hill, Wallace, Recendes, & Judge, 2017). Distinguishing between the bright side and the dark side is a recent advance in applying personality to organizational behavior (Kaiser, Lebreton, & Hogan, 2015). The bright side refers to people's behavior when they are on guard and engaged in self-monitoring. It is concerned with the dispositional qualities observed during social interaction when people are doing their best to get along and get ahead, such as in a job interview (Hogan & Fico, 2011). The FFM is a taxonomy of bright-side characteristics and reflects the themes observers use to describe others, especially in the early stages of a relationship: outgoing and assertive (extraversion), congenial and cooperative (agreeableness), reliable and rule abiding (conscientiousness), calm and steady (emotional stability), curious and worldly (openness). Over the past several decades, the overwhelming majority of applied personality research has been based on the FFM and therefore concerns the bright side only (Kaiser et al., 2015).

On the other hand, "the dark side" refers to the impression people make when they are "just being themselves"; when they let down their guard; when they stop self-monitoring; or when they are stressed, tired, or otherwise less vigilant about how they are being perceived (Kaiser et al., 2015). It often takes repeated exposures to these people for observers to recognize these dispositions. Dark-side tendencies originate in efforts to get along and get ahead but rest on unsound assumptions about how one expects to be treated or how best one can serve one's personal interests. These strategies neglect the needs of other people and lead to self-defeating behaviors that may secure minor short-term benefits but at the expense of significant long-term costs. For example, talking up one's achievements may impress others at the moment but over time may lead to a reputation of boastfulness and excessive self-promotion. Good social skills can compensate for dark-side tendencies, but if they manifest themselves repeatedly, they may disrupt relationships and corrupt judgment (Kaiser et al., 2015). The dark side comes from an interest in derailing the management. They are viewed as extensions of the bright-side dimensions past the point where the behavior is fully adaptable. There are positive and negative behaviors associated with high and low scores on all the dimensions of both the bright and dark side (Hogan & Fico, 2011; Smith et al., 2017).

As mentioned before, the bright side of personality, represented in many studies by the FFM, has been the dominant approach in research that examined the relationship between personality and work attitudes and behaviors. However, the study of the dark personality and its impact on the workplace have gained increasing attention in the past few years (Nübold et al., 2017). One of the ongoing issues in the study of the dark personality is what makes its characteristics different from other personality characteristics (Harms & Spain, 2015). There is a consensus that dark traits are those that lead individuals to derail in their daily lives (both personal and work) and that they are likely to emerge under periods of stress, when individuals lack the cognitive resources to inhibit their impulses and motives in order to adhere to social norms and expectations. In particular, characteristics that reflect a motivation to elevate the self and harm others are considered particularly dark. Jonason et al. (2012a) stated in this context that "Toxic employees, as embodied by the dark triad traits, present problems for any company, supervisor, and fellow employee. Learning how those high on the Dark Triad traits behave at work may permit preventive measures to be taken or, at least, what to expect from them" (p. 452).

An important and challenging issue is drawing the line between a "normal" and "abnormal" personality (Furnham, Richards, & Paulhus, 2013) because in the personality disorder literature, the terms "clinical" and "subclinical" are often contrasted. One way to apply the terminology is to define clinical samples as those composed of individuals who are currently under clinical or forensic supervision, while subclinical samples refer to continuous distributions in broader community samples (Furnham et al., 2013). Harms and Spain (2015) mentioned Hogan and Hogan's (2001) paper, according to which dark traits are distinguished from clinical pathologies that are not reflected in an inability to function in everyday life. In fact, it is believed that such characteristics may reflect specific evolutionary strategies and that dark personality characteristics may be functional at specific levels or in particular situations. It should also be restated that dark personality characteristics are not simply extreme variants of normal personality traits. Subclinical traits represent a middle ground between "normal" personality traits such as the FFM and "clinical" traits used to diagnose psychological pathologies. One might consider them personality quirks that do not greatly inhibit day-to-day functioning but may cause severe negative outcomes in particular circumstances, such as in leadership situations and social interactions (Gudmundsson & Southey, 2011; Harms, Spain, & Hannah, 2011). Individuals who score high on dark triad traits are socially malevolent with tendencies toward callousness, aggression, and manipulation (Furnham et al., 2013).

Scholars have suggested that in the constellation of the dark-side personality traits, psychopathy in particular, have played a significant role in the recent spate of widespread financial disasters, corporate and political corruption, and callous and unbridled greed (Griffin & Lopez, 2005; Mathieu, Neumann, Babiak, & Hare, 2015). When large corporations are destroyed by the actions of such personalities, employees lose their jobs and sometimes their livelihoods, shareholders lose their investments and sometimes their life savings, and societies lose key parts of their economic infrastructure. Capitalism also loses some of its credibility. Psychopaths in organizations present themselves as glibly unbothered by the chaos around them, unconcerned about those who have lost their jobs, savings, and investments, and lacking any regrets about what they have done. They cheerfully lie about their involvement in events, are very persuasive in blaming others for what has happened, and have no doubts about their continued worth and value. They are happy to walk away from the economic disaster that they have managed to bring about with huge payoffs and with new roles, advising governments how to prevent such economic disasters (Boddy, 2011).

Therefore, there is a strong need for more systematic scientific study of the dark triad traits in the workplace. An important reason for that is that such personalities exist in great numbers in the workplace, and ignoring them may limit our understanding of employees and managers' behaviors. Solas (2015) mentioned Babiak, Neumann, and Hare (2010), who found in one comprehensive study of corporate psychopathy based on seven companies, three US-based and four global companies with US subsidiaries, ranging in size from 150 to more than 40,000 employees worldwide, that 9 of the 203 managers and executives who took part were undoubtedly psychopaths (Hare, 1991). Moreover, the study showed that there were no significant differences in the general nature and structure of psychopathy in the corporate sample in comparison with that found in samples from the offender, psychiatric, and community populations.

Also, in recent years, there has been a generational rise in self-esteem and narcissism. This means that, in the future, narcissism in the workplace will become a more common phenomenon (Twenge & Campbell, 2008). While the rise in narcissism may appear to be a good thing, Twenge and Campbell (2008) mentioned several downsides to this rise. First, narcissists have great difficulty getting along with others: they lack empathy and cannot take someone else's perspective. Narcissists take more risks, experience more ups and downs in performance, and react more defensively to criticism. The narcissist's inflated self-concept can be damaging to organizations, especially in jobs requiring accurate self-assessment. Moreover, throughout the years, an increasing number of organizations have developed a "narcissistic culture" that often promotes a "win at all costs" mentality, which can end in immoral scandals, such as those that have occurred in some of the world's largest companies. The "narcissistic culture" of some of these companies is often mentioned as a key factor leading to the company's (or CEO's) unethical behavior and downfall (Twenge & Campbell, 2008). As a result, the interest in promoting ethical leadership in organizations has been steadily growing among organizations and researchers. Research on the topic can clarify the role of narcissists in today's organizations.

Another problematic personality in organizations is the "corporate psychopath." Boddy (2011) described these individuals as giving the impression that they are smooth, charming, sophisticated, and successful. However, they are destructive to the organizations for which they work. They destroy the morale and the emotional well-being of their fellow employees. They do this by humiliating them, lying about them, abusing them, using organizational rules to control them, not giving them adequate training, blaming them for mistakes made by themselves, and coercing them into unwanted sexual activities. Corporate psychopaths were found to be key contributors to conflict and bullying (Baughman et al., 2012) and further to high CWBs (Boddy, 2014). All of these increase the levels of employees' withdrawal from organizations, as employees seek to minimize their exposure to such unpalatable and stressful behaviors. Having good employees leave because of the nasty behavior of other employees should logically be detrimental to organizational success and contribute to organizational destruction, as the human resource is gradually undermined, depleted, and weakened (Boddy, 2011). There is definitely a need for more scientific research on the role of corporate psychopaths in work organizations.

This book covers each of the dark triad personalities and their implications for the workplace. The notion of studying a set of three traits attributed to people who are insensitive, malevolent, and pursue egoistic aims at the expense of their colleagues has been adopted universally (Bańka & Orłowski, 2012). While the three components of the dark triad share much in common, the main differences between them are that for narcissists, the focus of their activities is on themselves, the focus of Machiavellians in their activities is on political manipulations, and psychopaths focus their activities on hurting other individuals in their environment. It should be noted that in many instances, the term "psychopathy" in the workplace is used as a synonym for the dark triad personality because some researchers have assumed that the three dark personalities overlap (Paulhus & Williams, 2002). Thus, "psychopathy" can be used as an umbrella term to cover the dark triad. Therefore, in some of the following chapters, "psychopathy" is used as such an umbrella term, particularly when citing studies that applied this approach. This is especially true for the terms "corporate psychopathy" and "successful psychopathy," which in fact refer to the dark triad but have become established terms in themselves.

There are several shortcomings in the knowledge accumulated so far on the dark triad traits. The vast majority of the current research on the dark triad traits utilizes either student (for the study of narcissism and Machiavellianism) or incarcerated populations (for the study of psychopathy). Consequently, although a great deal is known about the nature of these traits, very little of this knowledge has crossed over into workplace research (Spain et al., 2014). Thus, it is crucial for organizational leaders and societal well-being that professionals understand the effects of the dark triad personalities in the workplace. This book attempts to elaborate on this issue and to provoke more studies on it.

Another important reason for studying the dark triad traits in the workplace is related to employee selection. A number of scholars have examined the ability of personality tests to predict individuals' decisions to engage in CWBs. Much of the existing literature is focused on using traditional personality traits, such as traits that make up the FFM, to predict CWBs (Wu & Lebreton, 2011). However, the FFM is not the only approach toward personality description. The clinical and psychopathological field has noted maladaptive individual differences as extreme variants of adaptive traits. The growing evidence for a spectrum model operationalization of personality should direct the attention of industrial psychologists to both adaptive and maladaptive forms of personality functioning (Rolland & De Fruyt, 2003). Recent studies have raised the possibility that it may be predicted that the perpetration of CWBs by individuals with aberrant personality traits such as the dark triad will vary (Wu & Lebreton, 2011). Thus, the study of the "dark side" of personality has an important role in helping organizations identify those with the potential for "derailment," deviant behaviors, and poor work performance (Khoo & Burch, 2008).

The goal of this book is to further unfold this stimulating, important, and innovative issue of the dark triad personalities in the workplace. The book argues that most of the explanations offered to CWBs are related to work situation and are based on the exchange theory approach. However, a basic argument in this book is that current theories do not satisfactorily explain the reasons behind negative behaviors in the workplace. Therefore, more attention should be paid to possible explanations related to personality. One of these explanations is the focus of this book. According to these explanations, bad personalities in the workplace, particularly in managerial positions, can be the cause of a significant amount of negative behaviors in the organization. The dark triad personalities are the core of this book.

For this purpose, the book reviews the following issues: What are the main characteristics of dark triad personalities? What are their main characteristics in general and in work settings (Chapter 2)? What are the main theories pertaining to dark triad personalities (Chapter 3)? Who are the corporate or successful psychopaths? What makes them successful (Chapter 4)? The book also covers the main negative behaviors of the dark triad personalities that evoked the interest in this issue, such as CWBs, unethical behavior, bullying, fraud, and more (Chapter 5). Other issues that are covered by the book are situational and organizational factors that create an environment that is friendlier for dark triad personalities' operations (Chapter 6). The main argument here is that while the work situation in itself cannot adequately explain negative behaviors in the workplace, it nonetheless operates toward creating a friendlier or more hostile environment for bad personalities.

Another important issue covered by the book is that of possible selection tools that can detect dark triad personalities (Chapter 7). The effect of dark triad leaders on the organization and its members is another issue that will be examined here (Chapter 8). A separate chapter is dedicated to characterizing those who seem more vulnerable to dark triad supervisors and coworkers (Chapter 9). The cultural aspects and differences among dark triad personalities in the workplace are also covered in this book (Chapter 10). The final chapter deals mainly with suggestions and directions for future research and proposes theories and explanations for these directions. Some practical perspectives regarding dark triad personalities in the workplace are also covered in this chapter (Chapter 11).

In contrast to the few books on this issue, most of which seem to be timely and important but are more practitioner oriented, the current book is more science and research oriented. The issue of dark triad personalities in the workplace is covered based on existing research on the topic and provides an updated contribution to this quite overlooked but provocative issue. Two final comments regarding the book should be mentioned. First, despite the growing attention on dark triad personalities in the workplace, not enough studies have been performed on this issue. The book is based on the leading exiting studies on the topic. Second, this book does not take a clinical approach to the issue or even a psychological one. The book looks at this phenomenon from a managerial and organizational perspective, following the dominant view of this book that dark triad personalities affect the managerial functioning of the organization. Therefore, the book is targeted toward academics and practitioners in management and organizational behavior and is not psychologically or clinically oriented.

References

Babiak, P., Neumann, C. S., & Hare, R. D. (2010). Corporate psychopathy: Talking the walk. *Behavioral Sciences & the Law*, 28(2), 174–193.

Bańka, A., & Orłowski, K. (2012). The structure of the teacher Machiavellianism model in social interactions in a school environment. *Polish Psychological Bulletin*, 43(4), 215–222.

Baughman, H. M., Dearing, S., Giammarco, E., & Vernon, P. A. (2012). Relationships between bullying behaviors and the dark triad: A study with adults. *Personality and Individual Differences*, 52(5), 571–575.

Berry, C. M., Carpenter, N. C., & Barratt, C. L. (2012). Do other-reports of counterproductive work behavior provide an incremental contribution over self-reports? A meta-analytic comparison. *Journal of Applied Psychology*, 97(3), 613–636.

Berry, C. M., Ones, D. S., & Sackett, P. R. (2007). Interpersonal deviance, organizational deviance, and their common correlates: A review and meta-analysis. *Journal of Applied Psychology*, 92(2), 409–423.

Berry, C. M., Sackett, P. R., & Tobares, V. (2010). A meta-analysis of conditional reasoning of aggression. *Personnel Psychology*, 63(2), 361–384.

Blau, P. M. (1967). *Exchange and Power in Social Life*. New York: Wiley.

Boddy, C. R. (2011). *Corporate Psychopaths: Organizational Destroyers*. London: Palgrave MacMillan.

Boddy, C. R. (2014). Corporate psychopaths, conflict, employee affective well-being and counterproductive work behavior. *Journal of Business Ethics*, 121(1), 107–121.

Boddy, C. R. (2016). Unethical 20th century business leaders: Were some of them corporate psychopaths? The case of Robert Maxwell. *International Journal of Public Leadership*, 12(2), 76–93.

Bowling, N. A., & Beehr, T. A. (2006). Workplace harassment from the victim's perspective: A theoretical model and meta-analysis. *Journal of Applied Psychology*, 91(5), 998–1012.

Bowling, N. A., & Burns, G. N. (2015). Sex as a moderator of the relationships between predictor variables and counterproductive work behavior. *Journal of Business and Psychology*, 30(1), 193–205.

Cohen, A. (2016). Are they among us? A conceptual framework of the relationship between the dark triad personality and counterproductive work behaviors (CWBs). *Human Resource Management Review*, 26(1), 69–85.

Fine, S., Horowitz, I., Weigler, H., & Basis, L. (2010). Is good character good enough? The effects of situational variables on the relationship between integrity and counterproductive work behaviors. *Human Resource Management Review*, 20(1), 73–84.

Fineman, S. (2006). On being positive: Concerns and counterpoints. *Academy of Management Review*, 31(2), 270–291.

Furnham, A., Richards, S. C., & Paulhus, D. L. (2013). The dark triad of personality: A 10-year review. *Social and Personality Psychology Compass*, 7(3), 199–216.

Furtner, M. R., Maran, T., & Rauthmann, J. F. (2017). Dark leadership: The role of leaders' dark triad personality traits. In *Leader Development Deconstructed* (pp. 75–99). New York: Springer, Cham.

Griffin, R. W., & Lopez, Y. P. (2005). "Bad behavior" in organizations: A review and typology for future research. *Journal of Management*, 31(6), 988–1005.

Gudmundsson, A., & Southey, G. (2011). Leadership and the rise of the corporate psychopath: What can business schools do about the "snakes inside"? *E-Journal of Social & Behavioral Research in Business*, 2(2), 18–27.

Hare, R. (1991). *The Hare Psychopathy Checklist Revised*. New York, NY: Multi-Health Systems Inc.

Harms, P. D., & Spain, M. S. (2015). Beyond the bright side: Dark personality at work. *Applied Psychology: An International Review, 64*(1), 15–24.

Harms, P. D., Spain, S. M., & Hannah, S. T. (2011). Leader development and the dark side of personality. *The Leadership Quarterly, 22*(3), 495–509.

Hershcovis, M. S., Turner, N., Barling, J., Arnold, K. A., Dupré, K. E., Inness, M., LeBlanc, M. M., & Sivanathan, N. (2007). Predicting workplace aggression: A meta-analysis. *Journal of Applied Psychology, 92*(1), 228–238.

Hogan, R., & Fico, J. M. (2011). Leadership. In W. K. Campbell & J. D. Miller (Eds.), *The Handbook of Narcissism and Narcissistic Personality Disorder: Theoretical Approaches, Empirical Findings, and Treatments* (pp. 393–402). New York: Wiley.

Hogan, R., & Hogan, J. (2001). Assessing leadership: A view from the dark side. *International Journal of Selection and Assessment, 9*(1–2), 40–51.

Jonason, P. K., Webster, G. D., Schmitt, D. P., Li, N. P., & Crysel, L. (2012a). The antihero in popular culture: Life history theory and the dark triad personality traits. *Review of General Psychology, 16*(2), 192–199.

Jonason, P. K., Slomski, S., & Partyka, J. (2012b). The dark triad at work: How toxic employees get their way. *Personality and Individual Differences, 52*(3), 449–453.

Kaiser, R. B., LeBreton, J. M., & Hogan, J. (2015). The dark side of personality and extreme leader behavior. *Applied Psychology: An International Review, 64*(1), 55–92.

Khoo, H. S., & Burch, G. S. J. (2008). The 'dark side'of leadership personality and transformational leadership: An exploratory study. *Personality and Individual Differences, 44*(1), 86–97.

Linton, D. K., & Power, J. L. (2013). The personality traits of workplace bullies are often shared by their victims: Is there a dark side to victims? *Personality and Individual Differences, 54*(6), 738–743.

Lutgen-Sandvik, P., Tracy, S. J., & Alberts, J. K. (2007). Burned by bullying in the American workplace: Prevalence, perception, degree and impact. *Journal of Management Studies, 44*(6), 837–862.

MacLane, C. N., & Walmsley, P. T. (2010). Reducing counterproductive work behavior through employee selection. *Human Resource Management Review, 20*(1), 62–72.

Mathieu, C., Neumann, C., Babiak, P., & Hare, R. D. (2015). Corporate psychopathy and the full-range leadership model. *Assessment, 22*(3), 267–278.

Michel, J. S., & Bowling, N. A. (2013). Does dispositional aggression feed the narcissistic response? The role of narcissism and aggression in the prediction of job attitudes and counterproductive work behaviors. *Journal of Business and Psychology, 28*(1), 93–105.

Moore, C., Detert, J. R., Klebe Treviño, L., Baker, V. L., & Mayer, D. M. (2012). Why employees do bad things: Moral disengagement and unethical organizational behavior. *Personnel Psychology, 65*(1), 1–48.

Nübold, A., Bader, J., Bozin, N., Depala, R., Eidast, H., Johannessen, E. A., & Prinz, G. (2017). Developing a taxonomy of dark triad triggers at work: A grounded theory study protocol. *Frontiers in Psychology, 8*, 1–10.

O'Boyle Jr., E. H., Forsyth, D. R., Banks, G. C., & McDaniel, M. A. (2012). A meta-analysis of the dark triad and work behavior: A social exchange perspective. *Journal of Applied Psychology, 97*(3), 557–579.

O'Boyle, E. H., Forsyth, D. R., & O'Boyle, A. S. (2011). Bad apples or bad barrels: An examination of group-and organizational-level effects in the study of counterproductive work behavior. *Group & Organization Management, 36*(1), 39–69.

Paulhus, D. L., & Williams, K. M. (2002). The dark triad of personality: Narcissism, Machiavellianism, and psychopathy. *Journal of Research in Personality, 36*(6), 556–563.

Quow, K. L. (2013). An introspective analysis of the etiological relationships of psychopathy in serial killers and successful business men. *Modern Psychological Studies*, 19(1), 67–81.

Robinson, S. L., & Bennett, R. J. (1995). A typology of deviant workplace behaviors: A multidimensional scaling study. *Academy of Management Journal*, 38(2), 555–572.

Rolland, J. P., & De Fruyt, F. (2003). The validity of FFM personality dimensions and maladaptive traits to predict negative affects at work: A six-month prospective study in a military sample. *European Journal of Personality*, 17(Supplement 1), S101–S121.

Salgado, J. F. (2002). The Big Five personality dimensions and counterproductive behaviors. *International Journal of Selection and Assessment*, 10, 117–125.

Schilpzand, P., De Pater, I. E., & Erez, A. (2016). Workplace incivility: A review of the literature and agenda for future research. *Journal of Organizational Behavior*, 37(1), S57–S88.

Schyns, B. (2015). Dark personality in the workplace: Introduction to the special issue. *Applied Psychology: An International Review*, 64(1), 1–14.

Schyns, B., & Schilling, J. (2013). How bad are the effects of bad leaders? A meta-analysis of destructive leadership and its outcomes. *The Leadership Quarterly*, 24(1), 138–158.

Smith, M. B., Hill, A. D., Wallace, J. C., Recendes, T., & Judge, T. A. (2017). Upsides to dark and downsides to bright personality: A multidomain review and future research agenda. *Journal of Management*, 0149206317733511.

Smith, S. F., & Lilienfeld, S. O. (2013). Psychopathy in the workplace: The knowns and unknowns. *Aggression and Violent Behavior*, 18, 204–218.

Solas, J. (2015). Pathological work victimization in public sector organizations. *Public Organization Review*, 15(2), 255–265.

Spain, S. M., Harms, P., & LeBreton, J. M. (2014). The dark side of personality at work. *Journal of Organizational Behavior*, 35(Supplement 1), S41–S60.

Twenge, J. M., & Campbell, S. M. (2008). Generational differences in psychological traits and their impact on the workplace. *Journal of Managerial Psychology*, 23(8), 862–877.

Van Iddekinge, C. H., Roth, P. L., Raymark, P. H., & Odle-Dusseau, H. N. (2012). The criterion-related validity of integrity tests: An updated meta-analysis. *Journal of Applied Psychology*, 97(3), 499–530.

Vardi, Y., & Weitz, E. (2004). Misbehavior in organizations: Theory. In *Research, and Management*. Mahwah, NJ & London: Lawrence Erlbaum Associates.

Wu, J., & Lebreton, J. M. (2011). Reconsidering the dispositional basis of counterproductive work behavior: The role of aberrant personality. *Personnel Psychology*, 64(3), 593–626.

2   The Dark Triad Personalities
Main Characteristics

As mentioned in the introduction, the dark triad is a constellation of three theoretically separable, albeit conceptually and empirically overlapping, personality constructs that are typically construed as interpersonally maladaptive: psychopathy, narcissism, and Machiavellianism (Smith & Lilienfeld, 2013). The narcissistic personality is marked by grandiosity, a sense of entitlement, and lack of empathy (Smith & Lilienfeld, 2013). Extreme self-aggrandizement is the hallmark of narcissism, which includes an inflated view of self; fantasies of control, success, and admiration; and a desire to have this self-love reinforced by others (O'Boyle, Forsyth, Banks, & McDaniel, 2012). Machiavellianism, another constituent of the dark triad, is associated with disregard for the importance of morality and the use of craft and dishonesty to pursue and maintain power (Smith & Lilienfeld, 2013). The Machiavellian personality is defined by three sets of interrelated beliefs: an avowed conviction in the effectiveness of manipulative tactics in dealing with other people, a cynical view of human nature, and a moral outlook that puts expediency above principle (O'Boyle et al., 2012). Psychopathy, the third element, has been described as impulsivity and thrill seeking combined with low empathy and anxiety (Spain, Harms, & LeBreton, 2014). Psychopathy is marked by a person's lack of concern for both other people and social regulatory mechanisms, impulsivity, and a lack of guilt or remorse when his or her actions harm others (O'Boyle et al., 2012).

According to many researchers, psychopathy includes two factors. The first is called primary or instrumental psychopathy (Lykken, 1995). This factor contains facets of psychopathy such as shallow affect, low empathy, and interpersonal coldness, and individuals with profound levels of these traits are sometimes referred to as "emotionally stable" psychopaths. Broadly corresponding to primary psychopathy are interpersonal and affective domains. Interpersonally, individuals are superficial, grandiose, and deceitful. Affectively, they lack remorse or empathy and do not accept responsibility. Hanson and Baker (2017) mentioned Babiak and Hare (2006), who call attention to "a predatory stare and empty eyes" in psychopaths that can unsettle observers, "suggestive of a primitive, autonomic, and fearful response to a predator."

The second factor is secondary or hostile or reactive psychopathy. It is composed of the socially manipulative and deviant facets of psychopathy and has been variously referred to as aggressive, impulsive, and neurotic psychopathy (Lykken, 1995; Jonason, Slomski, & Partyka, 2012a; Blickle & Schütte, 2017). Individuals with high levels of this factor tend to "act impulsively, "without thinking," without giving themselves time to assess the situation, to appreciate the dangers, to foresee the consequences, or even to anticipate how they will feel about their own actions when they have time to consider them (Lykken, 1995). This self-centered impulsivity factor indicates that such individuals seek thrills, lack diligence, and are unconcerned with deadlines or responsibilities. Others have applied a Four-Factor Model of psychopathy, consisting of interpersonal, affective, lifestyle, and antisocial factors (Williams, Paulhus, & Hare, 2007).

The frequently used approach, which is applied here, too, is to conceptualize the dark triad as being multidimensional, that is, composed of multiple traits (Wu & Lebreton, 2011). Indeed, most research on the dark triad personality in the workplace was based on the multidimensional model (Schyns, 2015; Furtner, Maran, & Rauthmann, 2017). The characteristics that are common to the three dark triad constructs are highly salient: they all include the tendency to deceive, manipulate, and exploit others for the pursuit of selfish gains. However, as mentioned earlier, each of these three constructs has unique characteristics (Lee et al., 2013; Wu & Lebreton, 2011). In fact, the somewhat modest correlations among measures of the dark triad (e.g., ranging from 0.25 to 0.50 in Paulhus and Williams, 2002) suggest that each contains a substantial amount of specific variance (Lee et al., 2013). This does not say that there is still a going on debate whether to treat the dark triad traits as unidimensional versus multidimensional. Some of this debate is presented in the following section. This book continues with the approach that each dimension should be treated separately despite the similarities among them. For this purpose, the following sections review in depth the main characteristics of each of the constituents of the dark triad.

Narcissism

The term "narcissism," originally developed by Freud (1914/1991), was derived from the story of Narcissus, who, according to mythology, fell in love with his own image in a reflecting pool. So moved was Narcissus by his own reflection that he did not eat, drink, or sleep, resulting in his demise. Freud incorporated this term into his psychoanalytic theory to identify individuals who exhibit excessive self-admiration because of an unhealthy relationship between their ego and libido (Freud, 1914/1991). Since Freud coined the term, narcissists have been regarded as people who love themselves too much for their own good (Boddy, 2011). Today, the term "narcissism" often refers to a psychological personality disorder in the *Diagnostic and Statistical Manual of Mental Disorders,* fourth edition (*DSM-IV*), or a subclinical version of the trait, which is often studied by personality and social psychologists (Jonason et al., 2012a).

Narcissism is a personality characteristic used to describe individuals ranging from those who can function normally in society to those who are clinically impaired by their grandiose perception of themselves and their willingness to exploit others (Wu & Lebreton, 2011). Central to the clinical description of pathological narcissism is a core dysfunction related to managing intense needs for validation and admiration. When individuals fail or struggle to effectively manage these needs because of either extreme or rigid behavior or impaired regulatory capacities, the frequent result is a number of negative psychological consequences that may be characteristically grandiose or vulnerable in nature (Wright et al., 2013).

The psychoanalytic tradition regards narcissism as a defense against feelings of insecurity, inadequacy, or other psychic wounds. While Hogan and Fico (2011) found this view excessively speculative, they contended that the dark-side tendencies originate in childhood. They framed the origins of these tendencies in terms of something resembling attachment theory. Hogan and Fico (2011) cited Millon and Grossman (2005), who noted that the narcissistic personality reflects the attainment of a self-image of superior worth, learned largely in response to admiring and devoted parents. Destructive narcissism is a reaction to prolonged abuse and trauma in early childhood or early adolescence. Narcissism is a defense mechanism, the role of which is to deflect hurt and trauma from the victim's "true self" into a "false self" that is omnipotent, invulnerable, and omniscient. This "false self" concept refers to individuals who present a self-concept that is not who they really are but rather a facade of who they believe society thinks they should be. The false self is used to obtain any form of attention, either positive or negative, to satisfy the narcissist's labile sense of self-worth. The false self is a "fabricated personality" that serves as a defense mechanism to avoid conflict or rejection (Herbst, 2014).

Thus, narcissists possess feelings of dominance, entitlement, and exploitation, as well as displaying exhibitionism. As such, narcissism has been associated with self-enhancement, which involves convincing oneself, as well as others, that one is worthwhile, attractive, competent, and lovable (Wu & Lebreton, 2011). Schyns (2015) cited Babiak and Hare (2006), who put it simply but clearly: "Narcissists think that everything that happens around them, in fact, everything that others say and do, is or should be about them" (p. 40). Narcissism is not necessarily pathological but has an independent developmental sequence that stretches from infancy to adulthood. In its healthy form, mature narcissism produces behaviors such as humor and creativity. However, pathological narcissism occurs when one is unable to integrate the idealized beliefs one has about oneself with the realities of one's inadequacies. Pathological narcissists spend the balance of their lives seeking recognition from idealized parental substitutes as an emotional salve for their own shortcomings (Rosenthal & Pittinsky, 2006).

It is useful to think of narcissism as having three components: the self, interpersonal relationships, and self-regulatory strategies (Brunell et al., 2008). As for the self, the narcissist self is characterized by positive "specialness" and uniqueness, vanity, a sense of entitlement, and a desire for power and esteem. In terms of personal relationships, narcissistic relationships contain low levels of empathy and emotional intimacy. In their place, there are many shallow relationships than can range from exciting and engaging to manipulative and exploitative. Narcissists have several additional interpersonal strategies for maintaining self-esteem that go beyond simply controlling others or taking credit from them. For example, narcissists seek the admiration of others. They also strive to associate with high-status individuals from whom they can gain status by association. They will brag, show off, and otherwise draw attention to themselves, or act colorfully to gain notoriety. When there is an opportunity for glory, narcissists will shine, but they will underperform when the opportunity for glory is not available. As for self-regulatory strategies, these are strategies for maintaining inflated self-views. For example, narcissists seek out opportunities for attention and admiration, brag, steal credit from others, and play games in relationships. When narcissists are good at this, they feel good; they report high self-esteem and positive life satisfaction. When they are unsuccessful, however, they evidence aggression and sometimes anxiety and depression (Brunell et al., 2008; Campbell, Hoffman, Campbell, & Marchisio, 2011).

As a scientific construct, narcissism appears widely in the social-personality, clinical psychology, and psychiatric literature. The social-personality literature conceptualizes narcissism as a normally distributed trait in the population, for which there is no qualitative cut-off (taxon) for elevated narcissism. As mentioned by Grijalva and Harms (2014), the *DSM* describes narcissism as a grandiose preoccupation with one's own self-importance, that is, the belief that one is special and more important than others. Additional diagnostic criteria for a narcissistic personality disorder (NPD) include "fantasies of unlimited success," "hypersensitivity to criticism," "entitlement," "exploitativeness," and "a lack of empathy." Narcissism, similar to other personality traits, exists along a continuum from high to low levels (Grijalva & Harms, 2014). Narcissism is related to other "normal" variables, such as Machiavellianism and psychopathy.

According to Campbell et al. (2011), the clinical and psychiatric literature conceptualizes narcissism as a NPD, which refers to a continuing and flexible character structure associated with grandiosity, lack of empathy, and a desire for admiration. According to the *DSM* advanced by the American Psychiatric Association and the *DSM-IV* version of it, there are nine specific symptoms of narcissism (e.g., "Shows arrogant, haughty behaviors or attitudes"; "Believes that he or she is 'special' and unique and can only be understood by, or should associate with, other special or high-status people [or institutions]" (American Psychiatric Association, 2000). To be diagnosed as having an NPD, an individual must have five of the nine traits. Moreover, narcissism must also cause distress or damage. If an individual feels good about him- or herself, has reasonable relationships, and is performing at work reasonably well, he or she would not be considered to have an NPD. These criteria result in a relatively low point of prevalence for NPD, while the prevalence of those with narcissistic symptoms (but without causing sufficient distress to cross the line into the clinical disorder) is much larger. This pattern of characteristics is sometimes known as subclinical narcissism (Campbell et al., 2011).

The core aspects of trait narcissism are similar to those of pathological narcissism: egotism; low concern for others; and dominant, aggressive, or manipulative behavior. However, trait narcissism is characterized by fewer neurotic and great self-enhancing tendencies than pathological narcissism (Treadway, Yang, Bentley, Williams, & Reeves, 2017). Derived from the presence of an over-idealized and grandiose self-concept, narcissists experience high, yet unstable, self-esteem, which drives their self-enhancing and narcissistic tendencies; these tendencies, however, may be maladaptive in the long term. While high self-esteem is often theorized and measured as stable, narcissism is a variant of unstable self-esteem, the general category of which is believed to explain many of the maladaptive reactions exhibited by individuals with high self-esteem (Treadway et al., 2017).

Barry and Kauten (2014) found in a sample of at-risk adolescents that pathological narcissism was associated with both reactive and proactive aggression, low self-esteem, anxiety, depression, social stress, and high contingent self-worth, even when controlling for nonpathological narcissism and exploitativeness. Pathological narcissism was also associated with negative perceptions regarding the quality of one's interpersonal relationships. Their findings showed that pathological and nonpathological factors were associated in opposite directions with self-esteem, anxiety, social stress, and perceived quality of interpersonal relationships. Nonpathological narcissism was also associated with perceived positive relationships, a sense of self-reliance, and low social stress. They concluded that neither of the two forms of narcissism stood out as clearly adaptive or advantageous, although nonpathological narcissism was suggestive of fewer emotional difficulties. Barry and Kauten (2014) suggested that perhaps the two forms capture different underlying characteristics that influence a more personally insecure form of narcissism versus a more outwardly boastful and exploitative form of narcissism, which would be consistent with emerging research on adults.

Narcissism in the Workplace

As already mentioned, narcissism generally takes the form of a grandiose sense of self-importance; a preoccupation with fantasies of unlimited success, power, or love; and an exhibitionist orientation. Narcissist individuals act as if they are entitled to receive the service of others and tend toward exploitive and manipulative behavior (Sankowsky, 1995). Campbell et al. (2011) discussed the confusion in research and practice concerning narcissism, which stems from the existence of multiple "flavors" or forms of narcissism. Based on the literature, they distinguished between *grandiose narcissism* (a.k.a. grandiose-agentic, phallic, etc. narcissism) and *vulnerable narcissism* (a.k.a. grandiose-vulnerable, hypersensitive, etc. narcissism). According to them, when one brings to mind the classic narcissist in the workplace, especially at the CEO level, one is likely to be thinking about a grandiose narcissist, someone who is (over)confident, extraverted, high in self-esteem, dominant, attention seeking, interpersonally skilled, and charming but also unwilling to take criticism, aggressive, high in psychological entitlement, lacking in true empathy, interpersonally exploitative and grandiose, or even haughty. In contrast, when one thinks of a narcissist who might intentionally seek psychotherapy, one is likely to think of a vulnerable narcissist: someone who is hostile thinks the world is unfairly stacked against him or her and is high in psychological entitlement but also has low self-esteem and is depressed and anxious.

Both of these forms of narcissism have different reported etiologies. Whereas the grandiose form seems to emerge in part from parental overvaluation, the vulnerable form seems to emerge from parental coldness. Both also have different nomological networks. Grandiose narcissism is linked to antisocial personality and psychopathy, while vulnerable narcissism is linked to borderline personality disorder. In the realm of impulsivity, whereas grandiose narcissism is linked primarily to sensation seeking and approach orientation, vulnerable narcissism is linked to a broad spectrum of impulse control problems. The more relevant form of narcissism in the workplace setting is that of grandiose narcissism, especially in terms of leadership and decision making (Campbell et al., 2011). The importance of narcissism to organizational research stems from the current socio-historical context, where a financial crisis is spurred in part by selfish or unethical business decisions, highlighting the importance of personality traits such as narcissism, which are associated with unethical and selfish behavior (Grijalva & Harms, 2014; Michel & Bowling, 2013).

The social skills of narcissists are strongly relevant to the workplace. Narcissists, although not generally interested in emotional closeness and intimacy, are typically very socially skilled. Their social relationships often serve the function of self-enhancement rather than of developing intimacy. In other words, narcissists need others to maintain their inflated self-views and have, therefore, developed skills at initiating relationships. For example, narcissists are energetic, socially extraverted, socially confident, and entertaining. During initial encounters, they are liked by others, but this initial liking dissipates over the course of time, resulting in a pattern in which narcissists have more frequent relationships but of shorter duration and with less emotional intimacy. In short, narcissism from the narcissists' perspective is about acquiring and maintaining self-esteem, power, and status with little concern for the well-being of others; this is often accomplished through the effective use of social relationships. Viewed by others, however, narcissists (at least in the short term) often appear sociable, self-assured, likable, and charming (Brunell et al., 2008).

Narcissists are independent and not easily impressed. They are the innovators, driven in business to gain power and glory. Productive narcissists are experts in their industries, but they go beyond it. They also pose critical questions. They want to learn everything about anything that affects the company and its products. They want to be admired, not loved, and are not troubled by a punishing superego, so they can be very aggressive in pursuit of their goals. Of all the personality types, narcissists run the greatest risk of isolating themselves at the moment of success. Moreover, because of their independence and aggressiveness, they are constantly looking out for enemies, sometimes degenerating into paranoia when they are under extreme stress (Maccoby, 2000). Although it clearly shares some overlap with both Machiavellianism and psychopathy, narcissism's unique contribution to the dark triad may lie in narcissists' sense of entitlement or superiority to others. They do not just feel good about themselves—they feel that they are inherently better and more deserving of the respect and admiration of those around them (Jonason et al., 2012a). Studies found that narcissists tend not to take advice and are biased toward their own judgment. They also assess others' advice as useless and inaccurate (Kausel, Culbertson, Leiva, Slaughter, & Jackson, 2015).

Psychopathy

In common usage, a psychopath is a person with a personality disorder characterized by extreme callousness who is liable to behave antisocially or violently to get his or her own way (Davidson, Higgleton, Sargeant, & Seaton, 1994). Psychologists define psychopathy as a particular constellation of antisocial behaviors and emotions, including shallow affect, low remorse, low fear, low empathy, egocentrism, exploitativeness, manipulativeness, impulsivity, aggression, and criminality (Jonason et al., 2012a; Wu & Lebreton, 2011; Lee et al., 2013). Board and Fritzon (2005) contended that psychopathy, as initially described by Cleckley (1941), is a form of personality disorder. Psychopathic personality disorder comprises two components, "emotional detachment," which includes traits such as superficial charm, egocentricity, and remorseless use of others, and "antisocial behavior," which includes socially deviant behaviors and weak behavior controls. Similar to the psychological construct of narcissism, that of psychopathy has been extensively studied by both clinical and personality psychologists.

Researchers argue that the construct of the psychopathic personality should not be contaminated with the factors of criminality and socially deviant behavior because these elements are correlates of psychopathy rather than its core characteristics (Boddy, 2011). This fits with the view of psychopathy held by leading researchers in the field, such as Hare (1999), who have stressed that there are psychopaths who do not engage in criminal behavior and can function well in society. Other researchers distinguish between unsuccessful psychopaths, those who have criminal convictions, and successful psychopaths, those who have no criminal convictions or engage in no illegal antisocial behavior. There is some empirical support for this viewpoint, especially from recent investigations of the concept of "successful" psychopaths (Board & Fritzon, 2005). "Successful" or "corporate" psychopaths are said to be people with psychopathic personality disorder patterns but without the characteristic history of arrest and incarceration. Corporate psychopaths are thus opportunistic corporate careerists who lack any concern for the consequences of their actions and are totally ruthless in their pursuit of their own aims and ambition (Board & Fritzon, 2005; Boddy, 2011; Fennimore & Sementelli, 2016; Cleckley (1941, 1988). The "successful" or "corporate" psychopaths as well as other aspects of psychopathy in the workplace are reviewed in length in Chapter 4.

Wu and Lebreton (2011) cited Cooke and Michie (2001), who presented a three-factor model, conceptualizing the multidimensionality of psychopathy. The latter authors argued that psychopathy consists of (1) an arrogant and deceitful interpersonal style, (2) a deficient affective experience, and (3) an impulsive and irresponsible behavioral style. In accordance with the first factor, highly psychopathic individuals believe they are superior to others and constantly engage in self-promoting behaviors. In addition, they are egocentric and put their own interests before those of others. Such people believe that rules do not apply to them and that they are deserving of special treatment, and they are often critical of those they believe pose a potential threat to them. The second characteristic is the psychopath's unique experience of affect. According to Wu and Lebreton (2011), researchers have suggested that a lack of guilt and the absence of a conscience are the telltale signs of a psychopath. In addition, psychopaths do not experience anxiety or fear to the same extent as others, tend to be malicious toward others, are unlikely to experience embarrassment, and tend to reside at the extreme end of the dishonesty and manipulativeness spectrum. The final factor highlights that psychopaths are impulsive and irresponsible. As such, they are described as thrill seekers, who often struggle to maintain long-term romantic, platonic, and work-related relationships. In particular, these individuals are ego driven and seek immediate gratification of their needs.

Psychopathy in the Workplace

Darwinian processes of natural and social selection combine to make the corporate psychopath a well-equipped predator in general (Solas, 2015) and in the workplace in particular. According to Boddy (2011), Hare (1991) is the leader of psychopathy research. Solas (2015) cited Hare (1999), who stated that "psychopaths are social predators who charm, manipulate and ruthlessly plow their way through life. Completely lacking in conscience and feeling for others, they selfishly take what they want and do as they please, violating social norms and expectations without the slightest sense of guilt or regret" (p. xi). Hare (1994, 1999) added that psychopaths themselves see no problem with their lack of conscience, empathy, or remorse and do not think that they need to change their behavior to fit in with the societal norms in which they do not believe. Non-criminal psychopaths, such as organizational psychopaths, can be referred to as being successful in as much as they have deployed their skills of lying, manipulation, and deception well enough to avoid detection. They can avoid the displays of antisocial personality that would get them into trouble with the law and can have successful careers (in terms of getting jobs and promotions in those jobs) (in Boddy, 2011).

Solas (2015) cited two studies that provided an important description of psychopaths in the workplace. First, a study by Board and Fritzon (2005) compared a sample of senior business managers and chief executives from leading companies (*n* = 39) with psychiatric inmates from Broadmoor Special Hospital (*n* = 1,085) in the UK. Clinically distinct signs of psychopathy showed that several psychopathic attributes are more prevalent among business leaders. The latter tended to demonstrate more superficial charm, insincerity, egocentricity, manipulativeness, grandiosity, lack of empathy, exploitativeness, independence, perfectionism, excessive devotion to work, rigidity, stubbornness, and dictatorial tendencies. However, the groups differed in the more antisocial aspects of the syndrome. Members of the business elite group were less likely to demonstrate physical aggression, consistent irresponsibility with work and finances, lack of remorse, impulsivity, suicidal gestures, affective instability, mistrust, and passive-aggressive behavior.

The second study, conducted by Babiak (2000), was a two-year longitudinal study of six organizations, which detected a common pattern of behavior or "career phases" (p. 289) among employees who surpassed the threshold for psychopathy on the Psychopathy Checklist—revised (PCL-R). This study found that in the first phase, psychopaths charm their way into the firm using a false, though eminently convincing, facade. Upon entry, they then quickly set about assessing the potential utility of each employee and establish a network of pawns and patrons. The third phase involves manipulating communication channels in order to bring them credit and perceived influence. Phase four entails victimizing former supporters who sought to expose their exploitative behavior. Those who reached the final phase had managed to realize their primary ambition of ascending to the top of the organization. Babiak's (2000) research also showed that although they possessed the same personality traits as other psychopaths, those found in the corporate sample did not exhibit antisocial acts or a lifestyle typically found in forensic samples.

Machiavellianism

The third component of the dark triad is Machiavellianism. Although somewhat related to narcissism and psychopathy, Machiavellianism is a trait in its own right (Jonason et al., 2012a). Its name was inspired by the writings of Niccolo Machiavelli, a 16th-century Italian political theorist who outlined the strategies that a new prince could use to establish and maintain political power (Lee et al., 2013). Jones and Paulhus (2009, 2014) drew attention to a neglected predecessor, namely, the 1st-century military strategist Sun Tzu. To themes that resemble Machiavelli's, Sun Tzu added planning, coalition formation, and reputation building. The strategies, highly pragmatic and devoid of traditional social virtues, eventually became associated with an opportunistic and deceptive "Machiavellian" personality (Jonason et al., 2012a). Wu and Lebreton (2011) cited in their review Wilson, Near, and Miller's (1996) definition of Machiavellianism: "A strategy of social conduct that involves manipulating others for personal gain, often against others' self-interest (p. 285)."

Thus, the term "Machiavellianism" describes a personality construct characterized by a cynical view of human nature and a deceitful and calculated interpersonal style (Christie & Geis, 1970). A person who is not concerned with conventional morality has no interpersonal affect and gross psychopathology, who has a low ideological commitment, and who is willing and able to manipulate others by any means, including the use of deceit, is called Machiavellian. Machiavellianism has also been described as a strategy of socially manipulating other people for personal gain (Boddy, 2011). The main characteristics of the Machiavellian personality are also demonstrated in the Mach-IV scale, developed by Christie and Geis (1970), which has been widely used to assess this construct. The Mach-IV scale is composed of 20 items that are phrased as recommendations, quasi-facts, or statements (e.g., "Anyone who completely trusts anyone is asking for trouble"). People who endorse such items have been found to (1) think in a cold, strategic, and pragmatic way; (2) have cynical, misanthropic, and negativistic views; (3) be emotionally detached and callous; (4) be agentically (e.g., for money, power, status) rather than communally (e.g., for love, family, harmony) motivated; and (5) use duplicity, exploitation, and manipulation tactics to push through their self-beneficial goals (Rauthmann, 2013) (a more thorough discussion of this scale is presented in Chapter 7).

Machiavellians were characterized as people who, in general, negatively perceive others as weak and untrustworthy, while their pragmatic morality enables them to follow the rule that "the aim justifies the means." The dominant symptom is coldness, implying emotional detachment, lack of empathy, and disregard of the needs and aims of a partner. Research showed that Machiavellians not only have a common perception system but also eagerly try to manipulate their partners and use lies, deception, and cheating in situations when it is profitable for them to do so and when it increases the chances of reaching their goals. It could be said that the Machiavellian is capable of acting unethically whenever it will pay off (Bańka & Orłowski, 2012).

Wu and Lebreton cited Christie and Geis (1970), who argued that individuals high in Machiavellianism can be identified using four key characteristics. First, these individuals lack empathy for others and are instead suspicious of them. This tendency toward suspiciousness may make these individuals less likely to be swayed by social influence because they anticipate exploitation and selfishness during interpersonal interactions. Furthermore, high Machiavellians perceive others as less cooperative and generous than do those low in Machiavellianism. Second, high Machiavellians have lower levels of affect when interacting with others. They not only experience difficulties in identifying their own emotions but also lack basic interpersonal skills. High Machiavellians tend to approach others with a sense of detachment and lack of emotional involvement. Thus, these individuals can approach problems logically without the interference of affective states. Because they are prone to emotional detachment, it has been suggested that high Machiavellians are less cooperative and compliant than low Machiavellians. Third, high Machiavellians possess an aberrant view of morality and are willing to engage in immoral and unethical acts that go against convention, including manipulating, deceiving, and exploiting others. Research has suggested that high Machiavellians are less likely to help others in emergency situations. Finally, high Machiavellians focus on their own agendas with no regard for others. Machiavellians are willing to do whatever is necessary to achieve their own goals and are goal rather than people oriented. These individuals are not motivated by concern for others but by their own goals; as such, they are willing to manipulate others for personal gain. High Machiavellians are also more ambitious, adept at lying, seek to dominate others, and are more likely to assume control over situations than low Machiavellians (Wu & Lebreton, 2011).

The Machiavellians in the Workplace

For Machiavellians, the ends justify the means. They show some behavioral patterns that are similar to those of psychopaths because both engage in manipulation and superficial charm combined with an emotionally detached affective style that allows them to avoid negative feelings about their own unethical actions (Belschak, Den Hartog, & Kalshoven, 2015). A defining characteristic of Machiavellians is their cynical worldview. They expect the worst from others, assume that others are cheating and lying and thus distrust others and their motives. This negative worldview and the resulting lack of trust in others around them may explain Machiavellians' increased level of negative feelings (stress, dissatisfaction) and their manipulative and amoral behavior (e.g., "strike before the other does"). Machiavellian employees are more likely not to trust others, including their leaders, and research has shown that lack of trust between leader and follower has a negative impact on the follower's attitudes and behaviors (Belschak, Muhammad, & Den Hartog, 2016).

Machiavellianism has been described as a strategy involving social manipulation of other people for personal gain (Boddy, 2011). They were found to demonstrate higher levels of political skill when they perceived themselves to have been socially undermined by their coworkers (Smith & Webster, 2017). Findings also showed that Mach leaders are adept at forming political alliances and collaborate with others to promote their own interests (Belschak et al., 2015). Machiavellians are seen as manipulators and cheaters who decrease the social capital of a group or an organization. For example, Machiavellianism is positively related to salespersons' willingness to lie. Obviously, manipulating, cheating, and lying do not come to mind as ethical behaviors for leaders. Non-Mach leaders hold that coercion and manipulation are not ethical sources of influence, and leaders who use these tactics are unlikely to be seen as attractive ethical models by their followers (Den Hartog & Belschak, 2012).

However, stating that a Machiavellian personality shows no concern for conventional morality and lacks interpersonal affect and gross psychopathology, has low ideological commitment, and is willing and able to manipulate others through any means, including lying and deceit, does not imply a lack of conscience as displayed by psychopaths, although it broadly resembles many definitions of psychopathy. Machiavellians reportedly pursue strategies that promote their self-interest, using deception, flattery, and emotional detachment to manipulate and exploit social and interpersonal relationships to their own ends (Den Hartog & Belschak, 2012). Mach leaders are skilled at creating a desirable image, and Machiavellianism was found to be positively related to charismatic leadership. Thus, Machs do not always engage in counterproductive behavior, deception, and manipulation. Rather, they are adaptable persons who may also invest in prosocial and pro-organizational acts if this benefits them. Machs will show pro-organizational behavior if they are encouraged by their leaders to do so and perceive that showing such behavior is instrumental to achieve their own ends (Belschak et al., 2015).

Similarities and Differences Among the Dark Triad Traits

One of the issues that evoked researchers' interest is the similarities and differences among the three traits. This issue has given rise to many debates as to whether the three traits should be treated as multidimensional because of the differences among them or merged into one construct because of the similarity among them. According to the prevailing approach, the dark triad consists of three overlapping but distinct personality variables: narcissism, Machiavellianism, and psychopathy (Boddy, 2011; Furtner et al., 2017).

Psychopaths differ from people classified as having a narcissist personality in that narcissists do have emotions and feelings, and thus a conscience, and are therefore troubled by their own behavior. Psychopaths, on the other hand, with their lack of emotions or conscience, are not. Machiavellianism, similar to corporate psychopathy, has no regard for moral standards and promotes the idea that the end justifies the means. It also advocates a cynical, political approach to management, including the use of a fraudulent persona when necessary and the use of force, if necessary, as a means to achieve desired ends. Corporate psychopaths have the ruthlessness, charm, and cunning to get to the top of any organization in which they are situated. Therefore, it is the corporate psychopaths who may be the successful ones in the organizational setting (Boddy, 2011).

Machiavellians may also achieve success, but they may not quite make it because they lack the total ruthlessness of corporate psychopaths. A Machiavellian personality does not imply that the individual has the lack of conscience displayed by psychopaths, but it has broad similarities to many definitions of a psychopathic personality (Boddy, 2011). While narcissism involves excessive self-aggrandizement and psychopathy involves an antisocial nature lacking in empathic concern, Machiavellianism is characterized by a manipulative, self-serving social strategy composed of three main components: cynicism, manipulation, and the view that the ends justify the means (Jonason et al., 2012a). Robertson et al. (2016) also discussed the similarities and differences among the three traits. According to them, all three dark triad traits share a lack of honesty and humility (e.g., sincerity and fairness), but each trait adds additional components. Machiavellian individuals are adept at skillful manipulation and are cynical about other people. The narcissism component of the dark triad emerged from the clinical research studies of individuals who lack empathy and display inflated self-worth and need for admiration. Individuals with high levels of psychopathy exhibit both high impulsivity and low anxiety about the consequences of their behavior.

According to Jones and Paulhus (2014), whereas psychopaths act impulsively, abandon friends and family and pay little attention to their reputation, Machiavellians plan ahead, build alliances, and do their best to maintain a positive reputation. The element of impulsivity is crucial in distinguishing psychopathy from Machiavellianism. When overlap was controlled in research studies, these assertions were supported: Machiavellians are strategic rather than impulsive, and they avoid manipulating family members (Barber, 1998) and any other behavioral tactics that might harm their reputation, such as feigning weakness. The key elements of Machiavellianism appear to be (1) manipulation, (2) callous affect, and (3) a strategic-calculating orientation. Narcissists may always be too obviously egotistical in their efforts to get promoted unopposed. Narcissistic behavior is marked by manipulation and callousness, very much like Machiavellianism and psychopathy (Jones & Paulhus, 2014).

Research that have specifically discussed and examined whether the three traits should be treated as unidimensional or multidimensional is not entirely conclusive, and this should be taken into account by scholars who study the dark triad. Jones and Figueredo (2013) concluded from the results of their two studies that both manipulation and callousness appear to be necessary and sufficient components of a malevolent personality. This assertion is supported by the fact that it was found that the latter two traits (i.e., the traits called the "dark core") accounted for all the non-within-scale inter-relationships in the dark triad. This malevolent core seems to be a common element in all antagonistic variables. Jones and Figueredo contended that while all malevolent traits have a dark core of covariance, it is their behavioral, attitudinal, and belief-related components that make them unique. For example, Machiavellians have a dark personality with a cold, calculating, long-term, and strategic style. Psychopathy is a dark personality with an impulsive and antisocial style, while narcissism is a dark personality with an egotistical style.

Rauthmann and Kolar (2012) examined the perceived "darkness" of the dark triad traits narcissism, Machiavellianism, and psychopathy. Their findings showed that narcissism was perceived more favorably than Machiavellianism and psychopathy. Their explanation to the finding was that some narcissistic attributes may alter people's perceptions such as narcissists' (1) charmingness, (2) physical attractiveness, and (3) relatively higher conscientiousness and achievement motivation. This could help explain narcissism's perceived desirability. Moreover, themes such as seeking attention, admiration, and status may be inherently more desirable than Machiavellian and psychopathic themes of exploitation and callousness. Their findings also showed that people's judgments of what pertains to others versus themselves differed. While all three traits were less desirable for the self than for others, this was interestingly reversed for consequences for others: people tended to judge the consequences of their own behavior as less detrimental to others than when others in general enacted the same behavior.

McHoskey, Worzel, and Szyarto (1998) found that Machiavellianism is associated with psychopathy in general and specifically with both primary and secondary psychopathy. They concluded that Machiavellianism is a global measure of psychopathy that assesses but confounds both the unique and common sources of variance associated with primary and secondary psychopathy. According to them, this finding provides a framework for understanding seemingly inconsistent findings in the literature on Machiavellianism that have precluded its integration with psychopathy. For example, the consistent positive association between Machiavellianism and anxiety has precluded its smooth integration with psychopathy because anxiety is an antithetical characteristic to psychopathy. However, recognizing the implications of the distinction between primary and secondary psychopathy in relation to anxiety and the nature of Machiavellianism relative to the distinction between primary and secondary psychopathy erode the mystery surrounding this association (McHoskey et al., 1998).

Wisse, Barelds, and Rietzschel (2015) found based on data collected from 306 pairs of Dutch employees and their direct supervisors (most worked in commercially oriented [service] organizations, e.g., shops, financial institutions, health care organizations) a positive relationship between employee narcissism and supervisor ratings of (all subscales of) employee innovative behavior. They also found that employee Machiavellianism was negatively related, and employee psychopathy was not related to supervisor ratings of employee innovative behavior. They contended that this testify to the importance of differentiating between the dark triad personality traits. One factor that may explain these differential findings is that Machiavellians and psychopaths, more strongly than narcissists, lack communal tendencies and interpersonal orientations and generate more negative perceptions in others. An interesting study conducted by Jonason (2014) on a sample of American employees found that narcissism and psychopathy were linked to political conservatism. Machiavellianism was associated with low rates of political liberalism, not political conservatism exactly. Jonason concluded that political conservatism is informed by traits, such as those of the dark triad, that predispose individuals to desire social dominance.

While these findings support some discriminant validity among the three traits, it should be noted that there is evidence to suggest otherwise. In their study, Bertl, Pietschnig, Tran, Stieger, and Voracek (2017) tested the factorial structure of the dark triad in a large community-based sample ($n = 2,463$). Structural equation modeling indicated that a better fit for a single latent dark core is obtained than when assuming that the dark triad traits are independent constructs. The researchers concluded that the assumption that the three traits represent conceptually distinct, but overlapping, constructs appears to be questionable. If indeed these traits could be best characterized as being distinct, yet overlapping, then modeling the dark triad as a three-trait hierarchical factor structure should show the best fit. However, their results indicate that this is not the case.

In addition, meta-analysis findings (Muris, Merckelbach, Otgaar, & Meijer, 2017) did not yield a compelling reason to include all three traits when studying their role in transgressive human behavior. The findings of Muris et al. showed that correlations among the dark triad constituents were quite substantial, suggesting conceptual redundancy. Therefore, while the dominant approach is to treat the dark triad as multidimensional, there is evidence that in some cases and samples, one dimension represents the concept better than three. This means that before researchers analyze their data, they would be best advised to examine the dimensionality of the concept in their specific data to decide whether they should treat the concept as multi- or unidimensional.

The Dark Triad and the Five-Factor Model

The relationship between the dark triad model and the Five-Factor Model (FFM) is important because each covers a different perspective of personality. As mentioned earlier, the FFM represents the bright side of personality, while the dark triad model represents the dark side (Hogan & Fico, 2011). Studies examining this relationship are important because they can lend empirical support for this contention. In addition, such studies can provide further information about the dimensionality of the dark triad. That is, if dimensions of the dark triad model are strongly related or overlap with specific dimensions of the FFM, this might support the redundancy of a given dark personality. A similarity in the relationship between dark triad traits and the dimensions of the FFM might indicate whether some of the dark triad traits are not independent constructs and should not be treated as such.

A meta-analysis study (O'Boyle, Forsyth, Banks, Story, & White, 2015) showed that the global traits of the FFM were consistently and meaningfully associated with the dark triad traits. The FFM explained between 30% and 63% of the variance in dark triad traits, and every global trait of the FFM showed at least one correlation greater than 0.20 with a dark triad trait. Agreeableness, in particular, proved to be a key predictor of dark triad qualities, with the greatest overlap with psychopathy and Machiavellianism; the second greatest overlap was found to be with narcissism. Global neuroticism, on the other hand, was relatively unrelated to the dark triad, particularly in the relative importance analyses. The study also found that the FFM profiles of Machiavellianism and psychopathy were remarkably similar. Based on this, the authors raised concerns about whether these constructs are merely two sides of the same coin. O'Boyle et al. contended that Machiavellianism is more likely to be subsumed under psychopathy than vice versa. According to them, many of the proposed factor structures for psychopathy possess clear components of Machiavellianism (e.g., callous affect, egocentricity, interpersonal manipulation), but other facets of psychopathy, such as carefree nonplanfullness and immunity to stress, are unlikely to be tapped by the current measures of Machiavellianism.

Douglas, Bore, and Munro (2012) found a negative relationship between the dark triad and the FFM domains of agreeableness and conscientiousness. This supports, of course, the notion that the two constructs represent the bright and the dark side of human personality. In addition, secondary psychopathy was positively correlated with neuroticism and negatively with extraversion, as they predicted. Contrary to the expectations of Douglas et al. (2012), no relationship was found between neuroticism and narcissism. Their findings also showed that agreeableness was a significant predictor of the dark triad. An important finding of their study was that a considerable overlap exists between the dark triad constructs. Primary psychopathy loaded onto the antisociality component and psychopathy loaded onto the emotionality component. These results indicate two distinct constructs of psychopathy. Narcissism loaded onto emotionality, extraverted risk taking, and antisociality. In contrast, Machiavellianism loaded onto emotionality and antisociality. They concluded that Machiavellianism could be an undifferentiated measure of psychopathy and that the notion that Machiavellianism is a member of the dark triad is redundant.

DeShong et al. (2017) found some overlapping relationships among the dark triad and FFM domain facet level correlations. Machiavellianism was consistently related to low agreeableness, low conscientiousness, and high neuroticism. At the facet level, Machiavellianism was negatively correlated with three facets of agreeableness (trust, straightforwardness, and altruism) and one facet of conscientiousness (dutifulness). It was expected that when the FFM facet relationships were directly compared across the dark triad, all the agreeableness facets would correlate with all the dark triad constructs. This prediction held true for all but one facet (tender-mindedness). Additionally, both Machiavellianism and psychopathy were strongly correlated with a number of other facets, which further indicates that Machiavellianism measures may, in fact, be assessing aspects of psychopathy. Overall, it appears that both of these constructs are associated negatively with the facets of agreeableness and conscientiousness. However, they appear to have some relationships across the other domains of the FFM that may help differentiate them. DeShong et al. (2017) found that psychopathy was consistently negatively correlated with the neuroticism self-consciousness facet and positively with the impulsiveness facet.

Finally, Grijalva and Newman (2015) raised a question whether narcissism overlap with the FFM traits. They contended that it possible that narcissism relates to counterproductive work behavior (CWB) in only a spurious fashion, such that the observed covariation between the two is due to their well-known common correlates. Indeed, according to them, evidence suggests that narcissism has substantial overlap with some components of the FFM. Their findings showed that narcissism has strong interpersonal implications, as demonstrated by its link to the two FFM traits (i.e., extraversion and agreeableness) that also have strong relational content. According to Wu and Lebreton (2011), there is evidence that certain aspects of narcissism are captured in the traits of the FFM, but the relatively modest bivariate correlations suggest that narcissism is not redundant with the global traits of the FFM.

The above theory and findings suggest that while the dominant approach, also applied in this book, is to treat the dark triad as multidimensional, there are theories and findings that imply that this issue is still not entirely resolved, and further research is needed to clarify it (Furtner et al., 2017).

References

American Psychiatric Association. (2000). *Diagnostic and Statistical Manual of Mental Disorders* (4th ed., text revision). Washington, DC: American Psychiatric Association.

Babiak, P. (2000). Psychopathic manipulation at work. In C. B. Gacono (Ed.), *The Clinical and Forensic Assessment of Psychopathy: A Practitioner's Guide* (pp. 287–312). Mahwah, NJ: Lawrence Erlbaum Associates, Inc.

Babiak, P., & Hare, R. D. (2006). *Snakes in Suits: When Psychopaths Go to Work*. New York: Regan Books.

Bańka, A., & Orłowski, K. (2012). The structure of the teacher Machiavellianism model in social interactions in a school environment. *Polish Psychological Bulletin, 43*(4), 215–222.

Barber, N. (1998). Sex differences in disposition towards kin, security of adult attachment, and sociosexuality as a function of parental divorce. *Evolution and Human Behavior, 19*(2), 125–132.

Barry, C. T., & Kauten, R. L. (2014). Nonpathological and pathological narcissism: Which self-reported characteristics are most problematic in adolescents? *Journal of Personality Assessment, 96*(2), 212–219.

Belschak, F. D., Den Hartog, D. N., & Kalshoven, K. (2015). Leading Machiavellians: How to translate Machiavellians' selfishness into pro-organizational behavior. *Journal of Management, 41*(7), 1934–1956.

Belschak, F. D., Muhammad, R. S., & Den Hartog, D. N. (2016). Birds of a feather can butt heads: When Machiavellian employees work with Machiavellian leaders. *Journal of Business Ethics*, 1–14.

Bertl, B., Pietschnig, J., Tran, U. S., Stieger, S., & Voracek, M. (2017). More or less than the sum of its parts? Mapping the dark triad of personality onto a single dark core. *Personality and Individual Differences, 114*, 140–144.

Blickle, G., & Schütte, N. (2017). Trait psychopathy, task performance, and counterproductive work behavior directed toward the organization. *Personality and Individual Differences, 109*, 225–231.

Board, B. J., & Fritzon, K. (2005). Disordered personalities at work. *Psychology, Crime & Law, 11*(1), 17–32.

Boddy, C. (2011). *Corporate Psychopaths: Organizational Destroyers*. London: Palgrave MacMillan.

Brunell, A. B., Gentry, W. A., Campbell, W. K., Hoffman, B. J., Kuhnert, K. W., & DeMarree, K. G. (2008). Leader emergence: The case of the narcissistic leader. *Personality and Social Psychology Bulletin, 34*(12), 1663–1676.

Campbell, W. K., Hoffman, B. J., Campbell, S. M., & Marchisio, G. (2011). Narcissism in organizational contexts. *Human Resource Management Review, 21*(4), 268–284.

Christie, R., & Geis, F. L. (1970). *Studies in Machiavellianism*. New York, NY: Academic Press.

Cleckley, H. (1941/1988). *The Mask of Sanity (5th ed.), Private Printing for Educational Use by Emily Cleckley 1988* (Formerly first published by C. V. Mosley Co. in 1941). Georgia: Augusta.

Cooke, D. J., & Michie, C. (2001). Refining the construct of psychopathy: Towards a hierarchical model. *Psychological Assessment, 13*, 171–188.

Davidson, G., Higgleton, E., Sargeant, H., & Seaton, A. (Eds.). (1994). *Chambers Pocket Dictionary*. Edinburgh: Chambers.

Den Hartog, D. N., & Belschak, F. D. (2012). Work engagement and Machiavellianism in the ethical leadership process. *Journal of Business Ethics, 107*(1), 35–47.

DeShong, H. L., Helle, A. C., Lengel, G. J., Meyer, N., & Mullins-Sweatt, S. N. (2017). Facets of the Dark Triad: Utilizing the Five-Factor Model to describe Machiavellianism. *Personality and Individual Differences, 105*, 218–223.

Douglas, H., Bore, M., & Munro, D. (2012). Distinguishing the dark triad: Evidence from the Five-Factor Model and the Hogan development survey. *Psychology, 3*(3), 237–242.

Fennimore, A., & Sementelli, A. (2016). Public entrepreneurship and sub-clinical psychopaths: A conceptual frame and implications. *International Journal of Public Sector Management, 29*(6), 612–634.

Freud, S. (1914/1991). On narcissism: An introduction. In J. Sandler, E. Person, & P. Fonagy (Eds.), *Freud's "On Narcissism: An Introduction."* New Haven, CT: Yale University Press.

Furtner, M. R., Maran, T., & Rauthmann, J. F. (2017). Dark leadership: The role of leaders' dark triad personality traits. In *Leader Development Deconstructed* (pp. 75–99). New York: Springer, Cham.

Grijalva, E., & Harms, P. D. (2014). Narcissism: An integrative synthesis and dominance complementarity model. *The Academy of Management Perspectives, 28*(2), 108–127.

Grijalva, E., & Newman, D. A. (2015). Narcissism and counterproductive work behavior (CWB): Meta-analysis and consideration of collectivist culture, Big Five personality, and narcissism's facet structure. *Applied Psychology: An International Review, 64*(1), 93–126.

Hanson, L., & Baker, D. L. (2017). "Corporate psychopaths" in public agencies? *Journal of Public Management & Social Policy, 24*(1), 21–41.

Hare, R. D. (1991). *The Hare Psychopathy Checklist Revised.* New York, NY: Multi-Health Systems Inc.

Hare, R. D. (1994). Predators: The disturbing world of the psychopaths among us. *Psychology Today, 27*(1), 54–61.

Hare, R. D. (1999). *Without Conscience: The Disturbing World of the Psychopaths among Us.* New York, NY: Guilford Press.

Herbst, T. (2014). *The Dark Side of Leadership: A Psycho-Spiritual Approach towards Understanding the Origins of Personality Dysfunctions: Derailment and the Restoration of Personality.* UK: Author House.

Hogan, R., & Fico, J. M. (2011). Leadership. In W. K. Campbell & J. D. Miller (Eds.), *The Handbook of Narcissism and Narcissistic Personality Disorder: Theoretical Approaches, Empirical Findings, and Treatments* (pp. 393–402). New York: Wiley.

Lykken, D. T. (1995). *The Antisocial Personalities.* Hillsdale, NJ: Erlbaum.

Jonason, P. K. (2014). Personality and politics. *Personality and Individual Differences, 71*, 181–184.

Jonason, P. K., Slomski, S., & Partyka, J. (2012a). The dark triad at work: How toxic employees get their way. *Personality and Individual Differences, 52*(3), 449–453.

Jones, D. N., & Figueredo, A. J. (2013). The core of darkness: Uncovering the heart of the dark triad. *European Journal of Personality, 27*(6), 521–531.

Jones, D. N., & Paulhus, D. L. (2009). Machiavellianism. In M. R. Leary & R. H. Hoyle (Eds.), *Handbook of Individual Differences in Social Behavior* (pp. 93–108). New York, NY: Guilford.

Jones, D. N., & Paulhus, D. L. (2014). Introducing the short dark triad (SD3): A brief measure of dark personality traits. *Assessment, 21*(1), 28–41.

Kausel, E. E., Culbertson, S. S., Leiva, P. I., Slaughter, J. E., & Jackson, A. T. (2015). Too arrogant for their own good? Why and when narcissists dismiss advice. *Organizational Behavior and Human Decision Processes, 131*, 33–50.

Lee, K., Ashton, M. C., Wiltshire, J., Bourdage, J. S., Visser, B. A., & Gallucci, A. (2013). Sex, power, and money: Prediction from the dark triad and honesty—humility. *European Journal of Personality, 27*(2), 169–184.

Maccoby, M. (2000). Narcissistic leaders: The incredible pros, the inevitable cons. *Harvard Business Review*, 69–77.

McHoskey, J. W., Worzel, W., & Szyarto, C. (1998). Machiavellianism and psychopathy. *Journal of Personality and Social Psychology, 74*(1), 192–210.

Michel, J. S., & Bowling, N. A. (2013). Does dispositional aggression feed the narcissistic response? The role of narcissism and aggression in the prediction of job attitudes and counterproductive work behaviors. *Journal of Business and Psychology, 28*(1), 93–105.

Millon, T., & Grossman, S. D. (2005). Personology: A theory based on evolutionary concepts. In M. F. Lenzweger & J. F. Clarkin (Ed.), *Major Theories of Personality Disorder* (2nd ed., pp. 332–390). New York, NY: Guilford Press.

Muris, P., Merckelbach, H., Otgaar, H., & Meijer, E. (2017). The malevolent side of human nature: A meta-analysis and critical review of the literature on the dark triad (narcissism, Machiavellianism, and psychopathy). *Perspectives on Psychological Science, 12*(2), 183–204.

O'Boyle Jr., E. H., Forsyth, D. R., Banks, G. C., & McDaniel, M. A. (2012). A meta-analysis of the dark triad and work behavior: A social exchange perspective. *Journal of Applied Psychology, 97*(3), 557–579.

O'Boyle, E. H., Forsyth, D. R., Banks, G. C., Story, P. A., & White, C. D. (2015). A meta-analytic test of redundancy and relative importance of the dark triad and five-factor model of personality. *Journal of Personality, 83*(6), 644–664.

Paulhus, D. L., & Williams, K. M. (2002). The dark triad of personality: Narcissism, Machiavellianism, and psychopathy. *Journal of Research in Personality, 36*(6), 556–563.

Rauthmann, J. F. (2013). Investigating the MACH—IV with item response theory and proposing the trimmed MACH. *Journal of Personality Assessment, 95*(4), 388–397.

Rauthmann, J. F., & Kolar, G. P. (2012). How "dark" are the dark triad traits? Examining the perceived darkness of narcissism, Machiavellianism, and psychopathy. *Personality and Individual Differences, 53*(7), 884–889.

Robertson, S. A., Datu, J. A. D., Brawley, A. M., Pury, C. L., & Mateo, N. J. (2016). The Dark Triad and social behavior: The influence of self-construal and power distance. *Personality and Individual Differences, 98*, 69–74.

Rosenthal, S. A., & Pittinsky, T. L. (2006). Narcissistic leadership. *The Leadership Quarterly, 17*(6), 617–633.

Sankowsky, D. (1995). The charismatic leader as narcissist: Understanding the abuse of power. *Organizational Dynamics, 23*, 57–71.

Schyns, B. (2015). Dark personality in the workplace: Introduction to the special issue. *Applied Psychology: An International Review, 64*(1), 1–14.

Smith, M. B., & Webster, B. D. (2017). A moderated mediation model of Machiavellianism, social undermining, political skill, and supervisor-rated job performance. *Personality and Individual Differences, 104*, 453–459.

Smith, S. F., & Lilienfeld, S. O. (2013). Psychopathy in the workplace: The knowns and unknowns. *Aggression and Violent Behavior, 18*, 204–218.

Solas, J. (2015). Pathological work victimization in public sector organizations. *Public Organization Review, 15*(2), 255–265.

Spain, S. M., Harms, P., & LeBreton, J. M. (2014). The dark side of personality at work. *Journal of Organizational Behavior, 35*(Supplement 1), S41–S60.

Treadway, D. C., Yang, J., Bentley, J. R., Williams, L. V., & Reeves, M. (2017). The impact of follower narcissism and LMX perceptions on feeling envied and job performance. *The International Journal of Human Resource Management*, 1–22.

Williams, K. M., Paulhus, D. L., & Hare, R. D. (2007). Capturing the four-factor structure of psychopathy in college students via self-report. *Journal of Personality Assessment, 88*(2), 205–219.

Wilson, D. S., Near, D., & Miller, R. R. (1996). Machiavellianism: A synthesis of the evolutionary and psychological literatures. *Psychological Bulletin, 119*, 285–299.

Wisse, B., Barelds, D. P., & Rietzschel, E. F. (2015). How innovative is your employee? The role of employee and supervisor dark triad personality traits in supervisor perceptions of employee innovative behavior. *Personality and Individual Differences, 82*, 158–162.

Wright, A. G. C., Pincus, A. L., Thomas, K. M., Hopwood, C. J., Markon, K. E., & Krueger, R. F. (2013). Conceptions of narcissism and the DSM-5 pathological personality traits. *Assessment, 20*, 339–352.

Wu, J., & Lebreton, J. M. (2011). Reconsidering the dispositional basis of counterproductive work behavior: The role of aberrant personality. *Personnel Psychology, 64*(3), 593–626.

3 The Origins of the Dark Triad

This chapter covers the origins of the dark triad personalities. As in many discussions on the development of other personalities, an important issue is whether or not a dark triad personality is genetic or the result of growing up in a certain environment. Questions that will be advanced here are what is the role of the environment in the development of dark triad traits? Are there any physiological characteristics specific to dark triad personalities? These issues, which are reviewed in this chapter, have implications regarding the possible means of dealing with dark triad personalities in the workplace. If genetics are dominant for developing these personalities, very little can be done about it. The only course of action is to avoid these malevolent personalities, and, if they are already present in the workplace, to find means to either dismiss them or neutralize them in a way that will minimize the potential damage they can cause. If a dark triad personality is more the result of the environment, perhaps awareness and professional treatment can reduce the negative behaviors and the devastating outcomes of dark triad personalities in the workplace. This chapter also discusses demographic differences among the dark triad personalities, particularly gender.

Evolutionary Theory and the Dark Triad

The dominant approach to explaining the development of dark triad personalities is the evolutionary theory. It has been suggested that in general, individual differences play an important role in the vast majority of social adaptive problems. An evolutionary perspective can provide a foundational theory through which workplace phenomena such as the dark triad can be examined with greater intricacy (Jonason, Wee, & Li, 2014b; Furtner, Maran, & Rauthmann, 2017). According to Furnham, Richards, and Paulhus (2013), the notion that dark triad personalities can flourish as social parasites has been in existence since Mealey's (1995) study, who pointed out that the evolutionary theory predicts such predatory subgroups. Furnham et al. cited Vernon, Villani, Vickers, and Harris (2008), who showed that all three dark personalities have substantial genetic components. Distinctive behaviors among the dark triad are already evident in juveniles aged 11 to 17 years (Furnham et al., 2013). To better understand the origins on adaptationist analysis related to the dark triad traits, it is necessary to present the concept of life history strategies (Glenn, Kurzban, & Raine, 2011).

The life history strategies theory, which is a mid-level theory derived from the evolutionary theory, describes trade-offs that must be made because of individuals' limited time and energy budgets. Effort allocated to solving one adaptive problem, for the most part, precludes the effort allocated to other adaptive problems. The major predicted life history trade-offs are (1) somatic effort (resources devoted to continued survival) versus reproductive effort (resources devoted to producing offspring), (2) parental effort versus mating effort, (3) quality versus quantity of offspring, and (4) future versus present reproduction. Although previously used to account for differences among species, the life history theory has proven useful also for understanding individual differences in human behavior (Glenn et al., 2011; Furtner et al., 2017).

According to the life history theory, individuals make trade-offs in their energy allocation to different life tasks, including physical growth and maintenance, mating efforts, and parenting and kin investment. Thus, the particular pattern of actual energy allocation depends on the harshness and unpredictability of the environment. Unpredictable environments with high mortality risks tend to produce fast life history strategies in which individuals mature early and produce more offspring but invest less in each offspring (somatic effort). This strategy is adaptive because it increases the probability of producing at least some surviving offspring (Jonason, Webster, Schmitt, Li, & Crysel, 2012). Alternatively, a relatively predictable environment with low mortality risks tends to produce slow life history strategies, in which individuals mature and reproduce at a later age, producing fewer offspring in which they invest heavily. Increased allocation of energy may be associated with a greater ability to obtain resources, status, and long-term mates (reproductive effort) (McDonald, Donnellan, & Navarrete, 2012).

Individuals have been found to vary in the relative amount of resource investment along each of these dimensions. Organisms that mature sexually and reproduce relatively early, produce a large number of offspring, and invest little in parental care are said to have a "fast" life history strategy. Organisms that develop late and delay reproduction, having fewer offspring and investing heavily in parental care, are said to have a "slow" life history strategy. The life history theory predicts that personality traits that facilitate a coordinated fast or slow life history strategy tend to be selected together and therefore co-occur. In general, a slow life history strategy is associated with secure attachments, supportive communication, support of and contact with family and friends, a psychological disposition for long-term planning, and long-term mating efforts. In contrast, a fast life history strategy is associated with less focus on planning for the future, short-term mating efforts, increased risk taking, reduced self-control, and a selfish disposition (Glenn et al., 2011).

Researchers have applied the life history theory to explain individual differences in the dark triad traits. All researchers agreed that individuals with dark triad traits have a fast life history strategy. Characterized by deficits in self-control, such individuals often exhibit short-term mating, selfishness, and other antisocial manifestations. The relatively "lighter" traits, Machiavellianism and narcissism, include facets that ameliorate the socially undesirable and costly aspects of having a fast life strategy. Hence, the latter two personalities can easily function socially, but psychopaths encounter greater difficulties (Furnham et al., 2013).

The extent to which individuals engage in aggressive or antisocial behaviors is also a relevant outcome of one's life history strategy. Fast strategies are typically applied in environments where the risk of mortality is high and resource availability is unpredictable. These environments tend to favor risky and impulsive behaviors. As a result, individuals faced with these challenges may be more prone to using criminality and violence to obtain material resources, status, and mates. Consistent with this, aggression, antisocial behavior, and unrestricted sexual attitudes have been shown to be associated with the dark triad traits. Consequently, researchers concluded that the dark triad represents a fast life strategy (McDonald et al., 2012). McDonald et al. (2012) contended that although the outcomes associated with fast life strategies are often viewed by society as undesirable, the life history theory views them as strategic responses to environmental conditions. Thus, behaviors associated with a fast life strategy may be adaptive concerning individual fitness, regardless of whether or not these behaviors impose costs on society.

In humans, prosocial behaviors, attitudes, and personality traits are evolutionarily stable strategies, but evolution also favors those who use more self-serving strategies. Such strategies—as measured by the dark triad— might be in response to environmental contingencies, or they could be a heritable, alternative life history strategy (Jonason, Li, & Czarna, 2013a). Evidence suggests that those who score high in the dark triad have a short-term, opportunistic or exploitive mating strategy, together with a strategic approach to friendship selection and a protean approach to social interactions (Jonason et al., 2013a). This has led some researchers to conclude that the dark triad traits are part of a fast life history strategy, geared toward maximizing immediate returns over delayed outcomes, as would be predicted by the trade-offs expressed in the life history theory. However, Jonason et al. (2013a) contended that maximizing immediate returns can be costly. For instance, the dark triad traits are associated with mate defection, an ostensible cost to the individual's fitness.

The dark triad may indicate a fast life strategy that is also based on immediate rewards and gratification (Jonason et al., 2012). From an evolutionary perspective, the dark triad traits are seen not just in terms of their problematic associations but in the case of some individuals also as adaptive mechanisms for meeting some of life's fundamental challenges (e.g., seeking status, finding mates, and protecting kin). According to Jonason et al. (2014b), these individuals have adopted an acutely agentic, short-term social strategy. The adoption of these strategies is related to factors such as parental abuse or lack of resources during childhood (Jonason et al., 2012).

An important question regarding the evolutionary theory and the dark triad is the relevance of this conceptualization to the workplace. Indeed, Jonason, Lyons, and Bethell (2014a; Jonason et al., 2014b) questioned whether evolutionary psychology really has anything to do with the workplace. In their view, the evolutionary psychological paradigm proposes that human behavior is founded on basic, evolved psychological mechanisms that developed to allow humans to operate in social groups toward relatively collective ends. The workplace is just such a group. The evolutionary theory is preferable over previous theories because of its generalizability or its ability to make future predictions through a-priori assumptions and context specificity. According to Jonason et al. (2014b), an evolutionary model does not seek to eliminate proverbial bad apples but instead to find the appropriate niches (i.e., jobs) for individuals based on the consideration of how their personality is designed to function. Thus, by carefully examining the features of such a strategy and how they interact with the environment, an evolutionary perspective could provide an even more sophisticated, and balanced, understanding of the manner in which dark triad personalities function in the workplace.

Some empirical findings support the life history theory for the dark triad. Among these, those of Jonason et al. (2014a) show that low-level maternal care leads to Machiavellianism and to the aspects of entitlement/exploitativeness and leadership/authority of narcissism when the intervening factor of secure attachment is absent. Low-level paternal care, in turn, was found to be related to secondary psychopathy and high-level paternal care to be associated with the entitlement/exploitativeness dimension of narcissism. Many of the features of psychopathy represent characteristics of a "fast" life history strategy. Men scoring higher on psychopathic traits have also been found to engage in more short-term mating behaviors, showing interest in seeking a short-term mate, to exhibit socio-sexual attitudes, and to have a greater number of sexual partners (Glenn et al., 2011).

McDonald et al. (2012) examined the relationship between the dark triad constructs and life history strategies in a sample of American students. They found that whereas measures of these two constructs contain some features that map to a fast life strategy, other features correspond to a slow life strategy. Fearless dominance, leadership/authority, and grandiose exhibitionism share attributes such as confidence, social dominance, self-esteem, and low anxiety, which are reflective more of a slow life strategy than of a fast life strategy. In contrast, impulsive antisociality, entitlement/exploitativeness,

Machiavellianism, unrestricted socio-sexuality, and aggression share attributes such as a lack of self-control and a willingness to exploit others, which seem to be clear indicators of a fast life strategy. McDonald et al. (2012) concluded that only certain elements of psychopathy and narcissism reflect a fast life history strategy. It could be argued that these are the core elements of the dark triad constructs and that the other elements simply reflect construct contamination. McDonald et al. (2012) emphasized that their results are intuitive and largely consistent with previous research evaluating the correlates of the lower order facets of psychopathy and narcissism.

Jonason, Koenig, and Tost (2010) found across two studies that the dark triad traits, in particular psychopathy, are linked to the life history strategy. Psychopathy appears to be the dark triad component that best reflects a fast life history strategy. This may be because those who score high in psychopathy, not in narcissism or Machiavellianism, report low levels of self-control. The researchers contended that psychopathy might better tap the fast life strategy than the other two components, despite prior evidence that has linked Machiavellianism to life history strategy, because it is a "darker" personality trait. Machiavellianism and narcissism may be "lighter" than psychopathy but may function to ameliorate the socially undesirable and costly aspects of a fast life strategy, thereby reducing the strength of the correlations between their measures.

Several researchers have explored the idea that psychopathy represents an evolutionary strategy consisting primarily of "cheating" behaviors. In this view, the emotional, cognitive, and behavioral features of psychopaths are seen as specified and organized mechanisms that, during the human history of evolution, facilitated a viable reproductive social strategy (Glenn & Raine, 2009). Psychopathy is a trait that has evolved in the gene pool rather than being selected out of the gene pool, which implies that it has some survival and reproductive advantages. Humans are a social species concerned with reputation; therefore, reciprocal altruism is beneficial for most of the population because cooperation can increase survival in the long term even if it reduces opportunities in the short term. While reciprocal altruism may be beneficial for most, a proportion of the population may use the "cheater" strategy in which they choose not to reciprocate and therefore choose self-interest over cooperation (Walker & Jackson, 2017).

A cheater strategy is frequency dependent. If too many individuals within the population used a cheater strategy, then the strategy would not be successful because it is based on the others' anticipation that goodwill is the natural state of affairs and that they, in turn, will receive goodwill. Because the cheater strategy involves taking advantage of others, psychopaths can act as "con artists" because of the anticipation of reciprocation. Potentially, the advantageous features of psychopathy include undue acquisition and maintenance of resources as a result of superficial charm, deception, lack of other-centered emotions, and a manipulative and parasitic lifestyle (Walker & Jackson, 2017). Many of the features of the psychopath's personality seem to describe characteristics that would be important in pursuing the evolutionary strategy of cheating: being manipulative, conning, and glib; not experiencing empathy, guilt, or remorse; being risk taking and sensation seeking; and engaging in instrumental and goal-directed aggression are all means by which psychopaths may gain advantage. To successfully pursue a strategy that primarily involves a behavior of cheating may require one or both of the following elements: (1) lack of emotions that normally guide moral behavior and (2) reward or pleasure from causing harm to others (Glenn & Raine, 2009).

According to Walker and Jackson (2017), the game theory, as exemplified in the prisoner's dilemma, has demonstrated that cheating can be an effective strategy if the associate does not cheat. The cheater strategy can be particularly useful to psychopaths in a corporate setting for climbing the corporate hierarchy because it can be associated with gaining status and acquiring financial benefits unfairly. Psychopaths have been described as "homo economus" because they are focused on gaining rewards and unconcerned with the social consequences, including possible punishment. While others may use aggression as an emotional reaction, psychopaths are more likely to use aggression proactively and without emotion. Psychopaths score higher on instrumental aggression and are less likely to inhibit violence in response to cues of distress. Aggression is simply a means to an end to ensure that they get what they want. Corporate psychopaths similarly prioritize self-interest, which may have destructive consequences, such as disruptions to the group functioning (Walker & Jackson, 2017).

A Psychobiological Perspective of the Dark Triad

Another perspective is that psychopathy, as well as the other two dark triad personalities, represents dysfunction and is the result of mutation (Glenn et al., 2011). All humans carry mutations, some of which are new but most of which are inherited from ancestors and may be passed through generations. Although mutations with highly harmful effects will be removed quickly from the gene pool, it may take many generations for those with only mildly harmful effects to become extinct. This results in an accumulation of old mutations that serves as a source of genetic variation among individuals because individuals vary in the number and type of mutations they carry (mutation load). It is hypothesized that this source of individual differences contributes also to differences in psychological traits and disorders. Because personality traits are the product of a large number of genes, there are many opportunities for disruption by random mutations. Traits that are universally and highly valued in a mate, such as emotional stability, kindness, conscientiousness, and intelligence, may be disrupted by these mutations. Given it is likely that psychopathy represents the extreme of a continuum of symptom severity, it may well be influenced by the cumulative effect of many minor dysfunctions at the micro-level of genes and brain development (Glenn et al., 2011).

Neurobiological evidence suggests that there are differences in the brains of psychopaths compared with those of normal individuals, particularly in regions that are important for guiding moral behavior. Reduced functioning in regions important for generating emotions such as fear, guilt, and empathy may mean that psychopaths are not deterred from harming others to gain an advantage. At the same time, increased functioning in regions associated with reward may lead psychopaths to take pleasure in causing harm to others. In addition, learning based on both reward and punishment information may be disrupted and thereby impair socialization (Glenn & Raine, 2009). According to Herbst (2014), one of the older biological theories is that for some unknown reason, the psychopath's brain structures mature at an abnormally slow rate, reflected in a developmental delay. Another body of theories based on the biological model is that psychopathy is the result of early brain damage and dysfunction, especially in the frontal lobes of the brain involved in, for example, long-term planning, socially appropriate behavior, and impulse control (Herbst, 2014).

Gao and Raine (2010) also suggested a neurobiological model of successful and unsuccessful psychopaths. According to them, when psychopathy is studied among community-dwelling psychopaths, excluding those in temporary employment agencies, they seem to show cognitive or emotional deficits that include deficient behavioral modulation, reduced heart rate, and electro-dermal reactivity and startle response potentiation impairments, which were also observed in incarcerated psychopaths. In contrast, studies of psychopaths in temporary employment agencies, in general, suggested intact brain volume and enhanced executive functioning among successful psychopaths. When college students with an elevated psychopathic personality were examined, they exhibited cognitive and emotional deficits similar to those of incarcerated psychopaths, although their impairments may have been less severe.

Gao and Raine (2010) further argued that other characteristics, including relatively intact emotional regulation, better decision-making capability, and intact somatic markers, may also enable successful psychopaths to succeed in life by using more covert non-aggressive strategies rather than overt aggressive approaches. In contrast, reduced prefrontal gray matter and amygdala volume and reduced heart rate stress reactivity may indicate a predisposition to the cognitive and affective deficits observed in unsuccessful psychopaths. Finally, fear conditioning deficits and impaired somatic markers are implicated in the unsuccessful psychopaths' failure to detect the cues linked to punishment, predisposing them to risky decision making, which culminates in arrests and convictions.

Recent brain imaging studies explored the neural correlates of moral decision making. Many of the structures identified appear to be associated also with psychopathy (Glenn & Raine, 2009). Anderson and Kiehl (2012) cited two neurobiological theories of psychopathy posited by Blair (2006) and Kiehl (2006). Both theories implicate components of the limbic system, a network of brain regions supporting the utilization of emotional information in behavioral regulation. Blair's model emphasizes primarily dysfunction in the amygdala as leading to the development of psychopathy. The amygdala is integral in forming associations between environmental cues and affective states and the activation of basic threat circuits. Blair (2007) emphasized the role of both the amygdala and the ventromedial prefrontal cortex in ongoing monitoring of behavior vis à vis established reinforcement expectancies. This expansion of the model accounts for the distinguishable forms of antisocial deviance observed in psychopathy.

Kiehl's (2006) paralimbic dysfunction model, relative to Blair's model, describes more widely distributed abnormalities throughout the brains of psychopaths. The anterior-superior temporal gyrus (temporal pole), anterior cingulate, posterior cingulate, orbitofrontal cortex, and insula and parahippocampal regions are intimately connected to primary limbic regions, including the amygdala, septal region, and substantia innominata. The paralimbic system refers to primary limbic structures, and this extended network of brain regions serves as a transition from subcortical structures to higher neocortical regions. Kiehl's model accounts for evidence that psychopaths present abnormalities in areas beyond the primary limbic structures, such as the anterior and posterior cingulate cortex, temporal pole, insula, and parahippocampal gyrus.

The Dark Triad as an Interaction Between Biological and Social Forces

Studies have indicated that psychopathy is the result of a combination of biological and environmental forces (Akın, Amil, & Özdevecioğlu, 2016; Herbst, 2014; Hare, 1999). Jonason et al. (2012) cited Vernon et al. (2008), who demonstrated that some evidence exists for both genetic and environmental causes of the dark triad traits, with almost 70% of the variability in Machiavellianism being accounted for by genetic factors. The biological theories on the origins of psychopathy are supported by research that has provided evidence of the biological and genetic bases of personality: Some forms of brain damage result in symptoms resembling psychopathy, but psychopathic behaviors may emerge early in children. Herbst (2014) cited Hare (1994, 1999), who stated that genetic factors contribute to the biological bases of brain function and to the basic personality structure, which in turn influence the way individuals respond to, and interact with, life experiences and the social environment. According to Herbst (2014), as a result of some unknown biological influences on the developing fetus, the capacity for developing internal controls and making emotional connections with others is adversely affected. This implies that these individuals' biological endowment—elements or raw material that environmental, social, and learning experiences mold into a unique individual—provides a poor basis for socialization and conscience information.

Furthermore, social factors and parenting practices influence the behavioral expression of the disorder. Parents may be a strong factor that influences psychopathy in adulthood. Psychopaths have differing backgrounds and varying predispositions that seem to suggest a unique etiology to their antisocial behavior. Studies in children and adolescents indicate that coercive parenting interactions, the absence of a positive and affectionate parent–child bond, neglect, inconsistent parents, and corporal punishment may all be potential risk factors contributing to psychopathy in adulthood. Some parents who abuse their children may harbor a genetic predisposition toward aggression, impulsivity, and similar traits, which they then transmit to their children, resulting in the correlation between early abuse and childhood aggression. A link has been suggested between abuse and psychopathic characteristics described as the factor one traits. Abuse in childhood may also elicit a diminished capacity for affective responding, thus causing the child to become desensitized to future painful or anxiety-provoking experiences (Quow, 2013).

The general agreement of the approaches supporting the idea of biological and environmental interplay is that some dysfunction of the amygdala and orbitofrontal cortex is probably involved, and the other developmental and environmental pathways of psychopathy are not fully understood. Boddy (2011) found that environmental factors such as early-stage parental rejection predict the early onset of violent criminality, which is emblematic of psychopathic behavior. Boddy further argued that the detection of brain abnormalities does not necessarily mean that a causal direction has been established. It could be that learning and environmental factors contribute to changes in brain chemistry over time. Psychopathy appears to start in childhood when it is associated with the same neurobiological factors as those found in adults. How it manifests itself appears dependent on the culture in which the child is raised. Childhood neglect, with an associated lack of sensory input in infancy, has, for example, been associated with physiological changes in brain size and metabolic activity in the orbitofrontal gyrus and amygdala.

Demographic Differences

Gender has captured the majority of researchers' attention in an attempt to explore differences among the dark triad personalities. Gender differences in the dark triad can be attributed to the differing evolutionary pressures presented to, and thus the divergent adaptive strategies developed by, each gender. Historically, whereas men's needs were met through a "hunter" approach, whereby they directly attained material goods, and sociality was useful but not essential, women's needs may have been more effectively met through social belongingness, serving to protect and provide for both themselves and their offspring. The profound lack of empathy associated with psychopathy could be adaptive for achieving overtly exploitative "male" goals, with relatively higher levels of empathy and narcissism better suited to meet socially exploitative "female" goals. Therefore, differential evolutionary pressures may account for divergent paths to the exploitative nature of dark triad personalities and, equally, different routes to emotional deficits (Jonason & Krause, 2013). Because the costs and benefits associated with life history trade-offs are not the same for men and women, the life history theory predicts gender differences in life history strategies; the gender required to invest more bioenergetic and material resources in offspring will have a relatively slower life history strategy. Because women are biologically obligated to invest more in their offspring than are men, this suggests that men would be more likely to have a faster life history strategy than women. The large gender differences observed in psychopathy may, therefore, correspond to differences between men and women in terms of their life history strategies (Glenn et al., 2011).

Supporting this explanation, Jonason et al. (2010) concluded, based on their two studies, that gender differences are consistent with life history strategy and parental investment theory. Their findings showed that the life strategy of men tends to be faster than that of women, possibly because men have a lower level obligation to offspring. Their findings also showed that men scored higher than women on the dark triad measures and tended to have a faster life history strategy than women. It should be noted, however, that some studies did not find any significant difference between men and women in the levels of primary, secondary, and total psychopathy scores (Akın et al., 2016). This finding introduces some ambiguity into the notion that men will be scored higher on psychopathy.

The study of gender differences covered not only psychopaths but also other personality constructs. In support of the life history theory, Jonason et al. (2013a) found that, across cultures, men generally benefit more and pay fewer reproductive costs than women as a result of pursuing a fast life history strategy. Furthermore, it appears that the dark triad facilitates the creation of a volatile socioecology for men more than for women. While men may benefit more than women from adopting such an approach to life, they must also pay the related costs. It is the manner in which individuals—men in this case—negotiate these costs and benefits that results in increased inclusive fitness. It may be that for men, these costs are not sufficiently high to reproductively exclude them. Routes taken by men and women differ somewhat in practice or the frequency of use.

According to Jonason et al. (2012), psychopathy is strikingly different from the other dark triad traits in terms of the degree to which men and women differ on the trait. Whereas narcissism and Machiavellianism display small to negligible gender differences, in most studies, gender differences in psychopathy are nearly universal and are moderate to large.

This, according to them, may be related to a combination of hormones, such as cortisol and testosterone, and that it is primarily a functional trait within humans. Some evidence supports this proposal; for example, men tend to be more sensitive to environmental cues involving antisociality, and psychopathy covaries within and across cultures with fast life history traits in men.

Jonason, Lyons, Bethell, and Ross (2013b) contended that having limited empathy might facilitate an antagonistic approach to life that is more characteristic of men. Not caring for the feelings of others might enable one to pursue a selfish, competitive, and aggressive approach to social and sexual issues. According to Jonason and Krause (2013), lower levels of empathy and increased externally oriented thinking facilitate the dark triad in women compared with men, and a particularly strong relationship exists between psychopathy and these emotional deficits. High levels of psychopathy in women may be predicted by elevated levels of emotional deficits, a more nefarious part of the dark triad personality cluster, because this was found to be specifically linked to the more socially aversive constructs of limited overall empathy and externally oriented thinking. Narcissism was found to be the least aversive and could even potentially suppress the effect of the darker traits in women. Therefore, there may be specific constellations of dark triad traits that form personality types that could be considered more or less socially aversive—or adaptive—depending on the goals and resultant behaviors involved. Jonason et al. (2013b) found that the link between the dark triad and limited empathy might primarily be through narcissism in women but through psychopathy in men. These alternative routes present the possibility that different outcomes might be associated with limited empathy in men and women. For instance, whereas men who are high in psychopathy and thus have limited empathy may enact a risky lifestyle, women who are high in narcissism may enact parasitic relationship styles.

In a study that is highly relevant to the work situation, Semenyna and Honey (2015) contended that dark triad men and women adopt different routes to dominance. In particular, whereas men may be more likely to seek power over others, women may be more likely to seek influence in more communal or at least less overt and physically aggressive ways. Consistent with these different routes to dominance, Semenyna and Honey found evidence that men tend more toward dominance striving and ruthless self-advancement, weak evidence that women tend toward coalition building, and no meaningful differences in prestige striving or dominant leadership between the genders. They concluded, based on their two studies, that if we were to predict dark triad traits, knowing the individual's sex would be much less informative than knowing her or his score on measures of dominance striving or ruthless self-advancement. Therefore, it would be an overstatement to claim that dark triad traits are male typical and even adaptive for men but not for women.

While gender seems to be the main demographic characteristic to attract the attention of scholars, Akın et al. (2016) found in a sample of employees in Turkey that single individuals exhibited significantly higher psychopathy levels than married individuals, suggesting that environmental factors might play a role in the shaping and development of psychopathy. They argued that the significantly lower level of psychopathy observed among married individuals in their study might be explained by the feelings of compassion and responsibility that develop as a result of marriage. More studies are needed to explore demographic differences among dark triad personalities.

The evolutionary approach provides a useful conceptual framework to understand the development of dark triad personalities. The theory and findings presented here clearly show that the theory seems to be highly relevant, mainly for psychopaths. This is not to argue that it is not relevant for the other personalities, narcissism and Machiavellianism. However, the relevance of the life history theory to the latter two dark personalities is still unclear. There is definitely a need for more research to examine this theory, not only among psychopaths but also among narcissists and Machiavellians. The same can be said regarding the neurobiological theory. There is stronger support for this theory regarding psychopaths than for the other two constructs. Here, too, more research is needed. However, it seems that the findings so far point to the possibility that narcissism and Machiavellianism are lighter forms of malevolent personalities than psychopathy. This should also be examined in future research, although an increasing number of research findings do support this contention.

Particular attention should be paid to the arguments presented in this chapter about the role of the environment in the development of dark triad personalities. It seems that all the theories mentioned point to the environment as playing an important role in originating these personalities, not in itself and not exclusively but in addition or together with the factors outlined. It is not surprising that the environment is an important component for dark triad personalities in terms not only of their development as such personalities but also of finding and creating an environment that is more or less suitable for their activities. The work setting provides an environment that, for reasons to be outlined in the following chapters, creates a friendly environment for dark triad personalities, that is, an environment in which they will feel more comfortable and safer in pursuing their goals. This argument is elaborated in the following chapters.

References

Akın, M., Amil, O., & Özdevecioğlu, M. (2016). Is your manager a psychopath? An evaluation of the relationship between the personality types of managers and workers and the levels of psychopathy. *Procedia-Social and Behavioral Sciences, 221*, 76–85.

Anderson, N. E., & Kiehl, K. A. (2012). The psychopath magnetized: Insights from brain imaging. *Trends in Cognitive Sciences, 16*(1), 52–60.

Blair, R. J. R. (2006). The emergence of psychopathy: Implications for the neuropsychological approach to developmental disorders. *Cognition, 101*(2), 414–442.

Blair, R. J. R. (2007). The amygdala and ventromedial prefrontal cortex in morality and psychopathy. *Trends in Cognitive Sciences, 11*(9), 387–392.

Boddy, C. (2011). *Corporate Psychopaths: Organizational Destroyers*. London: Palgrave MacMillan.

Furnham, A., Richards, S. C., & Paulhus, D. L. (2013). The dark triad of personality: A 10-year review. *Social and Personality Psychology Compass, 7*(3), 199–216.

Furtner, M. R., Maran, T., & Rauthmann, J. F. (2017). Dark leadership: The role of leaders' dark triad personality traits. In *Leader Development Deconstructed* (pp. 75–99). New York: Springer, Cham.

Gao, Y., & Raine, A. (2010). Successful and unsuccessful psychopaths: A neurobiological model. *Behavioral Sciences & the Law, 28*(2), 194–210.

Glenn, A. L., Kurzban, R., & Raine, A. (2011). Evolutionary theory and psychopathy. *Aggression and Violent Behavior, 16*(5), 371–380.

Glenn, A. L., & Raine, A. (2009). Psychopathy and instrumental aggression: Evolutionary, neurobiological, and legal perspectives. *International Journal of Law and Psychiatry, 32*(4), 253–258.

Hare, R. D. (1994). Predators: The disturbing world of the psychopaths among us. *Psychology Today, 27*(1), 54–61.

Hare, R. D. (1999). *Without Conscience: The Disturbing World of the Psychopaths among Us*. New York, NY: Guilford Press.

Herbst, T. (2014). *The Dark Side of Leadership: A Psycho-Spiritual Approach towards Understanding the Origins of Personality Dysfunctions: Derailment and the Restoration of Personality*. UK: Author House.

Jonason, P. K., Koenig, B. L., & Tost, J. (2010). Living a fast life: The dark triad and life history theory. *Human Nature, 21*, 428–442.

Jonason, P. K., & Krause, L. (2013). The emotional deficits associated with the dark triad traits: Cognitive empathy, affective empathy, and alexithymia. *Personality and Individual Differences, 55*(5), 532–537.

Jonason, P. K., Li, N. P., & Czarna, A. Z. (2013a). Quick and dirty: Some psychosocial costs associated with the dark triad in three countries. *Evolutionary Psychology, 11*(1), 172–185.

Jonason, P. K., Lyons, M., Bethell, E. J., & Ross, R. (2013b). Different routes to limited empathy in the sexes: Examining the links between the dark triad and empathy. *Personality and Individual Differences, 54*(5), 572–576.

Jonason, P. K., Webster, G. D., Schmitt, D. P., Li, N. P., & Crysel, L. (2012). The antihero in popular culture: Life history theory and the dark triad personality traits. *Review of General Psychology, 16*(2), 192–199.

Jonason, P. K., Lyons, M., & Bethell, E. (2014a). The making of Darth Vader: Parent—child care and the dark triad. *Personality and Individual Differences, 67*, 30–34.

Jonason, P. K., Wee, S., & Li, N. P. (2014b). Thinking bigger and better about "bad apples": Evolutionary industrial—organizational psychology and the dark triad. *Industrial and Organizational Psychology, 7*(1), 117–121.

Kiehl, K. A. (2006). A cognitive neuroscience perspective on psychopathy: Evidence for paralimbic system dysfunction. *Psychiatry Research, 142*(2), 107–128.

McDonald, M. M., Donnellan, M. B., & Navarrete, C. D. (2012). A life history approach to understanding the dark triad. *Personality and Individual Differences, 52*(5), 601–605.

Mealey, L. (1995). The socio-biology of sociopathy: An integrated evolutionary model. *Behavioral and Brain Sciences, 18*, 523–599.

Quow, K. L. (2013). An introspective analysis of the etiological relationships of psychopathy in serial killers and successful business men. *Modern Psychological Studies, 19*(1), 67–81.

Semenyna, S. W., & Honey, P. L. (2015). Dominance styles mediate sex differences in dark triad traits. *Personality and Individual Differences, 83,* 37–43.

Vernon, P. A., Villani, V. C., Vickers, L. C., & Harris, J. A. (2008). A behavioral genetics investigation of the dark triad and the big 5. *Personality and Individual Differences, 44,* 445–452.

Walker, B. R., & Jackson, C. J. (2017). Moral emotions and corporate psychopathy: A review. *Journal of Business Ethics, 141*(4), 797–810.

4 The Corporate Psychopath

As mentioned above, despite traditional views of psychopathy as being purely maladaptive, certain features of the disorder can predispose individuals for success in arenas characterized by physical or social risk, such as business, law, politics, high-contact or extreme sports, law enforcement, firefighting, and front-line military combat (Boddy, 2014). The realization that psychopaths are found at the top of organizations and seem to favor working with other people's money in large financial organizations led to the development of the corporate psychopaths theory of the global financial crisis. The theory suggests that corporate psychopaths rising to key senior positions in modern corporations where they are able to influence the moral climate of the entire organization and wield considerable power largely were a large component of the crisis. According to Boddy (2011), the corporate psychopaths theory of the global financial crisis maintains that changes in the manner in which people are employed have facilitated the rise of corporate psychopaths to senior positions and that the personal greed of psychopaths in those positions created the crisis. This theory is only one demonstration to the possible devastating effects of psychopaths in the workplace.

Boddy (2014) mentioned that corporate psychopaths were initially identified in Cleckley's book *The Mask of Sanity* (Cleckley, 1941/1988), introducing the recognition that subclinical psychopaths may have advantages over normal people and that psychopaths live in society. Cleckley described successful psychopaths as those who encompass an "outward appearance [conducive to] business or professional careers that continue in a sense [to be] successful, and which are truly successful when measured by financial rewards or even by the casual observer's opinion of real accomplishment" (p. 213) (Fennimore & Sementelli, 2016). These psychopaths, who live undetected in society and work seemingly unnoticed in organizations, have been described as "successful psychopaths." They have also been termed "subcriminal psychopaths," that is, psychopaths who, because of social skills gained as a result of their intelligence and advantageous family background, are able to avoid detection by legal entities and are typically involved in white-collar activities of an ethically questionable and legally borderline nature (Boddy, 2011). Successful corporate psychopaths have been characterized as self-serving, opportunistic, ego-centric, ruthless, and shameless yet also charming, manipulative, and ambitious (Gudmundsson & Southey, 2011). The nature of modern corporations is characterized by rapid change, constant renewal, and rapid turnover of key personnel. These changing conditions make psychopaths difficult to spot because constant movement makes their behavior invisible, and their extroverted personal charisma and charm make them appear normal and even suitable as ideal leaders (Boddy, 2011).

Researchers have espoused several other terms for subclinical psychopaths, including "industrial psychopaths," "organizational psychopaths," "corporate psychopaths," and "executive psychopaths" (Babiak, 1995; Boddy, 2011; Boddy, Ladyshewsky, & Galvin, 2010). The term "corporate psychopath" simply marries the terms "psychopath" from the psychological literature with "corporate" from the field of business to denote psychopaths who work and operate in organizational arenas (Boddy, 2011). In this chapter, the term "corporate psychopath" is used as consistently as possible. It is, however, unclear why the literature on what is termed "corporate" or "successful" psychopaths does not mention the other two components of the dark triad. One reason may be that the personality of those high in narcissism and Machiavellianism is not as destructive as that of psychopaths and does not always lead to damage to the organization. There is some consensus that in organizations, psychopaths are more damaging than those having the other two dark triad personality disorders (Griffin & Lopez, 2005; Mathieu, Neumann, Babiak, & Hare, 2015). This chapter will focus on the corporate psychopaths who has attracted most of the attention in managerial research on the dark triad. One of the goals of this chapter is to elucidate this profile of psychopaths and to clarify the role and the impact of corporate psychopaths in work organizations according to existing research.

From Psychopaths to Corporate or Successful Psychopaths

Of all the people with personality disorders, psychopaths are the most studied in psychology and psychiatry (Boddy, 2010a). Psychopaths are prone to instrumental violence, that is, violence used as a means for another purpose, such as robbery, to get what they want, and these violent criminal psychopaths tend to end up in prison. However, this is not the case with successful or corporate psychopaths. While research into the differences between successful and criminal psychopaths is still in its infancy, prior studies have indicated that antisocial behavior and impulsivity may be key discriminants between the two groups (Westerlaken & Woods, 2013). One explanation for the difference between the two is that successful or corporate psychopaths have better cognitive levels of executive functioning, located in the orbital-frontal cortex of the brain, and may retain the ability to control their impulses, allowing them to seek corporate rather than criminal careers (Boddy, Miles, Sanyal, & Hartog, 2015). Boddy (2011) mentioned Yang et al.'s (2005) finding that recent brain imaging of successful versus unsuccessful psychopaths reinforces the view that these are two distinct subgroups and that the corporate psychopaths exist as a separate category of psychopathy.

In addition, what facilitates the "success" of psychopathic individuals in the workplace versus psychopathic individuals in prison may be also the result of differences in life circumstances (e.g., socioeconomic status, physical appearance, social skills), as well as education and the opportunities presented to them (e.g., family, political or business connections, financial resources) rather than differences in personality, intentions, behavioral dispositions, and antisociality. Yet the impact of psychopathic manipulation can be equally destructive regardless of the milieu (Mathieu & Babiak, 2016a).

Psychopathy is viewed as existing on a continuum, and it is suggested that the variations along the continuum may distinguish "successful" (or noncriminal) psychopaths from criminal psychopaths. Westerlaken and Woods (2013) argued that successful psychopaths live and work within the community and are able to avoid interaction with criminal justice or mental health systems. According to Westerlaken and Woods (2013), successful psychopaths may have a subclinical form of psychopathy and therefore display relatively low degrees of antisocial behavior. Psychopaths who are successfully integrated into the general population are by definition harder to detect than are incarcerated criminals. Successful psychopaths are effective in as much as they have developed their skills of lying, manipulation, and deception sufficiently well to avoid detection and can avoid the display of antisocial behavior that would get them into trouble with the law. As a result, they can manage successful careers. They are described as subtle manipulators who are good at playing the emotions of others and at using people according to the value they offer them in terms of excitement, entertainment, and material gain (Babiak, 2000; Boddy, 2011).

While the underlying personality disorder or syndrome may be identical for those working in organizations and those in the general population, the manifestation of their psychopathic behaviors may differ. For example, successful psychopaths differ from their criminal counterparts in that they have higher levels of conscientiousness. Thus, the higher conscientiousness of successful psychopaths may assist in balancing the characteristics of impulsive and antisocial behavior, thereby allowing them to function acceptably within the community. Successful psychopaths can effectively function in many different occupations and can obtain high status positions, including leadership positions (Westerlaken & Woods, 2013). Successful psychopaths also differ from criminal psychopaths in their higher level of control of themselves and others and in their charming, polished, likeable, and even charismatic appearance. However, they are emotionally detached from the rest of humanity and view other people merely as objects to be used and abused as they see fit. Boddy (2011) argued that the way in which psychopathy is manifested in behavior depends on the psychopath's social environment and that family wealth may enable psychopaths to achieve their goals in a socially acceptable manner. Corporate psychopaths may well be such people, able to control any impulsive or antisocial tendencies to the extent of hiding them or rendering them seemingly lawful and so enable themselves to operate relatively undetected in social and corporate settings (Boddy, 2011). Searching to explain unethical, deviant, and criminal executive behavior, scholars have identified a number of corporate executive leaders who portray subclinical psychopathic traits.

Psychopathy does not imply that the individual has lost touch with reality but is, rather, a cluster of interpersonal, affective, lifestyle, and antisocial characteristics (Boddy, 2006). Organizational psychopaths do not resemble the psychopaths of popular imagination when you first meet them. They can appear to act as appropriately as anyone else, and they use this disguise of normality to gain the trust and support of others. According to Hare (1999), corporate psychopaths are clever and charming enough to elude detection and conflict with society and thus avoid being caught. Therefore, a revised version of the definition used for criminal psychopathy or antisocial personality disorder should be used for these more sophisticated psychopaths. One can easily expect that intelligent psychopaths from relatively privileged social backgrounds, who have taken advantage of good educational opportunities, will know that they can execute their self-serving behavior to a far better effect and with much less risk of detection in a corporate setting than in criminal activity (Boddy, 2011). They are able to use their charm to seduce and manipulate their victims and play games of corporate politics (Boddy, 2006). Therefore, criminal or antisocial definitions of psychopathy are probably inappropriate for defining functional or corporate psychopaths because they are able to control the overt manifestations of any antisocial impulses they may have and so seem to act normally (Boddy, 2011; Hare, 1999).

Corporate psychopaths can be described as simply psychopaths working in the corporate sector, possibly attracted by the potentially high monetary rewards, prestige, and power available to those who reach the senior managerial levels of large corporations. According to Boddy (2006), corporate psychopaths are defined as workplace employees who exhibit a score of 75% or more on the 20 traits in Hare's psychopathy checklist (Hare, 1991), modified by Deutschman (2005) for use in business research. The realization then developed that psychopaths may be working in industry and business at senior levels, where they may be theoretically expected to be responsible for various kinds of the corporate misbehavior. The presence of corporate psychopaths is important also because, according to the social learning theory, people learn vicariously by observing the behavior of others, especially the influential role models that they find credible. This implies that when unethical managers such as corporate psychopaths are present, their toxic behavior, such as rudeness, conflict, and bullying, will be magnified as it is learned, repeated, and copied throughout the organization (Boddy, 2014).

The Incidence of Corporate Psychopaths

As stated, psychopathy is a clinical personality disorder estimated to occur in 1% to 3% of the adult male and 0.5% to 1% of the adult female population (Westerlaken & Woods, 2013). A UK study found a 0.6% incidence with a statistical confidence level of 95%. This indicates that the actual incidence may be somewhere between 0.2% and 1.6% (Boddy, 2016a). These data correspond to the figure of 1% quoted by psychologists as the incidence level of psychopathy in North American society (Babiak & Hare, 2006). Assuming that the normal distribution of psychopaths throughout society is about the same figure, 1%, it can be expected to be found also in the working population. Furthermore, presuming that, on average, employees work closely with between 5 and 15 people in the workplace, it can be logically assumed that at any one time, between about 5% and 15% of employees are working with a psychopathic colleague, an assumption that is corroborated by the published evidence.

Indeed, a question raised in the literature and that has also attracted the attention of practitioners is the proportion of corporate psychopaths in organizations. The amount of data on this issue is inadequate, and there is definitely a need for more research in an effort to provide more information. The more accurate the estimate of the numbers and the rate of corporate psychopaths, the more accurate science will be in evaluating the magnitude of the problem. Babiak, Neumann, and Hare (2010), for example, found a psychopathy prevalence rate of 3.9% on the Psychopathy Checklist—revised (PCL-R; Hare, 2003) in their corporate sample, a rate that is significantly higher than that found in the general population (1%; Neumann & Hare, 2008), indicating that psychopaths are, in fact, likely not only to be present in organizations but perhaps also present to a higher degree than expected. It seems that the business world serves as a virtual magnet for psychopaths, suggesting that the base rate for psychopathy in the upper ranks of corporations may in fact be as high as 3% compared with 1% in the general population (Schyns, 2015; Smith & Lilienfeld, 2013). Boddy (2016b) mentioned Caponecchia, Sun, and Wyatt (2011), who found that 13.4% of their respondents reported, via a behavioral scale, that they worked with a colleague who was significantly psychopathic. Boddy (2016a) states that an Australian research study found that 5.75% of the employees were working with someone who could be classed as a corporate psychopath according to the psychopathy measure used. In another study in the UK, performed in 2011 among a more specifically defined sample of 304 white-collar workers and managers, 10.9% of the employees stated they currently work with a corporate psychopath (Boddy, 2014).

Boddy (2015) also mentioned Babiak and Hare (2006) who found in a study of nearly 200 senior executives that 3.5% were corporate psychopaths. Boddy cited Babiak et al.'s (2010) study in a convenience sample of 203 corporate professionals identified about 4% of senior managers being psychopaths. This is a higher incidence of psychopaths in corporations than would be expected than among the 1% incidence in the general population (Babiak et al., 2010; Babiak & Hare, 2006). Nine senior executives (4.4%) had very high psychopathy scores, and six (3%) scored sufficiently high to be qualified as psychopaths on a psychopathy scale. This indicates that these executives may well have been corporate psychopaths and provides support for the argument that corporate psychopaths can gain high corporate positions. According to Boddy (2011), although corporate psychopaths represent only about 1% of the workforce, because of their skills at manipulation, they may be such more prevalent at more senior levels of organizational leadership. Boddy contended that psychopaths represent 1% at the junior organizational levels, 2% to 3% at the middle management levels, and 3.5% at the senior management levels. These are substantial numbers of people, illustrating the extent of the influence of psychopaths in the workforce in relation to other employees. The issue is even more severe for organizations because they may be being demolished from within without even realizing that a psychopath is at work.

However, there are exceptions to these findings. A study among employees in Turkey examined whether the levels of psychopathy varied significantly among individuals who described themselves as employees, mid-level managers, and upper level managers (Akın, Amil, & Özdevecioğlu, 2016). The findings showed no significant differences among these three groups. Akın et al. (2016) concluded that although mid-level managers had higher levels of psychopathy than employees and upper level managers, this difference was not statistically significant. Whether or not this finding can be attributed to cultural variables constitutes an interesting future research agenda. In short, while further research is needed to provide more accurate figures for the incidence of psychopathy in the workplace, the existing figures are quite disturbing. The figures mentioned imply that the proportion of corporate psychopaths can reach 5% in managerial positions. The notion that about 10% of the employees are probably supervised by psychopath managers indicates that we are dealing with a serious problem that may cause serious damage to organizations and their employees. This is not a negligible phenomenon. Corporate psychopaths, as well as other malevolent personalities in the workplace, form an important issue that deserves more scientific research.

The Evolution of Corporate Psychopaths in Research

For decades, research on psychopathy focused almost exclusively on largely unsuccessful individuals. Only in the 1970s did researchers begin to examine potentially adaptive manifestations of the condition. The scientific roots of the corporate psychopath are found in studies in the psychology literature that have identified a subclinical type of psychopath. These "subclinical" psychopaths are not prone to violent and impulsive outbursts or criminal behavior; rather, they tend to be successful in society (Fennimore & Sementelli, 2016). The re-realization that psychopaths are working in the business and public sectors has influenced a shift in research from criminal toward corporate psychopaths. This change in direction was arguably aided by the recognition that it is the characteristics of individual managers that predispose them to wrongdoing, illegal acts, and immoral behavior (Boddy, 2016). However, formal research on the implications of psychopathy in the workplace has been lacking until recently (Smith, Watts, & Lilienfeld, 2014). The importance of this issue also stems from recent evidence demonstrating that psychopaths are destructive to the organizations for which they work and to their colleagues. Moreover, corporate psychopaths have empirically been shown to create a toxic workplace environment, typified by conflict, bullying, increased workload, low levels of job satisfaction, higher levels of withdrawal, and higher than necessary organizational constraints (Boddy, 2010a, 2010b, 2011). Such findings provide sufficient reason for extensive research on this issue.

The topic of psychopathy in business settings began to attract increasing research attention also because of the realization that a better understanding of successful psychopathy may help identify the factors that assist these individuals to successfully rise to the top of their organizations, while applying behavior-based criteria may detect only psychopaths who have had repeated legal and social difficulties (Fennimore & Sementelli, 2016). The importance of this issue also stems from the possibility that corporate psychopaths constitute perhaps the most significant threat to ethical corporate behavior worldwide, and the study of corporate psychopaths opens an important new direction for leadership research and the examination of leadership fraud. Psychopaths appear to be more adroit at getting to the top than other employees, and their incidence may be four times greater in senior positions than in junior ones (Boddy, 2016b).

The literature today on successful—that is, non-institutionalized—psychopaths (Furnham & Crump, 2016) is still small but growing. The study of corporate psychopaths is gaining credence, and the implications of their incidence within corporations are now being seriously considered. Many issues regarding corporate psychopathy arouse interest among industrial and organizational psychologists, such as whether individuals with psychopathic traits are represented in businesses to a greater (or lesser) degree than in the general society. If so, how do they present themselves in the selection or promotion processes? What kind of leaders will they be, and what is their long-term impact on the success or failure (financial or otherwise) of their companies? Despite a host of challenges that need to be overcome in an effort to find answers to these questions, the relatively few empirical studies conducted to date have uncovered some useful and perhaps provocative findings about corporate psychopathy, although an insufficient amount of research has been conducted on psychopaths in the work setting (Boddy, 2010b).

Conceptualizing Corporate Psychopaths

Researchers have suggested competing frameworks for the conceptualization and causes of successful psychopathy (Lilienfeld, Watts, & Smith, 2015; Steinert, Lishner, Vitacco, & Hong, 2017). Three such models are reviewed here. First, the *differential-severity model* proposes that noncriminal psychopaths represent less extreme examples of psychopathy. According to this model, antisocial behaviors of incarcerated psychopaths stem directly from the core personality traits of psychopathy. Hence, the social transgressions of the less severely affected individuals will be of a lesser magnitude and will occur at a lower frequency. That is, psychopathy is a unitary construct in which successful and unsuccessful psychopathy differ only in intensity. This model essentially equates successful psychopathy with mild to moderate levels of psychopathic traits, which in turn are assumed to be associated with lower negative outcomes for the individual (Lilienfeld et al., 2015). The model provides an incremental conceptualization of the link between psychopathy and success: the higher the level of psychopathy, the greater the degree of negative outcomes. As noted by Lilienfeld et al. (2015), this model has significant conceptual problems. First, the model adheres to a narrow conceptualization of success by equating it only with the absence of negative outcomes and ignoring the possibility that success may reflect superior functioning relative to most people. Second, the adoption of an additive model minimizes the potential interplay between psychopathic traits and their link to success, as well as the potential interaction between psychopathic traits and variables external to psychopathy that may influence success.

The second model, *the differential-configuration* model, presumes that psychopathy is an amalgam of two or more distinct traits rather than a unitary construct and that successful and unsuccessful psychopathy differ in their constituent traits (Lilienfeld et al., 2015). According to this model, the interpersonal-affective features of psychopathy are considered to be etiologically distinct from the component of antisocial behavior. Because these two trait dimensions are thought to reflect distinct etiologies, certain individuals could exhibit an elevation in one dimension but not in the other. Thus, a noncriminal psychopath would present elevated levels of interpersonal-affective traits but reduced or normal-range levels of traits related to antisocial deviance. According to this view, the specific configuration of high and low psychopathic traits determines whether a behavior will be successful or not. In certain configurations, behavior will tend to be more successful, but in other configurations, it will tend to be less successful, depending on the extent to which the configuration ameliorates the maladaptive outcomes of psychopathy (Lilienfeld et al., 2015). For example, it may be that high callousness and low impulsivity produce a more successful behavior than low callousness and high impulsivity because an individual is able to regulate his or her behavior better in the former instance than in the latter. Note the level of psychopathy for both scenarios is identical from the differential-severity (i.e., additive) perspective; thus, this model would fail to account for different patterns of behavior. In contrast, the differential-configuration model can account for different patterns of behavior because whether traits lead to success depends on other associated traits (Steinert et al., 2017).

Although the differential-configuration perspective can account better for the pattern of findings in the above example, any interpretation requires the assumption that psychopathy can be high even when callousness is low. However, this assumption introduces a major limitation. By assuming that differential configurations of core psychopathic traits can differentially predict success, one essentially alters the meaning of psychopathy. In essence, the differential-configuration model of successful psychopathy requires one to compromise the theoretical integrity of the construct of psychopathy because one must abandon the notion that psychopathy consists of a set of core traits that transcends successful and unsuccessful variants of psychopathy (Steinert et al., 2017).

The third model is the *moderated-expression model*. It defines successful behavior as an interaction between psychopathic traits and various moderating variables. According to this model, one or several compensatory processes alter the association between psychopathy and crime. The model suggests that criminal and non-criminal psychopathic individuals share both etiology and severity; however, intervening variables account for the alternative manifestations. This premise assumes a compensatory process by which the antisocial behaviors of incarcerated psychopaths are the consequence of their psychopathic personality (Hall & Benning, 2006; Wall, Sellbom, & Goodwin, 2013). These moderating variables are considered compensatory environmental factors or dispositional characteristics external to psychopathy and can attenuate the negative behavioral outcomes associated with high psychopathy. Possible compensatory factors include (but are not limited to) intelligence, exceptional talent, educational opportunity, socioeconomic status, highly effective socialization, or independent aspects of temperament (Hall & Benning, 2006; Smith, Lilienfeld, Coffey, & Dabbs, 2013).

This model has some advantages over the differential-severity model. Namely, the moderated-expression model is open to the intricate interplay between psychopathic traits and other moderating variables involved in reaching success, and it assumes that success is possible even with high levels of psychopathy, depending on the degree of buffering offered by the moderating variables. The model is also advantageous as compared with the differential-configuration model because it allows consideration of successful psychopathy regardless of the traits that are assumed to be the constituents of the core of psychopathy. Specifically, the model makes it possible to define which traits are core psychopathic traits and which are external to psychopathy based on theoretical preference and then considers whether the external traits serve as moderators of the link between the psychopathic traits and successful behavioral outcomes. The moderated-expression model thus maintains the theoretical integrity of the psychopathy construct provided that one explicitly states which traits are necessary to define the construct's essential nature (Lilienfeld et al., 2015; Steinert et al., 2017).

Several disadvantages of the moderated-expression model are noteworthy. First, the present conceptualizations of the model assume some form of buffering of the inherently maladaptive characteristics of psychopathy. As in the differential-severity model, the notion that moderating variables can counteract maladaptive qualities of psychopathy seems to focus on success in terms of achieving average, rather than superior, functioning relative to others. As in the differential-severity and differential-configuration models, a second disadvantage of the moderated-expression model is that it downplays the potential of the *context* to exert a moderating influence on the link between psychopathic traits and successful behavior. Instead, it overstates dispositional moderators and prior learning at the expense of situational moderators. Yet what is deemed successful in one situation may be considered unsuccessful in another. For example, traits of emotional callousness and interpersonal manipulation may be beneficial in certain competitive situations, such as in political or business arenas, but those same traits may be maladaptive in many cooperative situations, such as team sports or research collaborations (Steinert et al., 2017).

The approach of this book is that the model that explains best the phenomenon of corporate psychopaths is the moderated-expression model. Following the logic of this model, it can be argued that bright or well-disciplined individuals may recognize and avoid the pitfalls of serious antisocial behavior and instead express their psychopathic tendencies via socially sanctioned outlets, such as business. These individuals may even excel in their legal pursuits, in which case they may be considered truly successful psychopaths (Hall & Benning, 2006). This theory may explain why some psychopaths demonstrate severe antisocial tendencies and end up in prison, while others, who, as already mentioned, are sometimes referred to as successful psychopaths, are able to see that easier gains can be made by applying their ruthless skills in the commercial arena (Boddy, 2011).

The Motivation of Corporate Psychopaths

There are indications in research that the attractiveness of the business world to psychopaths can be found early in their educational background. Vedel and Thomsen (2017) examined whether there are pre-existing dark triad differences across academic majors. For this purpose, they surveyed a sample of newly enrolled students (n = 487) in different academic majors (psychology, economics/business, law, and political science), and their mean scores were compared. The findings showed that economics/business students scored higher on all dark triad traits than psychology and political science students. The differences were particularly large when economics/business students were compared with psychology students. Thus, the economics/business students were the "darkest" group, the psychology students were the "brightest" group, and the law and political science students were more similar than expected and fell somewhere in the middle. Vedel and Thomsen (2017) importantly mentioned that these personality group differences were already present at enrollment and therefore not due to socialization processes in the higher education institute.

Why do corporate psychopaths work for organizations and corporations? According to Boddy (2006), they do so because they are attracted to positions of power. Motivated by a desire to win what they see as being the "game" of life and by a desire for power and to gain wealth and prestige, organizational psychopaths gravitate to wherever these can be found, and this often means that they are drawn to large organizations. They are likely to be attracted to positions of influence and thus might be slightly over-represented in leadership and top management positions (Schyns, 2015). Organizational psychopaths can be found in positions that entail control over other people and where the opportunity for self-enrichment exists (Boddy, 2006). The destructive behaviors of corporate psychopaths are amplified because, through their skill of manipulation and the cultivation of power networks, they are able to move up the corporate hierarchy to gain positions of power and influence well above their actual managerial abilities (Babiak, 2000; Boddy, 2011).

Successful, subclinical, industrial psychopaths can be very successful at work. If they are clever and presentable, their superficial charm and boldness may benefit them well, particularly in business situations that are rapidly changing. Furthermore, stress may push people "over the line" from people with a "weak conscience" and taste for excitement into subclinical and even psychopathic behavior. Indeed, some of the psychopath's traits can be adaptive in work settings, such as the business world (Smith & Lilienfeld, 2013). What seems to make psychopaths "successful" at work is that they are good at creating an illusion of success at the expense of honest work (Chiaburu, Muñoz, & Gardner, 2013).

With attributes and qualities such as charisma, confidence, persuasiveness, and courage, the characteristics of successful corporate psychopaths could initially be confused with the espoused behaviors of effective charismatic leaders. However, corporate psychopaths take little heed of criticism, may commit to risky or unwise ventures, are unlikely to nurture future talent, do not create a harmonious team, and incur the loss of talented employees (Gudmundsson & Southey, 2011). Paradoxically, psychopathic managers often rise rapidly through the organizational ranks into positions of power. Gudmundsson and Southey (2011) mentioned Babiak (2000), who claimed that organizational chaos provides the necessary stimulation and breeding ground for corporate psychopaths, satisfying their thrill-seeking behavior, creating avenues for demonstrating their charm, and providing sufficient cover for their psychopathic manipulation and abuse of power. Structurally, the absence of institutionalized rules or formal limits on leader prerogatives, delegated authority, goal abstraction, the strict control that leaders have of the circulation of information, and reward systems that value lifting profits and stock prices above all else enables, and to some degree fosters, the deviant behavior of the corporate psychopaths, giving them the necessary latitude for destructive leadership behavior. It is easy to understand why some characteristics of the mischievous person are particularly attractive: they are stable extraverts or sanguine and are open to experience; their low level of agreeableness may make them seem courageous and able to confront poor performance, but their low conscientious scores may cause a problem unless they are particularly intelligent or their support is good (Furnham & Crump, 2016).

The Recruitment of Corporate Psychopaths

How do organizational psychopaths enter organizations? Corporate psychopaths look and dress like any other business people. They can be very persuasive and fun to be around and so are able to do well at recruitment interviews. Their charm in particular means that they come across well at job and promotion interviews and inspire people's confidence in them. This confidence means that they can easily enter and do well in organizations and corporations. These psychopaths present the traits of intelligence and success to which many people aspire (and they thus come across as proficient and desirable employees). The fact that they are accomplished liars helps them obtain the jobs they want (Boddy, 2015).

Another explanation of the way psychopaths penetrate work organizations is that corporations want to recruit employees who are energetic, charming, and fast moving because they expect such employees to bring their charm and energy to the workplace for the benefit of the company. Psychopaths may appear to be energetic and fast moving and can present themselves in a good light because of their ability to tell interesting, plausible, and flattering stories about themselves (Boddy, 2011). Corporate psychopaths are thus recruited into organizations because they make a distinctive positive impression during the first meeting (Babiak, 2000).

They appear to be alert, friendly, and easy to get along with and talk to. Corporate psychopaths present themselves as the type of people one would like to be friends with and to work alongside. They appear to possess good abilities and to be emotionally well-adjusted and reasonable, and these traits make them attractive to those in charge of hiring staff within organizations. According to evolutionary psychology, humans have a desire to be liked and approved of in order to gain social advantages and supportive relationships with parents and friends and to attract mates. Psychopaths are aware of this need and use it to present themselves as people who can help, befriend, and aid others. They make themselves attractive to know, and this facilitates the building of support networks for themselves (Boddy, 2006).

Up the Corporate Ladder

Penetrating the organization is only the first step for many corporate psychopaths. Corporate psychopathy theory posits that changes in the speed of personnel turnover within corporations make it easier for psychopaths to advance because there is not enough time for colleagues to recognize their destructive character traits. Psychologists argue that corporations, by using less structured and longitudinal methods of personnel assessment, facilitate their rise because the possible barriers to their advancement are removed. In such an environment, the superficial charm of corporate psychopaths, together with their ability to present a false persona of competence and commitment, makes them appear ideal leaders. This is particularly true for those higher in rank than the corporate psychopaths, who do not interact with them on a day-to-day basis and therefore do not know them well (Boddy et al., 2015; Furtner, Maran, & Rauthmann, 2017).

When in an organization, corporate psychopaths are very successful in promoting themselves with or without the support of the organizational environment because of their charm and ability to look friendly and even exciting (Boddy, 2011). They are reportedly good at ingratiating themselves with people by telling them what they want to hear. Being accomplished liars helps them obtain the jobs they want. Corporate psychopaths can continue their strategies for a long time before being discovered, during which time they establish groups of supporters and other defenses to protect their positions. The psychopathic traits of manipulativeness and cold-heartedness are the traits that are least discernible to others, and this can help psychopaths appear fun-loving and interpersonally attractive. The personal charm of corporate psychopaths means that they make a good impression at promotion interviews and can inspire senior managers' confidence in them (Babiak, 2000). All this poise and apparent attractiveness eases their rise through the ranks of management, giving them opportunities to exploit their work positions for their own ends (Boddy, 2011; Furtner et al., 2017). Organizational psychopaths who reach the top of organizations can be assumed to be highly intelligent, as well as manipulative. High intelligence in psychopaths seems to enhance their destructive potential (Boddy, 2006).

Corporate psychopaths are better equipped to rise to high corporate positions also because they are ruthless, unemotional, and without empathy, and they are fully prepared to lie and, for example, to claim the credit for the good work of other people as if it were their own achievement (Boddy et al., 2015; Boddy, 2016a). They also have fewer other time commitments and constraints because they have a lower number of emotional attachments to other people than normal people have. As mentioned earlier, they can also appear attractive candidates for hiring and promotion because they are extroverted, popular, likeable, and confidence inspiring, as well as being smartly and appealingly dressed. In line with this viewpoint, psychopathic managers have indeed been found to occupy leadership positions.

Another tactic used by corporate psychopaths for self-promotion after entering an organization is to identify a potential support network of patrons who can be flattered and befriended to help them ascend to senior jobs. They also identify pawns who can be used and manipulated as necessary as well as potential opponents who may try to block their rise if these people are not already undermined, disenfranchised, and emasculated (Boddy, 2011). Corporate psychopaths then manipulate their way up the corporate ladder, using pawns and shedding patrons as these people are superseded and no longer needed. Boddy (2015) cited Babiak and Hare's (2006) description of how corporate psychopaths advance. According to them, two factions develop in an organization when a corporate psychopath starts to ascend to power. One faction comprises the supporters, pawns, and patrons of the psychopath. The other faction consists of their detractors, those who realize they have been used and abused or that the company is in danger (Babiak & Hare, 2006). The result is a confrontation, stated Babiak and Hare, during which the detractors are outmaneuvered and ultimately removed and the psychopath ascends to power unopposed. In short, when they are inside organizations, corporate psychopaths have the personal and social abilities to rise to leadership positions. In support of this contention, Spencer and Byrne (2016) found in their study that senior-level managers possess greater levels of primary psychopathy than mid-level managers and low-level employees.

In short, successful psychopaths have all the necessary tools to convince organizations to hire them, to begin with, and then to promote them. After they have entered the organization, they start working to accomplish their personal goals, using their tactics and causing damage to the organization and its employees. Individuals with psychopathic traits successfully enter the mainstream workforce and enjoy profitable careers in organizations (especially in large corporations in the midst of rapid growth or chaotic change) by lying, manipulating, and discrediting their coworkers (Gao &

Raine, 2010). Although suggestions on how to be aware of and defend oneself against these predators are provided, it is extremely difficult to detect and keep a distance from sociopaths and psychopaths in business, regardless of how educated or astute one is through purposeful manipulation and damage to their relationships or social status within a group (Gao & Raine, 2010).

Corporate Psychopaths in Leadership Positions

The issue of psychopaths in public and corporate leadership positions has also gained some prominence in the popular press. Popular magazines, such as *Psychology Today*, in dealing with workplace issues and psychology, discuss the links between leadership and psychopathy. Against the background of recurring crises in the leadership of financial and commercial organizations, leadership has been described as being in a state of miserable failure (Boddy, 2016b). It has been reported that research into leadership is similarly in a state of crisis as it struggles to understand and explain the events around such phenomena as the global financial crisis and its continuing repercussions. Commentators on leadership have openly wondered why bad leaders are able to emerge in corporations and climb the corporate ladder to senior positions. It appears that this is possible because toxic leaders can, through careful manipulation of their image and presentation, appear to be glittering examples of ideal leaders who promise a golden future to the organizations they profess to serve (Babiak, 2000; Boddy, 2016a). As an example, Boddy (2016b) cited Lipman-Blumen (2004), who contended that toxic leaders emerge because they are unafraid to put themselves forward; they know how to appeal to the psychological needs of others for security, authority, inclusion, and acceptance. In doing so, they appear to be strong, capable, and determined, thus influencing others to follow and support them. According to them, recent research results suggest that in times of turmoil and uncertainty, people tend to back strong leaders who would be seen, in more normal times, as unacceptably authoritarian. In uncertain environments, followers prefer leaders who are confident, extrovert, assertive, and dominant.

According to Boddy et al. (2015), the corporate psychopathy theory has provided one means of understanding the increasing rise of psychopathic managers as toxic and bullying leaders in western capitalist organizations. With their conscience-free approach to life and willingness to lie to present themselves in the best possible light, corporate psychopaths are to some extent products of the modern business world. In particular, the increasing pace of business and the fast turnover of personnel, combined with the relatively shallow appointment procedures, which are unable to uncover their personality flaws, has allowed them to advance. Furthermore, Western business has promoted psychopathic managers because of their ruthless ambition to "get the job done." However, as they attain senior positions, corporate psychopaths become architects of ruthlessness as they create a culture of extremes. Their characteristics of being ultra-rational, financially oriented managers with no emotional concern for, or empathy with, other employees mark them as apparently useful to the style of capitalism that is only interested in making profit.

Corporate psychopaths seek leadership positions because of their desire to access the associated power, influence, prestige, and money. Gudmundsson and Southey (2011) cited Goldman (2006), who stated: "Trivializing pathologies and perceiving them as normal disturbances in the workplace is potentially quite detrimental in a volatile workplace already embroiled in bullying, toxic behaviors, aggression, violence, and what has recently been identified as organizational terrorism. Undiagnosed or mis-diagnosed pathologies in our leaders are a precursor to ever escalating organizational dysfunction" (p. 410). As the consequences of corporate psychopathic behavior are extreme, both financially for the organiza-tions and emotionally for those who work with them, it is important that leadership research continues its endeavor to understand this dark side of leadership.

Gudmundsson and Southey (2011) cited Pech and Slade (2007), who, having explored why organizations promote such leaders, suggested that organizational members tolerate these destructive practices because cul-turally and structurally complex cultures favor manipulative, egotistical, and self-centered managerial behavior. Furthermore, if these executives are delivering results and meeting corporate business objectives, these negative tendencies may be overlooked. Not surprisingly, the corporate psychopath is an elusive study target. Accordingly, there is little empirical work examining the interaction of successful corporate psychopaths and their environment. Studies of leader behavior found a positive relationship between corporate psychopathy and the laissez-faire leadership style, a type of leadership that has been identified as destructive in nature. A negative relationship was also being found between corporate psychopathy and transformational leadership, which is considered the most effective style (Mathieu & Babiak, 2016b). Babiak et al. (2010) found that senior executives who scored high on psychopathy were viewed as displaying both adaptive and maladaptive leadership behavior. It has also been suggested that psychopaths have an inclination toward white-collar crime, such as fraud, as well as toward irre-sponsible leadership, and that they ultimately cause their followers psycho-logical distress. However, relatively few insights are available from clinical psychopathy or industrial psychology studies to suggest how successful cor-porate psychopaths may behave in specific business situations. As research on destructive leadership continues to evolve, it is worthwhile heeding the warnings voiced by scholars researching corporate psychopathy. It should be noted that a thorough review of all dark triad personalities and leader-ship is presented in chapter 8.

The Devastating Effect of Corporate Psychopaths on an Organization and Its Employees

Because of the possible damages caused by possibly toxic leaders, the existence of leaders with personality disorders and their potential impact on corporate life has also emerged as a subject of interest for academics and practitioners in the field of business. Consequently, the relation between leaders with personality disorders and dysfunctional management has been increasingly reported in the literature (Cohen, 2016). When in leadership and managerial positions, the damage that corporate psychopaths cause to the organization is almost inevitable. Preliminary evidence suggests that the deleterious impact of psychopaths on individual organizational followers and on organizations as a whole is severe and that psychopaths at work are ultimately destructive. For example, some commentators have attributed the recent financial crises to the ruthless greed of corporate psychopaths. Psychopaths in corporations are associated also with low levels of corporate social responsibility and job satisfaction; with organizational withdrawal, bullying, and conflict in the workplace; and with heightened levels of organizational constraints. This has implications for human resources and the resource-based view of a firm regarding the management of psychopaths and minimizing staff turnover (Boddy, 2016a). The employment of corporate psychopaths in supervisory positions has been shown to be associated with lower job satisfaction, higher work–family conflict, and greater psychological distress in the employees they supervise (Mathieu & Babiak, 2016b). In the following, two main forms of damage to the organization are discussed: damage to the organization itself and damage to its employees.

Organizational Damage

Although corporate psychopaths are often regarded as stars and awarded for their short-term or apparent financial performance by those above them, the findings of Boddy et al. (2015) illustrate that their behavior is not aligned with the longer term success of their employing organizations. The researchers' findings showed that corporate psychopaths engage in fraud and are unconcerned with the organizational destruction that they create. Boddy et al. contended that their findings support earlier findings of quantitative studies, in which yelling, shouting, and the undermining of employees via public humiliations were all evident. Their findings also support the view that corporate psychopaths overstate their qualifications and abilities, claiming degrees from prestigious universities and management competencies that they do not possess. Furthermore, corporate psychopaths use divide-and-conquer tactics to maintain control of employees, unions, and boards while jeopardizing client service quality and organizational outcomes through their erratic and fickle management plans.

According to Boddy (2014), corporate psychopaths manifest their parasitic lifestyles by engaging in such behavior as claiming the successful work efforts of their colleagues as their own. Following the equity theory, this would infringe on the perceived fairness of the workplace and would therefore influence measures of workplace conflict. It may also be expected to influence counterproductive work behavior. Corporate psychopaths have been identified as agents of organizational chaos, and therefore, levels of uncivil behavior, such as rudeness, and of conflict are higher in the presence of corporate psychopaths than otherwise. Successful psychopaths are also assumed to have the greatest potential to transform a company's organizational culture to one of their liking, which others must follow or else leave the company. Psychopaths have a destructive effect on teamwork and job satisfaction and therefore on productivity. This jeopardizes the decision-making capability of the organizations for which they work and the example they set adversely influences the moral and ethical behavior of the entire organization (Boddy, 2011).

The cold-heartedness and manipulativeness of psychopaths are reported to be traits that are the least discernible to others, allowing psychopaths to gain other people's confidence and facilitating their entry into positions where they can gain the most benefits for themselves and do the greatest harm to others (Boddy, 2014). The types of organizational behavior in which a corporation managed by psychopaths indulges could include harsh treatment of employees, sudden termination of employment contracts, unhealthy and environmentally damaging production practices, dangerous working conditions, and the breaking of human rights conventions and the laws of employment. According to Boddy, this marks psychopaths who work in corporations as potential agents of organizational and environmental destruction.

Corporate psychopaths systematically and cold-bloodedly eliminate anyone standing in their way to the top of the organizational hierarchy, regardless of how valuable these people are to the corporation. Although they are not psychotic (delusional), they are ruthless and a source of danger for those around them and the companies that employ them (Boddy, 2011). The presence of corporate psychopaths in organizations affects the levels of employee satisfaction, as well as workplace conflict and bullying, firm performance, decision making by the management involving morality, and whether matters such as social responsibility are even considered. Boddy also contended, based on his research results, that employees who work in organizations where corporate psychopaths are present clearly take steps to minimize their exposure to adverse working conditions. They more frequently take sick leave when in fact they are not ill than people working in organizations where corporate psychopaths are not present. They also take longer breaks almost twice as frequently as allowed and leave work early more than twice as frequently. Finally, Boddy et al. (2015) found in their qualitative study that employees working with psychopaths are mistreated, loyal employees are fired or resign, resources are misallocated or stolen, business plans are capriciously rejected, management consultants are hired needlessly, and internal intellectual resources are abused or unused. Employee well-being decreases, organizational confusion replaces a sense of direction, organizational ethics decline, and the corporate's reputation is damaged.

Personal Harm

Psychopathy has long been associated with aggressive behavior and bullying (Boddy, 2016b). The literature relates to bullying as one of the main strategies of corporate psychopaths to achieve their goals when confronting individuals in the organization. For example, corporate psychopaths have been strongly associated with bullying, while the results of research on the dark triad have shown that bullying is most strongly related to psychopaths, followed by Machiavellians and then by narcissists in the third place. In particular, research results show that psychopaths in the corporate sphere are the source of between a quarter and more than a third of all workplace bullying. Furthermore, corporate psychopaths can engage in the bullying of numerous victims over many days and weeks (Boddy, 2016b). Recent research on the frequency of psychopathic bullying has indicated that workplace psychopaths may be responsible for 26% to 35% of all bullying (Boddy & Taplin, 2017). However, according to qualitative findings, workplace conflict and bullying may be considerably more frequent than currently estimated, when the highly skewed nature, and in particular the high frequency, of psychopathic bullying are taken into account. According to Boddy and Taplin (2017), the collection of actual numbers would be the most accurate and useful method to indicate the frequency of bullying.

Furthermore, the literature on psychopathy and bullying suggests that bullying can be used to intimidate others and scare them into confronting the corporate psychopath involved, thus allowing the corporate psychopath more leeway. Bullying is also used by corporate psychopaths to humiliate subordinates, possibly because many psychopaths enjoy hurting people, and to confuse and disorientate those who may be a threat to the corporate psychopath's activities (Boddy, 2014). It distracts attention from the corporate psychopath's activities that may otherwise be noticed by personnel whose work methods are normal. It seems likely, then, that bullying is associated with the presence of psychopaths. In support of this notion, Boddy (2014) found that people with high scores on a psychopathy rating scale were more likely to engage in bullying, crime, and drug abuse than others. Boddy (2014) also mentioned that employee well-being declines when the manager is not trustworthy and that as corporate psychopaths are characterized as liars, manipulators, and deceivers, they can be assumed to be untrustworthy.

Valentine, Fleischman, and Godkin (2016) found in a sample of sales personnel that bullying experiences and psychopathic attitudes were positively related. They also found that the positive associations identified with unethical corporate values and both bullying experiences and psychopathy underscored the negative normative impact of an unethical culture on employees. Significant negative associations were found between psychopathy and several issue-based ethical reasoning constructs. Valentine et al. concluded that covert bullying and latent psychopathy are pertinent to sales force behavior. Finally, Boddy et al. (2015) contended that corporate psychopaths rely on the good work of others, claiming their ideas, presentations, and plans as their own or rely on management consultants to do their work. Employees report that they hate to work in these environments and withdraw from these extreme workplaces via claiming high levels of sick leave and leave due to stress and by seeking alternative employment. A minority even withdraw from the workforce with no other job in hand.

This chapter concludes with somewhat pessimistic tone. Boddy (2006) discussed an interesting aspect regarding psychopaths, namely, why do organizational psychopaths not retire after they have become rich? This is because the literature concerning organizational psychopaths observed that organizational psychopaths do not retire when they become very wealthy, which is perplexing until the nature of organizational psychopaths is considered. According to Hare (1994, 1999), psychopaths' appetite for power and control is insatiable. In other words, they never feel that they have enough power, money, or prestige. This could be the reason why such people in the corporate world do not retire voluntarily regardless of how wealthy and successful they become. Playing the game of corporate power politics gives them a thrill, and nothing in their lives can replace that. Being emotionally shallow, they probably have few real friends or a family (promiscuity often ends in their divorce, and friends are discarded as they lose their usefulness) with whom they have emotional ties. A family day at the seaside is just not appealing to them compared with the satisfaction to be gained from another day of manipulating and abusing people at work. Speculation as to what drives organizational psychopaths includes the notion that they pursue wealth and status to compensate for an internal sense of worthlessness and despair. This may serve as a clue as to why they never consider themselves rich enough to retire; instead of an emotionally fulfilled life, they have an ever-extendable wallet that can never be full enough and a desire for power that can never be completely satisfied and would certainly not be satisfied by retirement (Boddy, 2006). This definitely does not sound optimistic for those in an organization who are waiting for corporate psychopaths to retire. They will do anything they can to hold on to their position.

References

Akın, M., Amil, O., & Özdevecioğlu, M. (2016). Is your manager a psychopath? An evaluation of the relationship between the personality types of managers and workers and the levels of psychopathy. *Procedia-Social and Behavioral Sciences*, 221, 76–85.

Babiak, P. (1995). When psychopaths go to work: A case study of an industrial psychopath. *Applied Psychology, 44*(2), 171–188.

Babiak, P. (2000). Psychopathic manipulation at work. In C. B. Gacono (Ed.), *The Clinical and Forensic Assessment of Psychopathy: A Practitioner's Guide* (pp. 287–312). Mahwah, NJ: Lawrence Erlbaum Associates, Inc.

Babiak, P., & Hare, R. D. (2006). *Snakes in Suits: When Psychopaths Go to Work.* New York: Regan Books.

Babiak, P., Neumann, C. S., & Hare, R. D. (2010). Corporate psychopathy: Talking the walk. *Behavioral Sciences & the Law, 28*(2), 174–193.

Boddy, C. R. (2006). The dark side of management decisions: Organizational psychopaths. *Management Decision, 44*, 1461–1475.

Boddy, C. R. (2010a). Corporate psychopaths and organizational type. *Journal of Public Affairs, 10*(4), 300–312.

Boddy, C. R. (2010b). *Corporate Psychopaths in Australian Workforce: Their Influence on Organizational Outcomes.* Perth: Curtin University of Technology.

Boddy, C. R. (2011). Corporate psychopaths, bullying and unfair supervision in the workplace. *Journal of Business Ethics, 100*(3), 367–379.

Boddy, C. R. (2014). Corporate psychopaths, conflict, employee affective well-being and counterproductive work behavior. *Journal of Business Ethics, 121*(1), 107–121.

Boddy, C. R. (2015). Organizational psychopaths: A ten-year update. *Management Decision, 53*(10), 2407–2432.

Boddy, C. R. (2016a). Unethical 20th century business leaders: Were some of them corporate psychopaths? The case of Robert Maxwell. *International Journal of Public Leadership, 12*(2), 76–93.

Boddy, C. R. (2016b). Psychopathy screening for public leadership. *International Journal of Public Leadership, 12*(4), 254–274.

Boddy, C. R., Ladyshewsky, R., & Galvin, P. G. (2010). The influence of corporate psychopaths on corporate social responsibility and organizational commitment to employees. *Journal of Business Ethics, 97*(1), 1–19.

Boddy, C., Miles, D., Sanyal, C., & Hartog, M. (2015). Extreme managers, extreme workplaces: Capitalism, organizations and corporate psychopaths. *Organization, 22*(4), 530–551.

Boddy, C., & Taplin, R. (2017). A note on workplace psychopathic bullying: Measuring its frequency and severity. *Aggression and Violent Behavior, 34*, 117–119.

Caponecchia, C., Sun, A., & Wyatt, A. (2011). Psychopaths' at work? Implications of lay persons' use of labels and behavioural criteria for psychopathy. *Journal of Business Ethics, 107*(4), 399–408.

Chiaburu, D. S., Muñoz, G. J., & Gardner, R. G. (2013). How to spot a careerist early on: Psychopathy and exchange ideology as predictors of careerism? *Journal of Business Ethics, 118*(3), 473–486.

Cleckley, H. (1941/1988). *The Mask of Sanity (5th ed.), Private Printing for Educational Use by Emily Cleckley 1988* (Formerly first published by C. V. Mosley Co. in 1941). Georgia: Augusta.

Cohen, A. (2016). Are they among us? A conceptual framework of the relationship between the dark triad personality and counterproductive work behaviors (CWBs). *Human Resource Management Review, 26*(1), 69–85.

Deutschman, A. (2005). Is your boss a psychopath? *Fast Company, 96*, 44–51.

Fennimore, A., & Sementelli, A. (2016). Public entrepreneurship and sub-clinical psychopaths: A conceptual frame and implications. *International Journal of Public Sector Management, 29*(6), 612–634.

Furnham, A., & Crump, J. (2016). A Big Five facet analysis of a psychopath: The validity of the HDS mischievous scale of sub-clinical psychopathy. *Scandinavian Journal of Psychology, 57*, 117–121.

Furtner, M. R., Maran, T., & Rauthmann, J. F. (2017). Dark leadership: The role of leaders' dark triad personality traits. In *Leader Development Deconstructed* (pp. 75–99). New York: Springer, Cham.

Gao, Y., & Raine, A. (2010). Successful and unsuccessful psychopaths: A neurobiological model. *Behavioral Sciences & the Law, 28*(2), 194–210.

Goldman, A. (2006). High toxicity leadership: Borderline personality disorder and the dysfunctional organization. *Journal of Managerial Psychology, 21*(8), 733–746.

Griffin, R. W., & Lopez, Y. P. (2005). "Bad behavior" in organizations: A review and typology for future research. *Journal of Management, 31*(6), 988–1005.

Gudmundsson, A., & Southey, G. (2011). Leadership and the rise of the corporate psychopath: What can business schools do about the "snakes inside"? *E-Journal of Social & Behavioral Research in Business, 2*(2), 18–27.

Hall, J. R., & Benning, S. D. (2006). The "successful" psychopath: Adaptive and subclinical manifestations of psychopathy in the general population. In C. Patrick (Ed.), *Handbook of Psychopathy* (pp. 459–478). New York: Guilford Press.

Hare, R. D. (1991). *The Hare Psychopathy Checklist Revised.* New York, NY: Multi-Health Systems Inc.

Hare, R. D. (1994). Predators: The disturbing world of the psychopaths among us. *Psychology Today, 27*(1), 54–61.

Hare, R. D. (1999). *Without Conscience: The Disturbing World of the Psychopaths among Us.* New York, NY: Guilford Press.

Hare, R. D. (2003). *Manual for the Revised Psychopathy Checklist* (2nd ed.). Toronto, Ontario, Canada: Multi-Health Systems.

Lilienfeld, S. O., Watts, A. L., & Smith, S. F. (2015). Successful psychopathy: A scientific status report. *Current Directions in Psychological Science, 24*(4), 298–303.

Lipman-Blumen, J. (2004). *The Allure of Toxic Leaders: Why We Follow Destructive Bosses and Corrupt Politicians: And How We Can Survive Them.* Oxford: Oxford University Press.

Mathieu, C., & Babiak, P. (2016a). Validating the B-Scan self: A self-report measure of psychopathy in the workplace. *International Journal of Selection and Assessment, 24*(3), 272–284.

Mathieu, C., & Babiak, P. (2016b). Corporate psychopathy and abusive supervision: Their influence on employees' job satisfaction and turnover intentions. *Personality and Individual Differences, 91*, 102–106.

Mathieu, C., Neumann, C., Babiak, P., & Hare, R. D. (2015). Corporate psychopathy and the full-range leadership model. *Assessment, 22*(3), 267–278.

Neumann, C. S., & Hare, R. D. (2008). Psychopathic traits in a large community sample: Links to violence, alcohol use, and intelligence. *Journal of Consulting and Clinical Psychology, 76*(5), 893–899.

Pech, R. J., & Slade, B. W. (2007). Organizational sociopaths: Rarely challenged, often promoted: Why? *Society and Business Review, 2*(3), 254–269.

Schyns, B. (2015). Dark personality in the workplace: Introduction to the special issue. *Applied Psychology: An International Review, 64*(1), 1–14.

Smith, S. F., & Lilienfeld, S. O. (2013). Psychopathy in the workplace: The knowns and unknowns. *Aggression and Violent Behavior, 18*, 204–218.

Smith, S. F., Lilienfeld, S. O., Coffey, K., & Dabbs, J. M. (2013). Are psychopaths and heroes twigs off the same branch? Evidence from college, community, and presidential samples. *Journal of Research in Personality, 47*(5), 634–646.

Smith, S. F., Watts, A., & Lilienfeld, S. (2014). On the trail of the elusive successful psychopath. *Psychological Assessment, 15*, 340–350.

Spencer, R. J., & Byrne, M. K. (2016). Relationship between the extent of psychopathic features among corporate managers and subsequent employee job satisfaction. *Personality and Individual Differences, 101*, 440–445.

Steinert, S. W., Lishner, D. A., Vitacco, M. J., & Hong, P. Y. (2017). Conceptualizing successful psychopathy: An elaboration of the moderated-expression model. *Aggression and Violent Behavior, 36*, 44–51.

Valentine, S., Fleischman, G., & Godkin, L. (2016). Villains, victims, and verisimilitudes: An exploratory study of unethical corporate values, bullying experiences, psychopathy, and selling professionals' ethical reasoning. *Journal of Business Ethics*, 1–20.

Vedel, A., & Thomsen, D. K. (2017). The dark triad across academic majors. *Personality and Individual Differences, 116*, 86–91.

Wall, T. D., Sellbom, M., & Goodwin, B. E. (2013). Examination of intelligence as a compensatory factor in non-criminal psychopathy in a non-incarcerated sample. *Journal of Psychopathology and Behavioral Assessment, 35*(4), 450–459.

Westerlaken, K. M., & Woods, P. R. (2013). The relationship between psychopathy and the full range leadership model. *Personality and Individual Differences, 54*(1), 41–46.

Yang, Y., Raine, A., Lencz, T., Bihrle, S., LaCasse, L., & Colletti, P. (2005). Volume reduction in prefrontal gray matter in unsuccessful criminal psychopaths. *Biological Psychiatry, 57*(10), 1103–1108.

5 Dark Triad Personalities and Counterproductive Work Behavior

It is argued that personality measurement has considerably more to offer than only the prediction of positive work-related outcomes (Guenole, 2014) and may also be capable of predicting negative behaviors. In this respect, the dark triad can definitely be considered personalities that predict negative behaviors based on the assumption that deviant workplace behaviors may be best predicted by deviant personality traits. Counterproductive work behaviors (CWBs) are considered deviant behaviors, and our understanding of them may thus be enhanced by viewing measures of deviant or aberrant personality characteristics as predicting them. As mentioned in the introduction, the main reason for studying dark triad personalities in the workplace is their expected relationship with CWBs. Workplace deviance and CWBs probably constitute the single most popular topic in the study of dark personalities in the workplace (Spain, Harms, & LeBreton, 2014).

Moreover, there is growing evidence that the dark triad may be useful in predicting some of the variance in CWBs unaccounted by the Five-Factor Model (FFM) or integrity tests (Wu & Lebreton, 2011). The FFM has been considered one of the personal predictors of CWBs (Wu & Lebreton, 2011). However, it is criticized because it does not fully summarize the existing personality traits, particularly antisocial ones, and for focusing on a positive personality model that may limit personality research. More specifically, a potential problem of the FFM is that the positive language used to describe its components leads to its being used mainly to describe positive personality traits and not the dark side of personalities (Youli & Chao, 2015). This approach leaves a lot of room for researching dark personality traits. The dark triad breaks the theoretical frame of the FFM personalities and makes personality theories more rigorous and complete. It is reasonable and important to compare positive and dark personality clusters in the empirical field of organizational behavior. The role of positive and negative personality traits should be considered equally important. Research should focus more on dark personality clusters to expand personality theories (Youli & Chao, 2015).

Although it has been noted that similarities between particular dark characteristics and the dimensions of the FFM do exist, dark personality characteristics are often composites of more elemental aspects of the personality, and correlations may be driven by construct overreach in the FFM measures (Harms & Spain, 2015). Thus, any associations are likely to oversimplify or obscure the complicated negative relationships between the two trait categories. An additional reason for questioning the FFM as a foundation for understanding dark traits and CWBs is that it represents an incomplete taxonomy of traits. Because evaluative terms (e.g., "evil" or "dangerous") were eliminated in the early stages of the psychological research that led to the FFM, many defining characteristics of the dark personality were not captured within this model.

This chapter first presents some of the accumulated knowledge regarding the relationship between the FFM and CWBs. In the same section, the contribution of the dark triad framework to a better explanation of CWBs, that is, its additive contribution to the explanation offered by the FFM, is reviewed. In the following sections, the relationships between each of the dark triad personalities and CWBs are discussed separately, following the approach taken by this book to review each of the dark triad traits as a unique construct, based on the multidimensional approach adopted here.

The Five-Factor Model, the Dark Triad Traits, and Counterproductive Work Behaviors

As mentioned earlier, much of the existing literature is focused on using traditional measures of personality traits, such as the FFM, to predict CWBs (Wu & Lebreton, 2011), and industrial psychologists have been relying heavily on it to examine maladaptive behavior in the workplace (Guenole, 2014). The five-factor compound technique essentially involves the computation of the linear composites of the five factor facets that are related to specific personality disorders (Guenole, 2014). It should be noted that in addition to the FFM, many scholars have also relied on integrity tests to predict CWBs (Wu & Lebreton, 2011). Wu and Lebreton cited Ones, Viswesvaran, and Schmidt (1993), who reported corrected criterion-related validity estimates for predicting CWBs of 0.39 for overt integrity tests and 0.29 for personality-based integrity tests. However, the issue of integrity tests are not further discussed here because it is not the aim of this book; rather, the focus is on the dark triad traits as an addition to the FFM for predicting CWBs (Youli & Chao, 2015).

The FFM consists of five related yet distinct traits that can be further refined into specific dimensions or facets. A short description of the content of the FFM is needed for a better understanding of its relationship with CWBs. **Extraversion** consists of at least four lower order facets, including social inhibition, sociability, dominance, and energy. **Neuroticism** includes both anxious distress and irritable distress. **Conscientiousness** consists of at least six lower order facets: self-control, attention, achievement motivation, orderliness, responsibility, and conventionality. **Agreeableness** includes antagonism, prosocial tendencies, and cynicism. Finally, **openness to experience** consists of facets such as openness and intellect (Wu & Lebreton, 2011).

In the following, conceptual arguments for the expected relationship between the FFM and CWBs are presented, some of them based on Kozako, Safin, and Rahim (2013). Extraversion is a positive facet of personality because individuals high in extraversion tend to be self-confident, dominant, active, and excitement seeking. They are less likely to experience anger and therefore are more likely to demonstrate lower levels of CWBs. Agreeableness is a tendency to be compassionate and cooperative rather than suspicious and antagonistic. It is manifested in an individual's ability to inhibit disagreeable tendencies and has also been linked with orienting sensitivity, as well as sensitivity to internal, affective, and external perceptions. Therefore, it is expected that people with higher levels of agreeableness will demonstrate lower levels of CWBs. Individuals with high-level conscientiousness tend to show self-discipline and aim for achievement beyond expectations. Conscientiousness is composed of numerous characteristics associated with high-level regulation. Therefore, a negative relationship is expected between conscientiousness and CWBs. Neuroticism is the personality trait related to a person's emotional stability. Because people with this trait are less stable emotionally, their judgement might be affected negatively, and they are expected to demonstrate higher levels of CWBs. People with a higher level of openness to experience are more interested in new experiences because of their curiosity and thus are more likely to become emotionally exhausted, and this, as in the case of neuroticism, causes them to perform more CWBs (Kozako et al., 2013).

The findings regarding the relationship between the FFM and CWBs show a stable and consistent negative relationship between conscientiousness and agreeableness and CWBs and less stable relationships with the other dimensions. Salgado (2002), in a meta-analysis, reported corrected correlations between emotional stability, agreeableness, and conscientiousness, ranging between –0.06 and –0.26. Berry, Ones, and Sackett (2007) reported in their important meta-analysis negative relationships between agreeableness and interpersonal deviance (corrected correlation = –0.36), and between conscientiousness and organizational deviance (corrected correlation = –0.34). Agreeableness was also negatively related to organizational deviance with a somewhat weaker relationship (corrected correlation = –0.25). Sackett, Berry, Wiemann, and Laczo (2006) found in their meta-analysis that each of the FFM dimensions was significantly and negatively correlated with CWB, with the exception of openness to experience, which was not significantly correlated with CWB. An important finding of Berry et al. (2007) in their meta-analysis was that the FFM had in general a stronger relationship with overall deviance than justice variables. In a US sample, Bolton, Becker, and Barber (2010) found that lower levels of agreeableness and conscientiousness predicted more reports of all CWBs. A lower level of agreeableness was also associated with more interpersonally directed behaviors, while a lower level of conscientiousness was associated with more organizationally directed behaviors.

However, Guenole (2014) reported some concerns regarding the predictive validity of traditional personality-based approaches for predicting CWBs because they often explain at most 5% to 10% of the variance in CWBs (and many other organizationally valued behaviors). For example, some researchers have noted the low criterion-related validities of the FFM and suggested that the incremental validity attributed to the FFM may be overestimated and that the actual estimates may, in fact, be closer to zero. Jonason, Wee, and Li (2014), as well as Youli and Chao (2015), claimed that the FFM tends to tap "positive" aspects of people's personality better than the "negative" or "darker" side. Wu and Lebreton (2011), drawing from research on personality, social, and clinical psychology, posited that CWB research could benefit from a more systematic integration of the three dark triad traits.

The importance of the dark triad personalities is demonstrated in their ability to predict a wide variety of socially important criteria (Lee et al., 2013). The dark triad model can provide considerable incremental validity beyond that of the factors of the FFM. Moreover, the diversity of the criteria predicted by the dark triad personalities suggests that their characteristics represent important aspects of human personality. All three dark triad elements involve a tendency to manipulate individuals in pursuit of selfish gains. Therefore, it should not be surprising if these traits show important correlations with measures of outright fraud, cheating, or theft (Lee et al., 2013) and with CWBs in general. This is, in fact, the main reason for the need to study the dark triad model in theory and practice: its ability to predict behaviors in the workplace, mostly negative ones, or, to use a more technical term, its predictive validity.

Several studies support the expected strong relationship between the dark triad model and CWBs, as well as the additive contribution of the dark triad, above and beyond the contribution of the FFM. DeShong, Grant, and Mullins-Sweatt (2015) examined the FFM and the dark triad model in terms of predicting interpersonal and organizational CWBs. Their findings, based on a sample of working students, showed that the FFM domains of agreeableness and conscientiousness are related negatively to interpersonal and organizational CWBs, while neuroticism is related positively to organizational CWBs. As predicted, however, all three constructs of the dark triad were significantly related to both types of CWBs. According to them, this indicates that individuals high in any dark triad trait tend to engage in a variety of negative workplace behaviors. However, their findings showed a better fit of the FFM model than the dark triad model.

Scherer, Baysinger, Zolynsky, and Lebreton (2013) found a negative relationship between agreeableness and conscientiousness and CWBs in two samples. They also found that neuroticism was significantly and positively correlated with CWBs, and subclinical psychopathy was significantly correlated with a reported likelihood of engaging in future CWB. Notably, subclinical psychopathy predicted unique variance in future CWB beyond that predicted by the FFM traits. A similar pattern of findings was reported by Cohen and Shoval (2018) in a sample of Israeli teachers, indicating that agreeableness and conscientiousness were negatively related to CWB. Extraversion and openness did not have a significant relationship with CWB, and emotional stability was negatively related to CWB. More important, Cohen and Shoval (2018) found that their one-factor measure of the dark triad was strongly and positively related to CWBs. The dark triad scale had an incremental contribution on top of the contribution of the FFM traits.

Grijalva and Newman (2015) contended that narcissism could explain a large portion of CWB beyond the FFM because both narcissism and CWB focus on the negative side of human nature. In their study, the researchers found that narcissism explains incremental variance in CWB beyond the FFM. Grijalva and Newman (2015) concluded that for organizations interested in preventing CWB via personnel selection, narcissism should be used in combination with the FFM predictors to maximize predictive accuracy. Judge, LePine, and Rich (2006) also reported that narcissism explained a greater amount of variance in workplace deviance than any of the constructs in the FFM. All these findings strongly support the importance of the dark triad in predicting CWBs, as well as the ability of the dark triad traits to provide an incremental contribution in addition to that of the FFM traits. Naturally, there is a need for more research on this relationship.

Other studies focused on the similarities and differences between the three dark triad traits in terms of predicting CWBs. This issue concerns the question whether the three dark traits can be combined into one factor that represents all three dark traits. Muris, Merckelbach, Otgaar, and Meijer (2017) found in their meta-analysis that psychopathy is the dominant trait appearing in explanations of various types of malevolent behavior. They contended, based on their findings, that focusing specifically on psychopathy as the core antecedent of transgressive behavior is more parsimonious than taking the full spectrum of the dark triad traits into account. According to them, as things stand, the concept of the dark triad is not as simple as it may appear. DeShong, Helle, Lengel, Meyer, and Mullins-Sweatt (2017) investigated the similarity between the dark triad constructs; the relationship between the dark triad elements; and three measures of workplace behaviors: CWBs, unethical workplace behaviors, and citizenship workplace behaviors. They found that it may be difficult to differentiate between the dark triad constructs, especially between those of psychopathy and Machiavellianism, because they are all significantly correlated with CWBs and unethical workplace behaviors, and none was related to citizenship workplace behaviors. These researchers concluded that there might be a need for more adequate measures of Machiavellianism to clearly distinguish its construct from those of psychopathy and narcissism.

These findings suggest that more research is needed on how to best conceptualize the dark triad, that is, as a one-, two-, or three-dimensional concept. However, it could be argued that researchers are moving toward a consensus that narcissism is the "lightest" of the triad and that while Machiavellianism and psychopathy are very similar, psychopaths are the "darkest" of the three personalities (Boddy, Miles, Sanyal, and Hartog, 2015). For example, Stanescu and Mohorea (2016) found, in a sample of 122 Romanian employees, that only psychopathy was strongly and positively related to self-reported CWBs. No significant relationships were found between Machiavellianism and CWBs or between narcissism and CWBs. Nonetheless, whether unidimensional or multidimensional, the findings reviewed strongly support the importance and the unique contribution of the dark triad for a better understanding of CWBs and as contributing above and beyond the explanation of the FFM. The following sections review the main theories and findings on the relationship between each of the dark triad personalities and CWBs.

Psychopathy and Counterproductive Work Behavior

As mentioned, the trait of psychopathy is associated with a willingness to exploit others. Psychopaths are comfortable dominating others and have no regard for the feelings of the people they hurt. Common behaviors among subclinical psychopaths include patterns of destructive, unethical, immoral, or even illegal behaviors coupled with superficial apologies (if any) that fail to convey any sense of remorse or regret. Extant research suggests that there may be differences between how "normal" individuals are pressured into rationalizing fraud and how psychopathic and criminal individuals seek out and rationalize their exploitation of predatory opportunities (Harrison, Summers, & Mennecke, 2016). Disregard for societal norms and antisocial behavior are consistent attitudes exhibited by psychopaths. Psychopaths believe they are above the social, moral, ethical, and legal principles that govern our society. They rarely experience shame, guilt, remorse, or regret. All this can very easily lead them to perform CWBs (Babiak, 2000; Harrison et al., 2016). The conceptual arguments in the following section, present first how organizational psychopaths can engage specifically in interpersonal-oriented CWBs when working with other individuals (CWB-I) and later how they can cause damage to the organization (CWB-O).

Psychopathy and Individual Counterproductive Work Behavior

Schutte et al. (2015), following clinical and subclinical research on psychopathy, suggested that individuals with psychopathic personalities are driven by a strong desire to get ahead and do so with a disregard for getting along; thus, individuals who score highly on self-centered impulsivity (SCI) are more likely to engage in CWB-I. Those rated high in psychopathy have been characterized as exhibiting a pattern of intrinsically antisocial behaviors that are based on judgments that their own wishes and well-being are of elevated importance while, at the same time, minimizing the rights and well-being of others. Psychopathy manifests itself when a person exhibits a lack of guilt or remorse for actions that harm others. Psychopaths are impulsive and have little concern for other people or social regulatory mechanisms. They do not form meaningful personal relationships and, consequently, lack empathy, guilt, and regret when their decisions hurt others. Psychopathy is demonstrated by callous and remorseless manipulation and exploitation of others (Babiak, 2000; Hare, 1991; Lee & Ashton, 2005).

Because corporate psychopaths have little or no conscience or concern or empathy for those who work with them, it is reasonable to assume that they are not driven by any notion of social responsibility or commitment to employees. Wu and Lebreton (2011) cited Boddy (2006), who suggested that psychopaths may hurt others by distracting them from a particular task. Thus, by drawing others' attention to a matter other than the task at hand (i.e., hostility amongst coworkers), psychopaths may be better able to pursue their own agendas (Wu & Lebreton, 2011). Their tendency toward distracting others from their agendas may be associated with the CWB-I type. Moreover, research has suggested that psychopaths gain satisfaction from harming others. According to Boddy (2011), bullying is used by corporate psychopaths as a tactic to humiliate subordinates because many psychopaths enjoy hurting people emotionally or physically. Bullying is also used by corporate psychopaths as a tactic to scare, confuse, and disorient those who may be a threat to their activities. It distracts attention from their activities, which might otherwise be noticed by fellow employees if they are functioning normally. Corporate psychopaths might also use their reputation as bullies to drive their rivals away and to keep their subordinates submissive and afraid to ask questions.

These arguments lead us to expect a strong relationship between higher levels of psychopathy and higher levels of CWB-I. For example, research performed by Schutte et al. (2015) examined the relations between two facets of psychopathy, Self-Centered Impulsivity (SCI) and Fearless Dominance, and interpersonally directed CWB (CWB-I). Their findings, based on a sample of German employees from a broad range of occupations, showed that SCI was positively and significantly related to others' ratings of CWB-I.

They also found that high levels of Fearless Dominance and interpersonal influence were significantly associated with undesirable interpersonal performance (CWB-I).

Psychopathy and Organizational Counterproductive Work Behavior

Psychopaths believe that norms and rules do not apply to them and fail to take responsibility for their own actions. They are also commonly described as risk taking, remorseless, and conscienceless. In addition, when encountering what most people would classify as stressful events, psychopaths do not engage in thoughtful processing and are indifferent to consequences. It has been reported that the possibility or risk of being caught typically prevents individuals from engaging in CWBs, but these disincentives may not pose a threat to psychopaths because they do not experience guilt or consider the consequences of their actions (Wun & Lebreton, 2011). This may lead those high in psychopathy to engage in CWB-O to a greater extent than non-psychopaths.

Fraud is a particular crime that psychopaths tend to commit according to Cleckley (1941/1988), one of the first writers and researchers on psychopathy. Psychopaths are not concerned with the impact their behavior has on the emotional, financial, physical, social, or professional well-being of others. The careless and destructive ways they treat others are viewed by them as being perfectly acceptable and appropriate. Their impulsivity has a largely narcissistic tone: they act because they "want to." Although they prefer to describe their lifestyles as spontaneous, unstructured, and free-spirited, their behavior is often hasty and reckless and triggered by a whim with the sole purpose of immediate egocentric gratification. Accordingly, those rated higher in psychopathy exhibit more amoral and antisocial behaviors. Therefore, it is expected that these individuals are more likely to rationalize acts of fraud (Harrison et al., 2016), leading to severe damage to any organization. For example, psychopaths are willing to falsify financial results to gain promotion, bonuses, and other benefits and even to commit outright fraud against the company that employs them (Boddy, 2006).

Furthermore, secondary psychopathy is associated with making impulsive, short-term decisions. Decisions made for short-term benefits when individuals do not consider future effects have been linked with unethical judgment (Harrison et al., 2016). Because psychopaths lack any sense of remorse, guilt, or shame, they are capable of making decisions that put lives at risk in situations where other managers would make different, safer decisions (Boddy, 2006, 2015). Psychopaths routinely are untruthful and willing to use dishonesty to their personal advantage. Nonetheless, psychopathy may confer some degree of social advantage because it is highly associated with decisiveness and willingness to take risks; therefore, psychopaths may thrive in businesses, chaotic environments, and leadership roles in which stress is high (Harrison et al., 2016).

Psychopaths have no emotional attachment to the company for which they work or to the people with whom they work and find it easy to sack people. According to Boddy (2006, 2015), because psychopaths have no conscience and are not concerned with the financial or emotional effects of their actions on other people, they are quite willing to fire staff if this would impress the stock market, which could be passed off as a cost cutting or organizational efficiency policy. Organizational psychopaths are concerned with their own enrichment and success, not those of the organization for which they work. Therefore, corporations and organizations that employ organizational psychopaths are more likely to experience failure than others.

Because of their traits, corporate psychopaths are potential agents of corporate misbehavior and misconduct and may pose a threat to business performance, mainly to corporate social responsibility, because of their focused self-interest (Boddy, 2011). Their presence in a large firm can affect the firm's ability to make decisions that are socially responsible or ethical. Furthermore, according to Boddy, corporate psychopaths have greater need for stimulation than normal people, which may lead them to take financial, legal, or moral risks that others would not. Historically, a number of failed organizations were linked to CEOs who were described as possessing psychopathic traits (Boddy, 2006, 2015). When an organization is infiltrated by corporate psychopaths, the result is often that a few people become wealthy, but everyone else suddenly finds themselves out of a job, without their promised pension or without an organization for which to work (Boddy, 2015).

Organizational psychopaths who get to the top of their organizations can be assumed to be highly intelligent as well as manipulative, and research indicates that the psychopaths' higher intelligence seems to enhance their destructive potential. Psychopaths within organizations may resort to violence against those who threaten to expose them. Corporate psychopaths, by deliberately generating hostility between groups of colleagues and coworkers, can create confusion in the workplace, which enables psychopaths to push through their own agendas at the expense of the organization's true interests. Because they have no conscience, psychopaths are not at all concerned with the consequences of their actions on the environment or on society. They have no sense of corporate social responsibility other than paying lip service to the concept when it portrays them in a positive light (Boddy, 2015).

Research findings supported the strong relationship between psychopathy and forms of CWBs.

Lyons and Jonason (2015), in a non-incarcerated adult sample, found that the "darker" aspects of the dark triad (i.e., both psychopathy subtypes and Machiavellianism) are associated with admissions of having stolen something. Their results provided tentative support for the idea that psychopathy and Machiavellianism are part of an evolutionary cheater strategy, sharing the core features of dysfunctional impulsivity, an evening chorotype ("night owl"), and a hostile interpersonal style. Thefts may be part of the same package, adaptive when the behavior is not too conspicuous, allowing the avoidance of punishment. When the researchers controlled for shared variance between the dark triad and impulsivity, secondary psychopathy alone emerged as a significant predictor of diverse thieving behavior, such as stealing from strangers, stores, and agencies; higher number of lifetime thefts; and higher frequency of stealing various items in the past 12 months.

Blickle and Schütte (2017), who examined two distinct factors of psychopathy (fearless dominance and SCI), found support for the distinction between the two factors. Their results demonstrated that SCI is toxic to the organization. In a sample of German employees, they found that SCI is directly associated with CWB-O. The findings did not show a strong relationship between fearless dominance and CWBs and led them to conclude that the toxic nature of fearless dominance is not guaranteed. Harrison et al. (2016) found that psychopathy had a strong effect on the fraud process through its effect on rationalization. The willingness to use any means to get what they desire and the brash attitude exhibited by people with high levels of psychopathy make this personality particularly germane to the rationalization of fraud behaviors. Psychopathy was found to have a strong effect on rationalization, and some consider it to be the most salient part of the fraud process. This finding indicates that individuals who rate higher in psychopathy are more inclined to rationalize fraudulent behavior and fulfill their own desires through enactment. While narcissism and Machiavellianism affect perceptions of capabilities, opportunity, and motivation that may make a fraudulent act more or less appealing, psychopathy directly affects the decision-making step that determines whether an individual will execute fraud behaviors (Harrison et al., 2016).

Narcissism and Counterproductive Work Behavior

Despite its image as the "lighter" dimension of the dark triad traits, there are arguments that the narcissism–CWB relationship seems to be the most promising bivariate association observed to date (Grijalva & Newman, 2015). Based on the host of negative and interpersonally toxic characteristics associated with narcissism, it is almost intuitive that narcissism is associated with CWBs. Narcissism has been shown to predict conflict, aggression, and bullying across a variety of contexts outside of organizations. In terms of conflict, narcissism predicts lower levels of accommodation in relationships. That is, narcissistic individuals are more likely to respond to partner negative behaviors in ways that are destructive rather than constructive for the relationship. Narcissism also predicts lower levels of forgiveness in close relationships and aggression and violence against individuals and groups. Narcissistic violence is typically in response to some provocation such as ego threat or social rejection. Based on this, narcissism is proposed to be a significant predictor of CWBs (Campbell, Hoffman, Campbell, & Marchisio, 2011).

Given that CWBs and narcissism have such a robust relationship, it is no wonder that narcissism is the driving force behind unethical behavior in the workplace (Grijalva & Harms, 2014; Grijalva & Newman, 2015). Narcissism is expected to be positively related to CWBs for at least two more reasons. First, because narcissists view themselves as highly important, they may often be willing to violate the rules to gain desirable outcomes for themselves. In other words, they are preoccupied with the desire to reap the benefits that they believe they rightly deserve. Second, narcissism overlaps conceptually and empirically with impulsiveness. Because CWBs often constitute specific instances of impulsive behaviors, we can expect narcissism to be positively related to CWBs (Michel & Bowling, 2013). The following section presents first how narcissists engage specifically in interpersonal-oriented CWBs when working with other individuals (CWB-I) and later how they can cause damage to the organization (CWB-O). Research findings regarding this relationship conclude this section.

Narcissism and Individual Counterproductive Work Behavior

Several scholars (Penney & Spector, 2002; Grijalva & Newman, 2015; Grijalva & Harms, 2014; Wu & Lebreton, 2011) turned to the theory of threatened egotism and aggression in the workplace context to explain the relationship between narcissism and CWBs. This theory proposes that narcissistic individuals are more likely to encounter information or situations that challenge their positive self-appraisals. In response to these challenges, or ego threats, these individuals are likely to experience negative emotions, such as anger, frustration, or hostility, that in turn lead to aggression. Narcissists have been shown to act out in exceptionally aggressive ways when their self-esteem is threatened. Thus, when threatened, narcissists may be more likely to respond with aggression than with other forms of behavior (Grijalva & Newman, 2015; Grijalva & Harms, 2014).

When the opportunity presents itself, narcissists do whatever is necessary to self-enhance, self-aggrandize, or inflate their own self-image. Their sense of self-importance, rebelliousness, and belief that they are special may lead narcissists to be inconsiderate toward others because they are ready to manipulate them to showcase their own superiority. Narcissists also tend to possess a negative view of others and focus on dominating and exploiting them. In fact, people high in narcissism are less likely to believe that they are engaged in counterproductive behaviors and yet are more likely to engage in deviant behavior in their quest for self-enhancement. Thus, when faced with an opportunity to outshine others, those high in narcissism may be willing to engage in all types of interpersonally directed CWBs (Wu & Lebreton, 2011).

Because of narcissists' tendency to focus on dominating others and their negative attitude, they may not be as willing to consider the interests of others or the relationships that may be damaged as a result of their desire to dominate others. For example, narcissism has been reported to be positively related to a number of self-reported perceptions of interpersonal transgressions. Narcissistic individuals tend to perceive themselves as victims, perceive negative intent during interpersonal interactions, and have a heightened sensitivity to negative interactions. These tendencies may lead them to be more likely to engage in CWBs such as hostility, obstructionism, or overt aggression directed toward other individuals. In addition, narcissists' increased likelihood to interpret interactions as transgressions may also lead to retaliatory behaviors (Wu & Lebreton, 2011).

Narcissism and Organizational Counterproductive Work Behavior

Narcissists' ego and sense of entitlement create the desire to boast and engage through other attention-seeking behaviors. Narcissists have a strong need for validation, and narcissism is commonly thought to be the result of a lack of socialization, characterized by a lack of empathy and consistency in their upbringing. Narcissists project a sense of grandiosity but have an inner fragility and low self-esteem. As mentioned earlier, aspects of narcissism include the willingness to exploit others, a sense of entitlement, and self-absorption. During initial encounters, narcissists are generally viewed favorably but are viewed more negatively and as prone to arrogance in subsequent interactions. Thus, in short-term interactions, such as those involving e-commerce transactions, those who have higher narcissistic traits are in general more successful in gaining the trust of others. Narcissism is goal oriented and aimed at gaining affirmation, while characterized by insensitivity to any social constraints. Narcissists often combine entitlement with a strong desire for success and achievement. Furthermore, narcissistic behaviors and fraud motivation are considered by auditors to be significantly and positively related to fraud risk assessments and unethical financial behavior (Harrison et al., 2016).

Although inwardly insecure, narcissists routinely overvalue their own contributions and abilities when describing them to others. Narcissists exaggerate their own abilities and try to portray themselves as being more important than they really are. Even within the context of private self-evaluations, narcissists' evaluations are quite exaggerated. This exaggerated and unrealistic self-view may reflect a maladaptive self-regulatory style because narcissistic tendencies are indicative of long-term patterns of psychological distress and dysfunction. While narcissists tend to outwardly display egotistical behaviors, their perception of an opportunity to successfully engage in fraud is driven by their personal insecurity. However, in the context of fraud decisions, narcissism has the least effect of the dark triad personality characteristics. According to another explanation, aspects of narcissism include entitlement and self-absorption, and narcissists are inter-personally exploitative and socially inconsiderate. Thus, they are likely to engage in behaviors that satisfy their sense of self-entitlement. Narcissists think they are owed more than others and will engage in behaviors, ethical or not, to realize this. In fact, when narcissists do not get what they believe they are entitled to, they are more likely to exhibit lack of empathy, become angry, and act amorally. Consequently, in an effort to be perceived as having a higher status, narcissists are more motivated to commit fraud (Harrison et al., 2016). As for research findings, substantial evidence shows that nar-cissism has been linked to CWBs and various specific unethical and exploit-ative behaviors, such as tendencies to cheat, lack of workplace integrity, and even white-collar crime. Narcissism predicts a varied range of CWBs, in particular aggression and bullying. While there are certainly many risk-factors for workplace aggression (substance abuse, emotional instability, negative feedback), individuals high in narcissism are particularly likely to bully other employees. Narcissism is also likely to be linked to an overly sex-ualized workplace. It predicts uncommitted sexual relationships, infidelity, and sexual coercion, each of which has potentially destructive consequences in an organizational context (Grijalva & Newman, 2015).

Campbell et al. (2011) mentioned two studies that directly investigated the link between narcissism and CWBs. Penney and Spector (2002) found that narcissism is related CWBs ($r = 0.27$) and that this relationship is medi-ated by employee anger. Similarly, Judge et al. (2006) found that narcissism predicted supervisor ratings of CWBs ($r = 0.24$) and explained variance in CWBs beyond the FFM of personality. Interestingly, the magnitude of these effects rivals the (uncorrected) validity of integrity tests in the prediction of CWB-type behaviors (Ones et al., 1993), signaling the possibility that nar-cissism might explain variance in CWBs beyond integrity tests. Michel and Bowling (2013) found that narcissism was a significant predictor of CWBs. Their findings also showed strong evidence that aggression moderated the narcissism–CWBs relationship, while dispositional aggression strengthened it. Wu and Lebreton (2011) mentioned Bushman and Baumeister's (1998) study, which examined interpersonal interactions between narcissists and other individuals and found a positive relationship between narcissism and threat hypervigilance, which then leads to aggressive behaviors. Harrison et al. (2016) found that narcissism was positively correlated with the moti-vation to commit fraud.

Penney and Spector's (2002) findings showed that individuals high in narcissism reported experiencing anger more frequently and engaging in more CWBs than individuals lower in narcissism. In addition, the relation-ship between the trait of anger and CWBs was also significant in indicating that individuals with higher anger levels were more likely to engage in CWB than individuals lower in anger. Penney and Spector concluded that their findings are consistent with the theory of threatened egotism. Their results were also supportive of the mediator hypothesis, suggesting that the reason narcissistic individuals engage in more CWB is that they are angry.

Machiavellianism and Counterproductive Work Behavior

The literature provides strong arguments and findings that high Machiavellians are prone to engage in a variety of CWBs. Machiavellianism has been described as the willingness to use manipulation and act immorally. A person rated high in Machiavellianism is characterized as holding cynical views of others and the belief that manipulation is a valid and useful method for attaining goals. Consequently, Machiavellianism has multiple dimensions and is associated with amorality, the desire to control, the desire for status, and a distrust of others. Those who are high in Machiavellianism use manipulative behaviors and believe others to be gullible and foolish (Harrison et al., 2016). High Machiavellians are willing to do whatever it takes to achieve their goals (Nelson & Gilbertson, 1991), and this can definitely include CWBs.

Wu and Lebreton (2011), based on the frustration-aggression hypothesis, have suggested that when frustrated by the inability to achieve a goal, individuals possessing certain personality traits such as Machiavellianism are more likely to engage in exaggerated hostile and aggressive behaviors. This suggests that Machiavellians do whatever it takes as long as the end justifies the means. Therefore, whereas high Machiavellians are prepared to be deceitful, aggressive, and exploitive, low Machiavellians are more likely to respond in a socially desirable manner. Social norms would typically dictate alternative, less devious means to attain one's goals. Because CWBs have been described as behaviors that are inconsistent with social norms, high Machiavellians may be more likely to engage in highly manipulative CWBs when facing impediments to achieving their goals (Wu & Lebreton, 2011). Furthermore, high Machiavellians are remorseless and willingly engage in hostile and unethical behaviors. They are prone to making unethical decisions and often assume that others would make the same choices. Individuals rating high in the Machiavellianism trait are more likely to lie to, steal from, cheat, and mislead others (Harrison et al., 2016).

Several specific conceptual arguments were offered to support the relationship between Machiavellianism and each of the forms of CWBs. These explanations are presented in the following section, and as in the previous sections, they are divided into CWB-I and CWB-O.

Machiavellianism and Individual Counterproductive Work Behavior

Castille, Kuyumcu, and Bennett (2017) applied the trait activation theory and argued that organizational constraints motivate Machiavellians to view their coworkers as threats that have to be marginalized. Focusing on Machiavellians' perceptions of resource constraints, they contended that constraints motivate Machiavellians to increasingly undermine their coworkers, resulting in reduced production workplace deviance. By undermining their peers in a context that promotes competition, Machiavellians may achieve higher relative status while causing damage to organizational well-being. Additionally, when Machiavellians perceive low resource constraints, they do not engage in social undermining and are no longer counterproductive.

Machiavellians begin interactions with a friendly demeanor and yet can switch to aggressive behaviors if this initial tactic does not help them to achieve their goals. High Machiavellians have also been reported to act in a manner that generates trust in others and subsequently switch to less socially acceptable tactics to maximize their personal gains. Because of this potential switch in attitude, if Machiavellians do not achieve their goals within a certain time period, they may engage in CWBs to do so, thereby leading to the possibility of increased CWBs by Machiavellians over time (Wu & Lebreton, 2011). Individuals with high levels of Machiavellianism can be good communicators and leaders. However, high Machiavellian individuals tend to distrust others, which is often manifested in paranoia and cynicism. While individuals with Machiavellian impulses may appear to be charismatic, they are skeptical of the intentions of others and are very cynical of other individuals (Harrison et al., 2016).

Machiavellians do not express concern for others or display any emotions during interpersonal interactions. Their verbal interactions with others are less controlled because they are impulsive and do not consider the impact of their behaviors on others; the consequence may be a greater likelihood of engaging in verbal CWBs. Yet high Machiavellians are able to tailor their communications to suit their conversation partners if they believe this will help them achieve their goals. Because high Machiavellians are adept at manipulating others, the targets of manipulative communications or behaviors may be less likely to recognize the true nature of these communications. Thus, when struggling to achieve their goals, high Machiavellians may be especially inclined to engage in manipulative and subtle forms of verbal CWBs (e.g., spreading rumors, gossiping) (Wu & Lebreton, 2011).

Dahling, Whitaker, and Levy (2009) cited Wilson, Near, and Miller (1996), who presented compelling evidence drawn from evolutionary psychology to argue that high Machiavellian individuals serve themselves best by engaging in frequent defection. That is, they hide their true nature within the group for as long as possible, while capitalizing on their exploitative skills, and then move to another unsuspecting group as the knowledge of their tendencies becomes widespread. Furthermore, Wilson et al. suggested that this tendency should encourage Machiavellians to change groups frequently, which implies that they are likely to show a high turnover and remain concerned with only their own personal benefit.

For Machiavellians, bullying may be a preferred way of influencing others. Bullying behavior may also be the result of the negative view of other people held by high Machiavellians. A higher level of Machiavellianism characterizes both perpetrators (who bully others) and bully victims (who bully others and are bullied). The strategy used by Machiavellians is such that when they enter relatively long-term relationships with people, such as in a working environment, they take into consideration their long-term interest. Because high Machiavellians are social manipulators, they are interested in presenting themselves as socially attractive. Therefore, they engage in aggression (including revenge) only to the degree that it is deemed profitable. Thus, Machiavellian employees bully others only when they reach the conclusion that such a behavior will be of benefit to them, that is, when the cost–benefit balance is in their favor (Pilch & Turska, 2015).

Machiavellianism and Organizational Counterproductive Work Behavior

Perhaps a more alarming ethical implication is the potential of Machiavellian behaviors to spread and take root in an organization. Rather than viewing high Machiavellians as just a few "bad apples" that can be plucked out of the organization, researchers and practitioners should note that opportunistic and unethical behavior consistent with Machiavellianism can become socialized, reinforced, and eventually ingrained in the corporate culture. Unethical behavior certainly can yield beneficial outcomes, and although these outcomes are perhaps not sustainable, they are sufficiently appealing that mechanisms such as co-optation, incremental exposure to corruption, and compromise can be used to normalize opportunistic corruption in organizations. This may especially be true for high Machiavellian managers, whose deceitful nature and skill with using influence tactics may encourage acquiescence and eventually rationalized support among others in the organization (Dahling et al., 2009).

Machiavellianism is thought to be a contributing factor to unethical business behaviors of various types, and individuals scoring high ratings on Machiavellianism are more likely to defraud others in an organizational context (Harrison et al., 2016). Machiavellians pose a threat to ethical behavior in many regards. Most obviously, high Machiavellians are unlikely to place much value on ethical behavior if it stands in the way of personal rewards, which makes it unlikely that they will emerge as ethical managers. The traits and behaviors associated with being a moral person and a moral manager, such as integrity, trustworthiness, showing concern for people, openness, and following ethical decision rules, are contradictory to the traits and behaviors associated with a high Machiavellian. Machiavellianism is composed of four dimensions: amorality, desire for control, desire for status, and distrust of others. Of these subdimensions, one can expect that distrust of others is most relevant when assessing opportunities to engage in fraud (Harrison et al., 2016).

Machiavellians are more willing to make unethical choices and to engage in destructive behaviors. Because of their manipulative skills and lack of guilt feelings, they are best served by secretly exploiting an organization while hiding their true nature as long as possible and changing organizations when exposed. Machiavellians, therefore, have a "natural" tendency to engage in exploitative behavior and CWBs (Belschak, Muhammad, & Den Hartog, 2016). Individuals with high levels of Machiavellianism believe that manipulation is a valid and useful mechanism for accomplishing their goals, and they often take pleasure in their ability to manipulate others. High Machiavellians have a control-oriented motivational orientation that is manifested in their aspiration for financial success. This aspiration motivates them to engage in behaviors and activities that promote their self-interest, regardless of the ethical nature of their acts. Consequently, these individuals are also more strongly motivated by both monetary and non-monetary rewards, such as ego and prestige, for committing an act of fraud (Harrison et al., 2016).

Befitting their cynical nature and strong desire for achievement and control, individuals with Machiavellian perspectives are more skeptical of the opportunities to perform acts of fraud, but they enjoy the act more than do others. Because of the multi-dimensional nature of Machiavellianism, distrust of others plays a critical role in Machiavellians' perception of opportunities to commit an act of fraud. Someone who rates high in the Machiavellianism dimension and views others through its paranoid lens considers everyone else to be self-serving and out to get the others. Thus, a perceived lack of trust and benevolence between individuals contributes to the view that there are fewer opportunities to take advantage of others, even for those with an increased desire to do so (Pilch & Turska, 2015). Two other subdimensions of Machiavellianism, the strong desire for control and the desire for status, also play a central role in the motivation to commit fraud. Whether motivated by financial concerns or ego-driven considerations, the desire for control and power plays a key role in motivating fraud behaviors (Harrison et al., 2016). However, because high Machiavellians are aware of those around them and suspect their intentions, they are wary of committing acts of fraud because of their distrust of others' intentions. Paranoia and lack of trust in others often make high Machiavellians hesitant to engage in unethical activities that others may witness (Harrison et al., 2016).

Research findings support the relationship between high Machiavellians and CWBs. According to Dahling et al. (2009), the exploitation of others that takes place before defection is clearly evident in research, linking Machiavellians with stealing and the use of tactics of influence. High Machiavellians are more likely to take advantage of opportunities to steal than low Machiavellians. Moreover, whereas high Machiavellians are equally willing to steal from a supervisor who trusted them versus one who distrusted them, low Machiavellians are less willing to steal from a trusting supervisor out of a sense of reciprocation. Similarly, research indicates that high Machiavellians engage in a variety of influence tactics, including strategic self-disclosure, ingratiation, and intimidation, to attain their desired ends. These tactics help them generate the perception of trust and cooperation that provides them access to resources prior to their final defection (Dahling et al., 2009).

High Machiavellians show a general propensity to engage in antisocial behavior. Positive relationships were also found between Machiavellianism and self-reported (0.25; P<.001) and coworker reported CWBs (0.21; P<.001) (Cohen, Panter, Turan, Morse, & Kim, 2014). High Machiavellians were found to have a high level of commitment to their careers but low levels of commitment to their current organizations, supervisors, and teams (Zettler, Friedrich, & Hilbig, 2011). According to researchers, this makes it easier for them to engage in activities that promote their own career at the expense of their organization or workgroup, including their supervisors. Pilch and Turska (2015) found that Machiavellianism was related to bullying among employees in Poland.

Harrison et al. (2016) cited Cooper and Peterson's (1980) findings that when working with others, high Machiavellians were much less likely to cheat than low Machiavellians, but the opposite occurred when they were working in isolation. This finding means that individuals with high levels of Machiavellianism may be more willing to engage in acts of fraud but distrust the individuals around them and are more skeptical of the opportunities available to them. That is, when high Machiavellians perceive the risk of getting caught as high, they pass on the opportunity. Castille, Buckner, and Thoroughgood (2016) found that employees high in Machiavellianism tend to report greater willingness to engage in unethical behaviors intended to promote their organizations' interests. Their findings showed that Machiavellian employees are willing to engage in high levels of unethical behaviors regardless of the social norms that define the organizational contexts in which they work. They concluded that Machiavellians, who are generally believed to act in ways contrary to organizational goals and interests, are willing to protect their organizations via unethical means provided that they view these activities as being self-serving.

An interesting view of the performance of Machiavellian employees was advanced by Belschak, Den Hartog, and Kalshoven (2015), who examined the relation between Machiavellians and organizational citizenship behavior (OCB). Based on the knowledge that Machiavellians are selfish, having relatively little concern for the welfare of others, it is argued that their decisions concerning engaging in OCB are calculated, and they engage in such behavior only if it is clearly advantageous for them, for example, if they can expect favors in return from indebted individuals. In particular, organizationally focused OCB (which does not target specific individuals or groups who may return favors) is likely to be shown more often by non-Machiavellians than by Machiavellians. Therefore, one can expect that Machiavellian employees are less likely to exhibit challenging OCB.

To sum up, theory and research provide strong support for the relationship between the dark triad traits and CWBs. Because this direction was overlooked for quite a long time, there is a need for much more research on this relationship, as well as more theory building. Moreover, the findings so far regarding the dark triad personalities and CWBs can be characterized as consistent but relatively modest. This implies that the relationship is more complex in the sense that it is not linear but compounded by mediators and moderators. This should not be surprising. The theory and evidence presented so far show that the dark triad personalities are brilliant people in general and will act unlawfully only when they think they have the best opportunity to do so without being caught. The dark triad personalities are predators but of the clever type. They always look around to make sure that the conditions for striking are optimal. What are these conditions? The answer to this question leads us to the next chapter.

References

Babiak, P. (2000). Psychopathic manipulation at work. In C. B. Gacono (Ed.), *The Clinical and Forensic Assessment of Psychopathy: A Practitioner's Guide* (pp. 287–312). Mahwah, NJ: Lawrence Erlbaum Associates, Inc.

Belschak, F. D., Den Hartog, D. N., & Kalshoven, K. (2015). Leading Machiavellians: How to translate Machiavellians' selfishness into pro-organizational behavior. *Journal of Management, 41*(7), 1934–1956.

Belschak, F. D., Muhammad, R. S., & Den Hartog, D. N. (2016). Birds of a feather can butt heads: When Machiavellian employees work with Machiavellian leaders. *Journal of Business Ethics*, 1–14.

Berry, C. M., Ones, D. S., & Sackett, P. R. (2007). Interpersonal deviance, organizational deviance, and their common correlates: A review and meta-analysis. *Journal of Applied Psychology, 92*(2), 409–423.

Blickle, G., & Schütte, N. (2017). Trait psychopathy, task performance, and counterproductive work behavior directed toward the organization. *Personality and Individual Differences, 109*, 225–231.

Boddy, C. R. (2006). The dark side of management decisions: Organizational psychopaths. *Management Decision, 44*, 1461–1475.

Boddy, C. R. (2011). *Corporate Psychopaths: Organizational Destroyers*. London: Palgrave MacMillan.

Boddy, C. R. (2015). Organizational psychopaths: A ten-year update. *Management Decision, 53*(10), 2407–2432.

Boddy, C., Miles, D., Sanyal, C., & Hartog, M. (2015). Extreme managers, extreme workplaces: Capitalism, organizations and corporate psychopaths. *Organization, 22*(4), 530–551.

Bolton, L. R., Becker, L. K., & Barber, L. K. (2010). Big Five trait predictors of differential counterproductive work behavior dimensions. *Personality and Individual Differences, 49*(5), 537–541.

Bushman, B. J., & Baumeister, R. F. (1998). Threatened egotism, narcissism, self-esteem, and direct and displaced aggression: Does self-love or self-hate lead to violence? *Journal of Personality and Social Psychology, 75*(1), 219–229.

Campbell, W. K., Hoffman, B. J., Campbell, S. M., & Marchisio, G. (2011). Narcissism in organizational contexts. *Human Resource Management Review*, 21(4), 268–284.

Castille, C. M., Buckner, J. E., & Thoroughgood, C. N. (2016). Prosocial citizens without a moral compass? Examining the relationship between Machiavellianism and unethical pro-organizational behavior. *Journal of Business Ethics*, 1–12.

Castille, C. M., Kuyumcu, D., & Bennett, R. J. (2017). Prevailing to the peers' detriment: Organizational constraints motivate Machiavellians to undermine their peers. *Personality and Individual Differences*, 104, 29–36.

Cleckley, H. (1941/1988). *The Mask of Sanity (5th ed.), Private Printing for Educational Use by Emily Cleckley 1988* (Formerly first published by C. V. Mosley Co. in 1941). Georgia: Augusta.

Cohen, A., & Shoval, L. (2018). *The dark triad personality and the Big Five model in their relationship to counterproductive work behaviors.* Manuscript submitted for publication.

Cohen, T. R., Panter, A. T., Turan, N., Morse, L., & Kim, Y. (2014). Moral character in the workplace. *Journal of Personality and Social Psychology*, 107(5), 943–963.

Cooper, S., & Peterson, C. (1980). Machiavellianism and spontaneous cheating in competition. *Journal of Research in Personality*, 14(1), 70–75.

Dahling, J. J., Whitaker, B. G., & Levy, P. E. (2009). The development and validation of a new Machiavellianism scale. *Journal of Management*, 35(2), 219–257.

DeShong, H. L., Grant, D. M., & Mullins-Sweatt, S. N. (2015). Comparing models of counterproductive workplace behaviors: The Five-Factor Model and the dark triad. *Personality and Individual Differences*, 74, 55–60.

DeShong, H. L., Helle, A. C., Lengel, G. J., Meyer, N., & Mullins-Sweatt, S. N. (2017). Facets of the dark triad: Utilizing the Five-Factor Model to describe Machiavellianism. *Personality and Individual Differences*, 105, 218–223.

Grijalva, E., & Harms, P. D. (2014). Narcissism: An integrative synthesis and dominance complementarity model. *The Academy of Management Perspectives*, 28(2), 108–127.

Grijalva, E., & Newman, D. A. (2015). Narcissism and counterproductive work behavior (CWB): Meta-analysis and consideration of collectivist culture, Big Five personality, and narcissism's facet structure. *Applied Psychology: An International Review*, 64(1), 93–126.

Guenole, N. (2014). Maladaptive personality at work: Exploring the darkness. *Industrial and Organizational Psychology*, 7(1), 85–97.

Hare, R. (1991). *The Hare Psychopathy Checklist Revised.* New York, NY: Multi-Health Systems Inc.

Harms, P. D., & Spain, M. S. (2015). Beyond the bright side: Dark personality at work. *Applied Psychology: An International Review*, 64(1), 15–24.

Harrison, A., Summers, J., & Mennecke, B. (2016). The effects of the dark triad on unethical behavior. *Journal of Business Ethics*, 1–25.

Jonason, P. K., Wee, S., & Li, N. P. (2014). Thinking bigger and better about "bad apples": Evolutionary industrial—organizational psychology and the dark triad. *Industrial and Organizational Psychology*, 7(1), 117–121.

Judge, T. A., LePine, J. A., & Rich, B. L. (2006). Loving yourself abundantly: Relationship of the narcissistic personality to self-and other perceptions of workplace deviance, leadership, and task and contextual performance. *Journal of Applied Psychology*, 91, 762–776.

Kozako, I. N. A. M. F., Safin, S. Z., & Rahim, A. R. A. (2013). The relationship of Big Five personality traits on counterproductive work behavior among hotel employees: An exploratory study. *Procedia Economics and Finance*, 7, 181–187.

Lee, K., & Ashton, M. C. (2005). Psychopathy, Machiavellianism, and narcissism in the Five-Factor Model and the HEXACO model of personality structure. *Personality and Individual Differences*, 38(7), 1571–1582.

Lee, K., Ashton, M. C., Wiltshire, J., Bourdage, J. S., Visser, B. A., & Gallucci, A. (2013). Sex, power, and money: Prediction from the dark triad and honesty: Humility. *European Journal of Personality*, 27(2), 169–184.

Lyons, M., & Jonason, P. K. (2015). Dark triad, tramps, and thieves. *Journal of Individual Differences*, 36(4), 215–220.

Michel, J. S., & Bowling, N. A. (2013). Does dispositional aggression feed the narcissistic response? The role of narcissism and aggression in the prediction of job attitudes and counterproductive work behaviors. *Journal of Business and Psychology*, 28(1), 93–105.

Muris, P., Merckelbach, H., Otgaar, H., & Meijer, E. (2017). The malevolent side of human nature: A meta-analysis and critical review of the literature on the dark triad (narcissism, Machiavellianism, and psychopathy). *Perspectives on Psychological Science*, 12(2), 183–204.

Nelson, G., & Gilbertson, D. (1991). Machiavellianism revisited. *Journal of Business Ethics*, 10(8), 633–639.

Ones, D. S., Viswesvaran, C., & Schmidt, F. L. (1993). A meta-analysis of integrity test validities: Findings and implications for personnel selection and theories of job performance. *Journal of Applied Psychology*, 78, 679–703.

Penney, L. M., & Spector, P. E. (2002). Narcissism and counterproductive work behavior: Do bigger egos mean bigger problems? *International Journal of Selection and Assessment*, 10(1–2), 126–134.

Pilch, I., & Turska, E. (2015). Relationships between Machiavellianism, organizational culture, and workplace bullying: Emotional abuse from the target's and the perpetrator's perspective. *Journal of Business Ethics*, 128(1), 83–93.

Sackett, P. R., Berry, C. M., Wiemann, S. A., & Laczo, R. M. (2006). Citizenship and counterproductive behavior: Clarifying relations between the two domains. *Human Performance*, 19(4), 441–464.

Salgado, J. F. (2002). The Big Five personality dimensions and counterproductive behaviors. *International Journal of Selection and Assessment*, 10, 117–125.

Scherer, K. T., Baysinger, M., Zolynsky, D., & LeBreton, J. M. (2013). Predicting counterproductive work behaviors with sub-clinical psychopathy: Beyond the Five-Factor Model of personality. *Personality and Individual Differences*, 55(3), 300–305.

Schutte, N., Blickle, G., Frieder, R. E., Wihler, A., Schnitzler, F., Heupel, J., & Zettler, I. (2015). The role of interpersonal influence in counterbalancing psychopathic personality trait facets at work. *Journal of Management*, in press.

Spain, S. M., Harms, P., & LeBreton, J. M. (2014). The dark side of personality at work. *Journal of Organizational Behavior*, 35(Supplement 1), S41–S60.

Stanescu, D. F., & Mohorea, L. (2016). "Welcome to the dark-side": A correlational analysis of the dark-triad of personality with counterproductive work behavior and work locus of control. *Pannon Management Review*, 1, 47–58.

Wilson, D. S., Near, D., & Miller, R. R. (1996). Machiavellianism: A synthesis of the evolutionary and psychological literatures. *Psychological Bulletin*, 119, 285–299.

Wu, J., & Lebreton, J. M. (2011). Reconsidering the dispositional basis of counterproductive work behavior: The role of aberrant personality. *Personnel Psychology*, 64(3), 593–626.

Youli, H., & Chao, L. (2015). A comparative study between the dark triad of personality and the Big Five. *Canadian Social Science*, 11(1), 93–98.

Zettler, I., Friedrich, N., & Hilbig, B. E. (2011). Dissecting work commitment: The role of Machiavellianism. *Career Development International*, 16(1), 20–35.

6   The Predators' Environment
Work-Setting and Personal Factors

It has been argued in the literature that personality effects can be overshadowed by strong situational demands (Spector, 2011); that is, people are free to engage in behaviors consistent with their personalities only when the environment is not overly constraining (Cohen, 2016). For example, norms can either inhibit or reinforce an individual's personality tendencies (Spector, 2011; Smithikrai, 2008). Individuals who score high on any element of the dark triad may be willing to engage in unethical behavior. However, the question of the circumstances under which they will actually do so remains open (Spain, Harms, & LeBreton, 2014). One of the arguments posited here is that dark triad personalities are very watchful before they act. In other words, they check their environment very carefully to make sure that the surrounding conditions are appropriate for action and relatively friendly in terms of a low probability of being detected. More specifically, it is argued that the relationship between dark triad personalities and counterproductive work behaviors (CWBs) is mediated and moderated by variables that, based on the person–organization fit theory, represent a friendly or unfriendly environment for the dark triad traits (Vardi, 2001).

Because narcissism, Machiavellianism, and psychopathy are positively but only modestly related to CWB, it has been suggested that the role of contextual factors in strengthening this relationship should be examined (Palmer, Komarraju, Carter, & Karau, 2017; O'Boyle, Forsyth, Banks, & McDaniel, 2012). As employees operate within an organizational context, it is imperative to examine the effects of the individual's perception of organizational factors on the relationship between dark triad traits and CWB. For example, it is more adaptive for individuals to display their dark triad traits in certain organizational contexts (e.g., short-term jobs involving risk) than in others. Similarly, individuals scoring high on the dark triad report greater satisfaction in jobs that provide autonomy and prestige but not too much competition.

There is a gap in the research on the interplay between dark personalities and the organizational environment that can potentially nourish toxicity or the behavioral expression of their traits (Schyns, 2015). Individuals high in any of the dark triad traits may be willing to engage in unethical behavior, but the question remains as to the circumstances under which they will actually do so. For example, given that high-Machiavellians are willing to manipulate people but may not be able to do so, do they truly demonstrate negotiation skills? Might the need of narcissistic leaders to make themselves look good be manifested in attempts to obtain advantages and recognition for their team if they identify closely with it? These are open questions that need further investigation (Spain et al., 2014). In short, research is needed to understand the conditions under which the dark personality does or does not translate into negative behaviors. This chapter discusses the factors that represent what can be termed as the predators' organizational environment. In addition, this chapter also discusses personal characteristics of the dark triad that might cause to different behaviors and reactions in the workplace.

The Importance of the Environment for the Dark Triad Personalities

Behavior results from the interaction between environmental pressure and individual intrinsic quality. People display different behaviors under different circumstances because they seek to meet the needs of their environment (Youli & Chao, 2015). In the case of the dark triad, relatively little is known about how (i.e., the underlying explanatory processes) and under what circumstances (i.e., the boundary conditions of these processes) abusive supervision is related to workplace deviance (Michel, Newness, & Duniewicz, 2016). Executive behavior does not occur in a vacuum but in contexts and settings. Just as it could be said that form without function has little meaning, neither does the consideration of an executive's personality and make-up without considering the manner in which these are expressed in the working environment. In sharp contrast to the view that it is what the executive does "that gets results," it might be more illuminating to explore how (1) the internal context mediates what the executive is able to do, and (2) the context may define the executive's success and failure. In the case of dark triad managers, contextual conditions can either induce or restrict their toxic behavior. Heavier emphasis on the contextual determinants of leadership behavior, a topic somewhat neglected in the literature, is needed and may help reduce the incidence of excessive toxic leadership (Michel et al., 2016).

More important, environmental factors can explain the differences in the stability and consistency of results when dark triad personalities are used to predict outcome variables. The dark triad personalities are more deeply influenced by environmental factors (Cohen, 2016; Cohen & Shoval, 2018; Youli & Chao, 2015); therefore, it is necessary to explore them in depth (Youli & Chao, 2015). However, Nübold et al. (2017) contended that, to date, the dark triad has exclusively been conceptualized and investigated in its trait-like form, ignoring evidence for the malleability and short-term fluctuation in personal states, influencing the expression of one's personality in a specific moment. Because of the predominant view of the dark triad as a compilation of stable traits, situational cues eliciting dark triad behavior have not been considered of interest so far and research has failed to address the role of situational factors in eliciting momentary expressions of dark personality characteristics.

Attempts to identify the roots of the dark triad personality have thus focused on very broad, generic explanations, such as evolutionary, behavioral, genetic, socio-ecological, neuro-biological, and motivational foundations. Nübold et al. (2017) argued that the usual approach of people with an adaptive personality, according to which they perceive situations as opportunities to express their personality, may be problematic for the dark triad personality. Whereas some situations may allow for or even encourage the expression of dark personality characteristics because they may be beneficial in that moment (e.g., self-aggrandizement in a job interview), other situations may trigger dark personality states because specific needs and motives are not fulfilled (e.g., the need for power). Thus, a comprehensive taxonomy of situational triggers of specific personality characteristics, including the dark triad, has to be established. Yet the situational context has received little consideration in terms of its interaction with psychopathic traits in producing successful behavior.

In sum, any model that seeks to achieve a general framework for conceptualizing successful psychopathy needs to consider the role of the situational context in determining when and where psychopathy may result in success or failure (Steinert, Lishner, Vitacco, & Hong, 2017). For instance, whereas emotional callousness or a manipulative tendency might help an individual succeed in a competitive business context, the same traits might hinder success in an informal interpersonal interaction. Similarly, psychopathic grandiosity may protect the individual from anxiety or threats to his or her self-esteem in a work context where high levels of critical evaluation prevail, thus permitting the individual to better persevere in completing difficult tasks for which he or she will eventually be rewarded. However, grandiosity in such a context may limit the individual from engaging in behavior that permits professional development or learning when the criticism is valid (Steinert et al., 2017). These examples suggest that the manifestation and expression of the same psychopathic traits could lead to different outcomes, depending on the situation characteristics.

Identifying the possible triggers of dark personality behavior at work and building a taxonomy of these triggers is important for theoretical and practical reasons. At the theoretical level, a more comprehensive understanding of the triggers of dark personality behavior and their potential interconnections is crucial for acquiring knowledge of the nomological network and common mechanisms that may be associated with specific groups or categories of triggers. Moreover, identifying triggers of dark personality expressions at work has also practical implications because organizations strongly benefit from detailed knowledge of the situations that may "make people snap." Organizations and human resources professionals will be able to design evidence-based interventions that will help prevent employees from expressing their dark tendencies, thus preventing harm to organizations and their members in the short and long terms. These actions may include not only job design and selective placement but also training and coaching interventions that sensitize employees to potentially dangerous situations and help them manage themselves better and regulate their dark impulses and increase their ability to cope with others' dark behaviors. Such interventions would allow better relationships and work ethics within their organizations (Nübold et al., 2017). The following section discusses the specific factors that affect the willingness of dark triad personalities to act.

Specific Settings That Trigger or Constrain the Dark Triad's Behavior

Based on the existing literature, the specific factors that might affect the relationship between dark triad personalities and their behavior, particularly CWBs, are divided into personal and contextual.

Personal Factors

An interesting condition that might affect the relationship between the dark triad and CWBs is intelligence (O'Boyle, Forsyth, Banks, & Story, 2013). A meta-analytic review of empirical studies of the relation between dark triad traits and general mental ability showed that individuals who are more intelligent than others are not very likely in general to exhibit personality traits that condone a manipulative, socially aversive style of interaction. Furthermore, although aspects of the dark triad traits are related to impulsivity, short-sightedness, and deficits in abstract reasoning, it has been observed that these aversive personality traits are not more prevalent or pronounced in those who were less cognitively advanced. Individuals whose personalities include such dark traits as Machiavellianism, narcissism, and psychopathy are neither brute dullards nor evil geniuses, on average. According to O'Boyle et al. (2013), this is an interesting finding considering the general assumption that dark triad personalities are cleverer than ordinary individuals. Research should take into account the difference between intelligence and perceptions of intelligence. Narcissists, for example, have been found to rate their intelligence higher than non-narcissists and have higher levels of self-confidence in achieving goals. Thus, individuals who perceive that they possess the necessary capabilities to successfully perform acts of fraud will be more persistent in their actions and will anticipate their success (Harrison, Summers, & Mennecke, 2016).

Grijalva and Harms (2014) advanced another potential mediator based on the theory of threatened egotism and aggression. Accordingly, individuals who are high in self-esteem and are hypersensitive to threats to their self-esteem are more likely to experience negative emotions (e.g., fear, anger, frustration, hostility), which subsequently lead to aggressive outbursts. The workplace is full of potential self-esteem threats—poor performance reviews, competition from coworkers, difficulty mastering new technologies, failed projects—and highly narcissistic individuals are hypervigilant against perceived threats and are predisposed to interpret ambiguous stimuli as threatening. Thus, the positive relationship between narcissism (and probably the other two dark traits) and CWBs may be at least partially explained by narcissists' lashing out at their company or coworkers because of negative emotions triggered by threats to their self-esteem (Harrison et al., 2016). Therefore, according to Grijalva and Harms (2014), building on the theory of threatened egotism and aggression, when narcissists experience threats to their self-esteem they experience and frequently act on anger because of impulse control deficiencies, even though their CWBs may cause negative long-term consequences if they are caught.

Hogan and Fico (2011) tend to follow the same line of reasoning. According to them, narcissists overestimate their ability, often in the face of contradictory facts. They cited Kruger and Dunning (1999), who attributed their exaggerated belief in their ability to a deficit in cognitive ability, to a lack of what they call the capacity for meta-cognition, that is, the ability of individuals to be aware of how they think about their performance. This overestimation can be regarded as self-deception: it starts with the inability to face up to the inevitability of death and then generalizes to an inability to face any important reality. Role theorists call it a lack of role distance, the inability to regard oneself with ironic detachment. Others might see it as pluck and courage, an unusual ability to persevere in the face of reversals and misfortune. According to Hogan and Fico, this may be related to a lack of capacity for introspection. Introspective tendencies are normally distributed, and many highly successful people are constitutionally incapable of introspection. Narcissists are known to attribute failure to circumstances and success to their own abilities, which is consistent with the failure of introspection. This and the other already mentioned explanations can be generalized to all the dark personalities.

Contextual Factors

Situational factors may affect the emergence of dysfunctional behavior (Cohen, 2016). Most people are able to manage dysfunctional tendencies most of the time, but stress, work overload, fatigue, high emotion, and lack of social vigilance can increase the probability of maladaptive behavior. Furthermore, dysfunctional behavior is more likely to appear in situations that are ambiguous, where leadership positions have too little structure and allow executives too much discretionary power. Finally, organizational culture can potentiate dysfunctional behavior. Thus, personality, situational, and organizational influences interact to influence the emergence of dysfunctional behavior in any given performance or interpersonal context (Grijalva & Harms, 2014; Nelson & Hogan, 2009). The following section presents specific contextual factors mentioned and examined in the dark triad research.

The stability of an organization's external environment is an important dimension, influencing the destructive force of the leader and the workplace. If the external conditions are unstable, toxic behavior is facilitated. If not, the tolerance for extreme internal toxicity is much reduced. Examples of external environmental disturbance would be a collapse in the organization's market, a local disaster, an emergency alert, threat of a public humiliation or government inspection, the threat of an external inquiry, extensive media pressure, and high-profile stakeholder pressure (Walton, 2007). There is an important and urgent need for research on this factor.

Vardi (2001) mentioned organizational climate and organizational ethical climate as important variables that affect misbehavior in organizations. According to Vardi (2001), ethical climates are embedded in the organizational climate, which, in turn, is embedded in the organizational culture and thus affect behavior differently. The organization's culture, as demonstrated in its climate, provides the collective norms that guide behavior. The norms of what constitutes appropriate behavior and what does not are shared and are used to monitor behavior. In a culture where the values and norms are directed toward deviation, organizational misbehavior will become normative. There is definitely a solid basis for assuming that these two variables will affect the relationship between the dark triad and CWB and that dark triad personalities will be more inclined to perform CWB in a culture that is characterized as being more negative in terms of its climate and ethics.

Michel et al. (2016) developed and tested a model of workplace aggression that explained how and under what circumstances abusive supervision is related to employee workplace deviance. Rooted in the affective events theory and consistent with existing theories (e.g., fairness theory, frustration aggression theory, social cognitive theory, social information processing theory), they found that work-related negative affect mediates the relationship between abusive supervision and workplace deviance. This mediation process occurs where perceived abusive supervision is associated with higher work-related negative affect, and higher work-related negative affect is related to higher deviant behavior. They mentioned that this indirect outcome is conditional upon employee- and organization-based aggressiveness. Employees who apply socially unorthodox and antisocial beliefs (i.e., higher aggressive beliefs and attitudes related to social discounting bias) when interpreting and responding to events but not other forms of aggressive beliefs and attitudes (e.g., hostile attribution bias, potency bias) are more likely to deviate from the social norm and respond more negatively to abuse and engage in greater deviant and abusive supervision. Organizational deviance was stronger in participants who possessed a social discounting bias but no other facets of aggressive beliefs and attitudes. Michel et al. (2016) concluded that there are several aggression-related predispositions that influence the likelihood of deviance following abuse from a supervisor.

According to Grijalva and Harms (2014) and Campbell, Hoffman, Campbell, and Marchisio (2011), one unexplored potential generative mechanism is perceived organizational justice and its effect on narcissistic behavior. Perceptions of organizational justice are important because they are a leading antecedent of CWB. Grijalva and Harms (2014) proposed that because narcissists believe that they are better than others and deserve special treatment, when they receive external feedback that conflicts with their positive self-image, such as being denied a promotion or being reprimanded by a supervisor, they attribute the undesirable feedback to unfairness. Past research theorized that narcissists' self-esteem maintenance repertoire includes intrapersonal self-regulation processes, which are used to form biased interpretations of social feedback and performance outcomes, such as selectively focusing on some environmental stimuli while ignoring others, as well as recalling past events selectively or in a distorted form. Therefore, highly narcissistic individuals are more likely to report organizational injustice and psychological contract breach because their perceptual biases lead them to perceive themselves and their performance much more positively than do objective observers, leading to a discrepancy between their high expectations and reality. Little research has been done in this area, and future research should consider the fruitful area of the relationship between dark triad personalities and organizational justice.

Palmer et al. (2017) noted the role of perceived organizational support in the dark triad–CWBs relationship. "Perceived organizational support" refers to the employees' perception that their organization values their contributions and cares about their well-being. Based on the social exchange theory and person–situation interactionism, they theorized how perceived organizational support may inhibit the frequency with which narcissistic, Machiavellian, and psychopathic employees engage in various types of CWB. According to the social exchange theory, employees select behaviors by weighing the costs and benefits they expect to receive. It is possible that individuals high in narcissism (i.e., self-aggrandizing), Machiavellianism (i.e., manipulative), and psychopathy (i.e., lacking empathy) engage in CWB because they share a common "core of darkness," which includes callous affect and manipulation. Palmer et al. contended that perceived high organizational support may enhance the narcissist's sense of self-importance and reduce ego threat. They also argued that perceived organizational support is likely to reduce the element of provocation on the part of prime psychopathic employees and that they have more favorable perceptions of the organization is likely to reduce their unprovoked CWB. Similarly, they reasoned that

Machiavellians who perceive organizational support as high will view their organizations as less threatening and opt for conniving behind the scenes instead of using risky overt tactics (i.e., CWB). Thus, a more positive perception of the organization may inhibit the natural tendencies of employees who are characterized by the dark triad traits and result in their perpetrating a reduced amount of CWB compared with other trait-equivalent employees having a more negative perception of organizational support.

Campbell et al. (2011) mentioned the importance of narcissists' perception of psychological contracts with their employers. A psychological contract represents the beliefs, perceptions, and informal obligations between an employer and employee. Psychological contracts are often formed during recruitment and initial interviews and may later be remembered as promises and thus give rise to expectations. Employees who perceive a psychological contract breach are likely to become demotivated and resentful (Cohen, 2015). Responses to a breached contract may include reduced loyalty, commitment, and organizational citizenship behavior (OCB). Campbell et al. contended that, given narcissists' sense of entitlement, it would not be surprising to see increased perceptions of breach among narcissists, another mechanism potentially responsible for the influence of narcissism on reduced levels of OCB and increased levels of CWBs.

In sum, it seems that the contextual factors mentioned emphasize the role of the exchange theory as well as justice perceptions as important mediators or moderators in the relationship between the dark triad traits and CWBs. The following section presents more integrative models of the factors that influence the decision of dark triad personalities to perform CWBs.

Integrative Model of the Contextual Factors

Padilla, Hogan, and Kaiser (2007) described several contextual factors that support destructive leadership. They suggested such four key factors: instability, perceived threat, cultural values, and the absence of checks and balances and institutionalization. In times of instability, as was also mentioned by Walton (2007), leaders can enhance their power by advocating radical changes to restore order. Leaders taking power in unstable environments are also granted more authority because instability demands quick action and unilateral decision making. However, when decision-making becomes centralized, it is often difficult to reverse the situation. Instability provides dark triad personalities a friendlier environment in which to operate. Threat related to structural and organizational instability is perceived as imminent. When people feel threatened, they are more willing to accept assertive leadership. Threat increases followers' support and identification with charismatic leaders, particularly non-participative leaders. According to Padilla et al. (2007), two points should be mentioned in the context of environmental threats. First, objective threats are not essential; all that is needed is a perception of threat. Second, leaders often perpetuate the perception of threat or an external "enemy" to strengthen their power and motivate followers. Dark triad personalities feel more comfortable in an environment with higher perceptions of threat.

Cultural values constitute another contextual factor that contributes to destructive leadership. Culture concerns preferences for certain social conditions and therefore shapes emergent leadership. "Dark leaders" are likely to emerge in cultures that endorse the avoidance of uncertainty, collectivism (as opposed to individualism), and high power distance. Uncertainty avoidance involves the extent to which a society feels threatened by ambiguous situations; in such societies, people look to strong leaders to provide hope. Another element mentioned by Padilla et al. is the absence of checks and balances and institutionalization. Strong organizations tend to have strong institutions and strong countervailing centers of power. Systems without such dispersal of control (e.g., corporations lacking an independent board overseeing) allow individuals or parties to seize power. Although leaders need discretion to do their work, discretion may allow destructive leaders to abuse their power. The concept of managerial discretion suggests that destructive leadership is most likely in senior positions (where there is less supervision), in younger and smaller organizations with limited governance mechanisms, and in high-growth and rapidly transforming industries (Padilla et al., 2007).

Padilla et al. (2007) concluded that it is hard for destructive leaders to succeed in stable systems where the institutions are strong and adequate power and control checks and balances are in force (Walton, 2007). Conducive environments contribute to the emergence of destructive leadership, and destructive leaders and colluding followers are sometimes able to take over. When destructive administrations achieve power, they consolidate their control by undermining existing institutions and laws. They do so by replacing constructive institutions with those aimed to enhance central control, eliminating rivals and dissidents, manipulating the media, and exploiting educational systems, using propaganda to legitimize the process. The new policies soon become ingrained in the culture; people carrying out unconscionable orders sanctioned by a higher authority eventually accept the situation as normal.

Steinert et al. (2017) in their review of possible factors that affect the success of the dark triad proposed three types of moderators: structural, environmental, and contextual, which could influence the impact of psychopathic traits on success. Structural moderators are enduring internal characteristics, such as temperament, personality dispositions, or schemas that are distinct from core psychopathic traits but may modify the behavioral activity that they generate. Structural moderators have either genetic or environmental origins. Examples of potential structural moderators include gender, attractiveness, interpersonal acumen, addiction, and intelligence. Additionally, they contended that traits that are not ubiquitously and unequivocally agreed upon as core traits of psychopathy by most (if not all) researchers (e.g., impulsivity or disinhibition, boldness, and antisocial tendencies) may be considered potential structural moderators of psychopathy.

Environmental moderators are developmental experiences that may interact with core psychopathic traits to manifest specific behavioral outcomes. Although some core psychopathic traits are thought to be the outcome of genetic predispositions resulting from underlying structural or functional brain deficits (e.g., emotional callousness), the type of behavior generated by such deficits is likely to be shaped by various learning processes throughout one's life. According to Steinert et al. (2017), potential environmental moderators include social economic status, level of parental involvement, physical abuse, and peer antisociality. The authors defined contextual moderators as current situational factors that determine whether a behavior will produce positive or negative outcomes for the individual. The link between a behavior, the situational context in which a behavior is expressed, and how others interpret the behavior can determine whether that behavior will result in positive or negative consequences for the individual. Contextual moderators can be conceptualized in an objective or subjective manner, and this, in turn, will decide how they are operationalized. Steinert et al. (2017) cited examples of potential contextual moderators of the association between psychopathy and success and these include perceived threat or dangerousness and work demands. More speculative contextual moderators include the presence of strong behavioral norms, conditions that promote anonymity or transparency, and the presence of authority (Steinert et al., 2017).

Finally, a comprehensive model of the factors that moderate and mediate the relationship between the dark triad traits and CWBs was advanced by Cohen (2016). The model proposes a comprehensive conceptual framework explicating the relationship between the dark triad personalities and CWBs. Cohen advanced this model in response to the claim made by Harms and Spain (2015) regarding the lack of well-developed theoretical models to guide research and practice related to the conditions under which the characteristics of the dark personality should matter most and the potential moderators of their effects. Cohen's (2016) model includes mediators and moderators to explain the relationship between the two concepts. The model suggests that perceptions of organizational politics (POPs) and accountability mediate the relationship between the dark triad construct and CWBs. The model also advances four moderators. First, political skill is expected to moderate the relationship between the mediators mentioned and the dark triad. Second, three organizational factors—organizational transparency, organizational policies, and organizational culture—are expected to moderate the relationship between the two mediators and CWBs. The following section elaborates on Cohen's

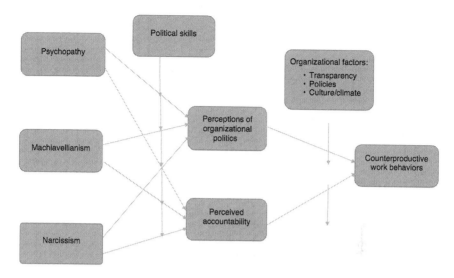

Figure 6.1 Research model
Source: Cohen, 2016.

model (Figure 6.1). The main propositions of this model are also included in the following section.

As shown, the model suggests that POPs and accountability mediate the relationship between the dark triad personality and CWBs.

Perceptions of Organizational Politics as Mediator

Rosen and Levy (2013) adopted Schneider's (1987) framework to explain the effect of politics on organizations. Schneider argued that employees are attracted to organizations where their perceived fit is good, and employers select employees who are a good fit for the organization (e.g., based on their perceptions as well as the selection tools), and employees who are not a good fit with the organization leave for organizations where they are a better fit. Furthermore, Schneider maintained that employees tend to gravitate toward organizations that are a good match for their individual traits (e.g., people who are high in the dark triad construct and have a high level of political skills may be more likely to work in highly political organizations).

Rosen and Levy (2013) contended that political environments are, by definition, characterized as having members who seek to maximize self-interests, often at the expense of others. This, in fact, is quite typical of the psychopaths' behavior in the organizational setting, as mentioned by Boddy (2010a), who argued that a political environment is ideal for the cunning and manipulative talents of psychopaths in organizations. In such an environment, it is easier for them to hide their lack of effort because performance appraisals are not as objective because they are not directly linked to external and objective performance indicators such as profits. Politics also plays a larger part in performance appraisals and promotions and therefore is advantageous to those who are cunning and manipulative, such as psychopaths.

Dark triad personalities are inclined, more than others, to sense the political opportunities in their organization. They are also more qualified to do so because they are always attracted to environments that provide them with a more convenient setting for their operations. Witt and Spector (2012) explained the process by which psychopaths adapt to the political setting. In their view, POPs are actually an assessment of the social nuances of the organizational context, providing cues that communicate the expected norms of behavior (Cialdini & Trost, 1998; Ehrhart & Naumann, 2004).

In agreement with the social cognitive theory, Witt and Spector (2012) further contended that perceptions of high levels of politics in an organization are likely to indicate that self-interested behavior leads to rewards and the norms of loyalty to the organization and treating others with respect are scarce. Accordingly, workers in highly political organizations may follow suit by exploiting others in the organization. Hence, they are likely to have a high level of tolerance for self-interest as a method of achieving advancement and a corresponding belief that political behavior is normatively appropriate. Consequently, those who perceive high levels of organizational politics are likely to conclude that refraining from expending effort on activities that may not enhance their career progression (i.e., low task and adaptive performance) is not inappropriate and is likely to go unpunished. In such environments, workers may be motivated to relax their personal standards through the psychological processes of displacement or diffusion of responsibility and may disregard or even distort the consequences of their actions.

Thus, workers who reduce the effort they expend on their tasks withhold organization-relevant adaptive behaviors. For example, they may exert effort to build competencies that enhance their own career mobility even at the expense of ignoring competencies that are of benefit to the organization. This focus on their own career building can lead to expending reduced effort on required tasks, being absent from work, engaging in self-serving activities (e.g., learning new skills), and eventually leaving when career-enhancing opportunities present themselves (Witt & Spector, 2012).

Consequently, a highly political environment seems to be the setting where dark triad personalities feel very comfortable to operate in order to achieve their goals. Because dark triad personalities are always looking for an environment perceived as friendly in terms of enabling them to achieve their goals, they are more inclined and more qualified to identify political opportunities in every setting in which they operate. Being more sensitive than others to the contextual cues of their setting and the political opportunities this setting offers, they are more capable of reading and understanding them.

This kind of rationale leads one to expect a positive relationship between POPs and CWBs. An environment perceived as highly political presents many opportunities for those high in the dark triad construct to achieve their goals. Contextual cues, such as high levels of politics in a given setting, signal that perpetrating CWBs paves the way to success. Highly political environments indicate that person-targeted CWBs may lead to resource acquisition and career success. Dark triad personalities, by their nature, are more aware of these clues and opportunities and perform more CWBs in order to achieve their goals.

Thus,

Proposition 1: Perceived organizational politics mediates the relationship between the dark triad construct and CWBs. The relationship between the dark triad personality and perceived politics is positive, and the relationship between perceived politics and CWBs is positive as well.

Accountability as a Mediator

Accountability is necessary for the effective operation of any enterprise (Hochwarter, Perrewé, Hall, & Ferris, 2005). It is based on the need of organizations to exert some degree of control over the behavior of their employees (Ammeter, Douglas, Ferris, & Goka, 2004). Without accountability, there can be no basis for a social order that sustains the social systems in organizations as we know them (Tetlock, 1992). Left to operate according to their own discretion, many people focus on advancing their own interests rather than the interests of the larger social group (Kaiser & Hogan, 2006). Accountability mechanisms can range from formal (e.g., performance evaluation systems, financial reporting procedures, laws and regulations) to informal (e.g., feeling of loyalty to an organization) (Ammeter et al., 2004; Kaiser & Hogan, 2006).

Ammeter et al. (2004) presented the definition of accountability proposed by Frink and Klimoski (1998), where accountability is viewed as the perceived need to justify or define a decision or action to some audiences who have no potential reward or sanction power and where such rewards and sanctions are perceived as contingent on accountability conditions. In recent years, scholars have focused on the concept of "felt accountability," which describes one's perceived need to justify actions and judgments to others (Hochwarter, Parker, Ellen, & Ferris, 2014). As such, accountability is a perception based on shared expectations about a potential requirement to explain one's actions or beliefs regarding an organizational issue to a constituency for reasons such as social desirability.

Based largely on phenomenological principles, it has been argued that accountability perceptions are subjective, with responses linked to person-centric cue interpretations rather than agreed-upon absolutes (Hochwarter et al., 2014). Because assessments of accountability are based, in part, on perceptions of subjective external conditions, individuals may perceive and experience those subjective conditions differently. Felt accountability can thus be defined as an implicit or explicit expectation that one's decisions or actions will be deemed important or noteworthy and will be subject to evaluation by salient others, based on the belief that there exists a potential for one to receive either rewards or sanctions (Hochwarter et al., 2005).

Boddy (2010a) argued that control and public scrutiny, which are more common in the public sector, may serve as barriers to psychopaths in organizations. Boddy contended that psychopaths in organizations have little or no conscience and therefore are not driven by any idea of social fairness or social responsibility, which, in turn, should, in theory, limit the development of corporate social responsibility within the corporations for which they work. Indeed, Boddy (2010a) found in a sample of white-collar employees in Australia that the presence of psychopaths is negatively and significantly associated with perceived levels of corporate social responsibility within organizations.

Witt and Spector's (2012) views on POPs are relevant here, too. Perceived accountability constitutes an assessment of the social nuances of the organizational context, providing cues that communicate the expected norms of behavior. As in the case of politics, the underlying idea is that individuals observe and model the actions of others and simultaneously link these actions with information about environmental incentives. These contextual cues enable individuals to interpret events and understand norms and make decisions accordingly. Hence, contextual cues lead to the development of socially constructed realities, which indicate what behaviors are acceptable, appropriate, and expected and therefore required for survival and advancement.

Perceptions of high levels of accountability are likely to indicate that self-interested behavior is controlled and might lead to preventive action being taken by the organization. Martin, Brock, Buckley, and Ketchen (2010) contended, for example, that the presence of job standards, such as productivity goals and accountability to meet those goals, is also likely to reduce time banditry. If effective controls are in place, individuals have a harder time engaging in counterproductive acts. Those high in psychopathy are also sensitive to these kinds of clues and might be more careful before considering and performing CWBs. Consequently, psychopaths who perceive a high level of accountability are likely to conclude that it would be better for them to refrain from CWBs that might put them at risk of exposure. Thus,

Proposition 2: Perceived accountability mediates the relationship between the dark triad personality and CWBs. The relationship between the dark triad personality and felt accountability is negative, and the relationship between felt accountability and CWBs is negative.

Political Skills as a Moderator

Ferris et al. (2005) contended that the research on organizational politics, although extensive, has failed to evaluate the political skill of the influencer, yielding inadequate information about why efforts to exert an influence succeed or not. Ferris et al. argued that politically skilled individuals convey a sense of personal security and calm self-confidence that attracts others and gives them a feeling of comfort. Highly politically skilled people know precisely not only what to do in different social situations at work but also how to do it in a manner that disguises any ulterior, self-serving motives and appears to be sincere.

Ammeter et al. (2004) discussed the definition proposed by Ferris, Kolodinsky, Hochwarter, and Frink (2001) of political skills as a construct of interpersonal style that combines interpersonal perceptiveness or social astuteness with the capacity to adjust one's behavior to different situational demands in a manner that inspires confidence, trust, sincerity, and genuineness and effectively influences and controls the responses of others. Ferris et al. contended that political skill is a multi-dimensional concept composed of four dimensions: (1) social astuteness—individuals possessing political ability are astute observers of others and are keenly attuned to diverse social situations; (2) interpersonal influence—politically skilled individuals have a subtle and convincing personal style that exerts a powerful influence on those around them; (3) networking ability—an individual with strong political skills is adept at developing and using diverse networks of people; and (4) apparent sincerity—politically skilled individuals appear to others as having high levels of integrity, authenticity, sincerity, and genuineness.

Treadway, Ferris, Duke, Adams, and Thatcher (2007) found that politically skilled employees were able to disguise their self-serving behavior. Treadway, Shaughnessy, Breland, Yang, and Reeves (2013) found a relationship between political skills and bullying. They contended that politically skilled employees are more capable of understanding both the social context within which they operate and the motivations of other participants in that context. As a result, politically skilled employees may be more competent at choosing contexts and victims that help them gain the scarce resources or create the broad coalitions needed to achieve their personal objectives. Treadway et al. (2013) argued that politically skilled bullies are more adept at understanding the social context of the workplace, gauging others' intentions and motivations, and calibrating their behavior to match these contextual demands. Thus, it is expected that politically skilled bullies are able to use their bullying behavior to build broad coalitions of supporters and pools of resources that will facilitate their own job performance. Furthermore, because of their ability to read the social context of the workplace, they are less likely to be viewed as bullies by their superiors and powerful others.

A different conceptual framework relevant for the dark triad construct was presented by Wallace (2015), which is focused mostly on narcissism but may also be relevant also to the other two dark triad dimensions. According to Wallace, the context relevant to explaining this relationship is ego threat. Organizations are riddled with ego-threatening situations with which employees must contend on a regular basis. Wallace mentioned two theories which, together, suggest that employees respond to ego-threatening situations via self-enhancing or self-protecting behavior. Wallace contended that narcissists, who are hypervigilant to ego threats, are more likely to engage in these self-preserving behaviors than non-narcissists. Her study proposed a contingency model, suggesting that narcissism can be functional or dysfunctional depending on the ability of the narcissistic individual to minimize threat through the use of self-maintenance mechanisms, resulting in either favorable or unfavorable performance-related outcomes. When faced with a threat, if they are politically skilled, those high in narcissism will engage in self-maintenance mechanisms effectively, leading to positive outcomes. Conversely, if they lack political skill, when threatened, those high in narcissism will engage in ineffective self-maintenance mechanisms, resulting in negative outcomes.

Interaction of Political Skills and Perceived Organizational Politics

Politically skilled individuals possess a high degree of social astuteness, interpersonal influences, networking ability, and the ability to project sincerity (Rosen & Levy, 2013). Rosen and Levy (2013) mentioned the contention of Ferris et al. (2007) that political skill reflects a pattern of social competencies, providing individuals with the ability to assess social cues, match behavior to fit situations, and attain goals using interpersonal influence. Elaborating this contention, Rosen and Levy (2013) argued that because political contexts are marked by ambiguous reward structures, politically skilled employees, because of their ability to influence others, are likely to view this situation as less threatening and may see it as an opportunity to capitalize on their unique skills. Thus, heightened social perceptiveness and the ability to influence others are likely to lead politically skilled employees to feel that they have greater control over their environment (Rosen & Levy, 2013).

Politically skilled workers are endowed with intuitive shrewdness and an understanding of people and interactions in addition to their ability to perceive other people and situations accurately and access information through their networks in the organization. Thus, they can navigate political environments more efficiently because their heightened understanding of people and environments provides them with knowledge about the performance required to achieve desired outcomes (Rosen & Levy, 2013). A political environment is an unfair setting in which decision making is influenced by political games. In such an environment, individuals who have political savvy (i.e., politically skilled individuals) are able to read the rules of the game, and thus their perception of the situation is less uncertain (Kimura, 2013). Indeed, Rosen and Levy (2013) found that politically skilled employees were less likely to perceive that their psychological contracts have been breached when engaging in politics at work and therefore are better fitted for organizations high in politics.

Based on these arguments, it is reasonable to expect that personalities scoring high in the dark triad construct and who operate in highly political organizations are aware of the fact that their environment makes it easier for them to act as they please to achieve their goals. However, the level of political skills varies among people, including among those scoring higher in the dark triad construct. Higher levels of political skill enable high-scoring employees in the dark triad construct to understand and manipulate their political environment better, as well as to identify better the opportunities offered by their organizational environment.

Because of their higher levels of political skills, demonstrated in skills such as social astuteness and networking ability, these employees recognize the political advantages in their environment considerably more easily than those whose level of political skills is low. As a result, the relationship between the dark triad personality and perceived organizational politics is expected to be stronger for those high in political skills than those low in these skills. Thus,

Proposition 3: The relationship between the dark triad personality and perceived organizational politics is stronger among those higher in political skills than those lower in these skills.

Interaction of Political Skills and Accountability

Ammeter et al. (2004) contended that highly politically skilled people are able to actively influence and control their accountability both in degree and type. That is, using skills such as interpersonal influence and apparent sincerity, they can exercise influence not only over the level or degree of accountability but also over the issues for which they are actually held accountable (behaviors or actual outcomes) and perhaps even over those by whom they are held accountable. According to Ammeter et al. (2004), examples of this are seen in corporate annual reports after a company has undergone a downturn. Here, the CEO (who is primarily responsible for crafting reports) uses appropriate language and instances to demonstrate that the performance outcome (downturn) was beyond the company's control and that the firm continued to show responsible behavior and worked hard in an effort to remedy the situation. It is more than reasonable to expect that those higher in the dark triad personality with high political skills are able to actively influence and control their own accountability more than those lower in political skills. Using skills such as interpersonal influence and apparent sincerity, they are more successful in convincing others in the organization, as well as even themselves, that they are accountable only for the organization's positive outcomes, not for the negative ones. Thus,

> *Proposition 4: The relationship between the dark triad personality and perceived accountability is weaker among those higher in political skills than those lower in these skills.*

Organizational Factors as Moderators

Three organizational factors are advanced here as moderators in the relationship between POPs and perceived accountability and the dependent variable, CWBs. The moderators are organizational transparency, organizational policies, and organizational culture or climate.

Organizational Transparency as a Moderator

Transparency is the availability of information about an organization or actor that allows external agents to monitor the internal workings or performance of that organization or actor (Grimmelikhuijsen & Welch, 2012). Ferry and Eckersley (2015) argued that transparency initiatives indeed help to reduce corruption because they represent an important mechanism through which citizens can access information that has not been edited or shaped by powerful political actors. "Transparency" has become a buzzword used to describe the notion of accuracy, truth, and the full disclosure of relevant information (Cicala, Bush, Sherrell, & Deitz, 2014). According to Cicala et al. (2014), based on the agency theory, transparency focuses on the enhanced ability of principals to monitor and potentially control agents' actions. Cicala et al. cited Zuboff (1988), who argued that transparency reinforces and increases managers' power and control over subordinates. They contended that from this perspective, the focus is within the organization and examines manager–employee relations. They found that salespersons' perceptions of managerial use of behavioral information, obtained through technological means, have a mediating effect on the relationship between managerial access to such information and the likelihood of unethical salesperson behavior.

Cicala et al. (2014) cited Turilli and Floridi's (2009, p. 105) definition that transparency is "the possibility of accessing information, intentions, or behaviors." According to Turilli and Floridi (2009), transparency is a pre-ethical condition for enabling or impairing other ethical practices or principles. Transparency is also defined as the willingness to hold oneself (and one's actions) open to inspection in order to receive valid feedback (Ellis, Caridi, Lipshitz, & Popper, 1999). Transparency can be achieved by technical and cultural means. The former can be reached by small-scale organizational designs that let everyone see how things are done and understand the role of each person in getting it done, exemplified by lack of defensiveness

(Ellis et al., 1999). The characteristics of transparency most frequently mentioned in the relevant literature are openness, disclosure, sharing, and free flow (Horne, 2012). Harvey, Martinko, and Gardner (2006) argued that a transparent organizational context can promote authenticity because transparency reduces the likelihood of biased attributions by clarifying the causes of outcomes. Harvey et al. further contended that this may help explain ethical failings caused by ambiguity and reduce transparency created by the size and complexity of many organizations, thereby increasing the potential of inauthentic behavior resulting from biased attributions.

In short, transparency throughout the organizational structure is a necessary condition for reducing the potential of illicit dealings. Ambiguity often stems from unclear articulation of required role expectations, work methods, or performance contingencies. In ambiguous contexts, employees have only a limited understanding of the appropriate work behaviors necessary for fulfilling the demands of their work roles (Rubin, Dierdorff, & Bachrach, 2013). Procedures such as record-keeping and reporting can be used by organizations to document key aspects of its compliance efforts and to monitor its programs for effectiveness. Even the reporting of minor incidents within an organization can serve a useful purpose in that it underlines a zero-tolerance policy for questionable behaviors. Failure to report such occurrences may lead to the perception that such irregularities will be tolerated (Luo, 2005).

How can transparency be related to CWB? Johns (1999) contended that self-serving behavior is most likely when cause–effect relationships are unclear; when it is difficult to predict future events or the consequences of decisions; or when cues regarding effective action are weak, vague, or contradictory. These are the main characteristics of organizational uncertainty. According to Johns, under uncertainty conditions, wishful thinking is feasible, and social censure for self-serving is less likely to be anticipated. In addition, ambiguity allows motives to have an undue impact on perceptions. Weak, vague, or contradictory conditions connote self-justification, self-presentation, and information bias. Johns contended that self-serving reactions are more likely under ambiguous task conditions and less likely when the reality of the situation is difficult to dispute. In short, ambiguity and uncertainty, as opposed to transparency, provide a perfect environment for dark triad employees who are willing to act. Indeed, Yang and Diefendorff (2009) found a relationship between perceived ambiguity and CWBs.

Interaction of Transparency with Perceived Organizational Politics and Accountability

Propositions 1 and 2 state that POPs and accountability mediate the relationship between the dark triad construct and CWBs, so that POPs are positively related to CWB and accountability is negatively related to it.

However, the model advanced here argues that these relationships are moderated by organizational transparency. The relationship between POPs and CWBs are weaker for those scoring high in the dark triad traits who operate in organizations higher in transparency. Kaptein (2008) contended that low visibility or transparency in organizations diminishes the possibility of controlling the environment and therefore widens the scope of unethical conduct. According to Johns (1999), organizational politics is most likely to occur under conditions of vague goals and complex tasks and at the higher levels of the organization. Each of these conditions introduces uncertainty into elements such as decision and performance criteria, leading to the occurrence of the blame laying and smoke screening that often characterize politics.

All these conditions constitute an ideal setting for those scoring high in the dark triad and operate in a political climate. It is more than reasonable to speculate that those high in the dark triad dimensions prefer to operate in the dark, where they cannot be traced and cannot be blamed. Low levels of transparency provide such an ideal setting for them. Because ambiguities allow flexibility in interpretation, they can be used strategically by those who are in the best position to take advantage of this interpretative power (Best, 2012). Smith and Lilienfeld (2013) mentioned Babiak (1995, 2000), who speculated that an organizational climate of chaotic transition, which contains stimulation and excitement, may be conducive to psychopathic individuals to achieve success.

According to Kaptein (2008), transparency was found to be important not only for its potential to expose unethical conduct but also for acting as a deterrent because of the perceived probability of getting caught. Peers, peer perceptions, and frequent contact with peer groups strongly influence ethical decision-making and behavior by virtue of the feedback, overview, disclosure, and the diminished room for misinterpretation and dishonesty that accompanies them. The organizational value of transparency is defined as the degree to which employee conduct and its consequences are perceptible by those who can act upon them (i.e., colleagues, supervisors, subordinates, and the employees concerned). Those scoring high in the dark triad construct, who perceive themselves as operating in a political environment, hesitate to perform CWBs in organizations with higher levels of transparency. An organizational environment where information about behaviors is available and can be tracked is not preferred by dark triad personalities because it increases the probability that they will be exposed.

Similar logic is relevant to organizational transparency as a moderator in the relationship between perceived accountability and CWBs. As mentioned previously, perceptions of high levels of accountability are likely to indicate that self-interested behavior is controlled and may lead to preventive action on part of the organization. Those who both score higher in the dark triad construct and perceive low accountability and who operate in a low-transparency organization would be more inclined to perform

CWBs because they believe that the environment is safe for such actions and the probability of their being caught is sufficiently low. Those with low perceived accountability operating in organizations high in transparency hesitate much more because there is a higher probability that they will find themselves in a situation where they will be traced and will have to explain some of their CWBs.

> *Proposition 5: The positive relationship between perceived organizational politics and CWBs is weaker among those operating in organizations with high levels of transparency than among those working in organizations with low levels of transparency.*
> *Proposition 6: The negative relationship between perceived accountability and CWBs is weaker among those working in organizations with higher levels of transparency than those operating in organizations with lower levels of transparency.*

Organizational Policies as a Moderator

An important perspective found in the literature on formal organizations is that the behavior of individuals is a function of the external constraints placed on them by the organization (Parilla, Hollinger, & Clark, 1988). As mentioned by Parilla et al. (1988), the use of formalized policies and rules has long been recognized as a fundamental means of obtaining control in bureaucratic organizations (Weber, 1947). In the Weberian model, written rules and policies serve as a mechanism through which members learn what is expected of them. Policies can directly affect employee behavior, and in our case, they might have a direct bearing on the CWBs of dark triad personalities. Parilla et al. (1988) exemplified the importance of policies for preventing theft, arguing that the treatment of employee theft as a matter of policy serves two deterrence-related functions. The most obvious of these is the communication of threat. An anti-theft rule or policy is a formal announcement that theft of organizational property is considered a serious matter and will be punished as such. Second, the presence of a theft policy increases the likelihood that supervisors will react when theft is discovered, thereby increasing the actual certainty of punishment. In addition, formalized rules tend to legitimize the use of management sanctions because they constitute a fair public warning as to the type of behavior that will result in punishment (Parilla et al., 1988). Employees are sensitive to stated company policies. A formal organizational policy about ethical behavior is a viable means by which firms can influence ethical conduct (Bellizzi & Hasty, 2001).

A broader perspective on organizational policies was provided by Fine et al. (2010), who defined security control norms as an overall measure of the perceived formal or informal means of deterring CWBs (i.e., security controls) and the actual pervasiveness of CWBs in the organization (i.e., security norms). Typical security controls include the monitoring of behaviors via physical control systems (e.g., guards, cameras, and police), which are designed to make employees aware of the likelihood of getting caught, and sanctioning or punishing such behaviors, intended to make employees aware of the consequences of getting caught. Fine et al. contended that informal sanctions are difficult to measure directly, and perceived controls and norms are arguably more appropriate than actual controls in predicting CWBs. Their findings supported their argument.

Fine et al. (2010) provided two conceptual explanations for the relationship between norms of security control and CWBs. Social learning theory describes how people's behavior is learned by observing and imitating the behaviors of others and how these behaviors can be positively reinforced by rewards and negatively by punishments. According to the second theory, that of social information processing, individuals develop attitudes about their surroundings that are in line with normative group behaviors and their typical consequences. For example, employees who observe their managers or coworkers engage in dishonest behaviors without being noticed or being punished by the company will probably conclude that these behaviors are acceptable and may start to adopt these behaviors themselves (Fine et al., 2010).

Several studies have supported these claims. According to Salin (2003), if there are no policy against bullying, no monitoring policy, and no punishments for those who engage in bullying, it might be interpreted that the organization accepts it, and a potential perpetrator will perceive the costs and dangers of bullying as very low. Peterson (2002) found that employees of organizations with a low perceived emphasis on adherence to company rules and laws would be more likely to engage in deviant behavior related to the misuse of organizational property. However, clear policies against such behaviors (e.g., sexual harassment) significantly reduced this behavior (Gruber, 1998).

Interaction of Organizational Policies with Perceived Organizational Politics and Accountability

As in the case of organizational transparency, the model proposed here argues that organizational policies moderate the relationship between POPs and accountability and CWBs. The relationship between POPs and CWBs is weaker for those scoring high in the dark triad construct, who operate in organizations with clear policies against CWBs, as well as sanctions to be applied when violation occurs. Naturally, the organizational history should very clearly show that sanctions were applied in the past against violators. Clear policies followed consistently by the organization increase the controlled environment, narrowing the scope of unethical conduct. While organizational politics is most likely under conditions of vague goals and complex tasks (Johns, 1999), strict organizational policies regarding CWBs introduce certainty and clarity into the decision-making processes in the organization. This, in turn, narrows the scope of politics in the decision-making process in the organization.

Clear and applied organizational policies create a very unfriendly setting for those scoring high in the dark triad construct who operate in a political climate. It is only reasonable to predict that they would prefer to operate in an organizational setting without or with very vague organizational policies regarding CWBs that are rarely applied by the organization. Formal and applicable organizational policies provide a very unfriendly setting for them. Those scoring high in the dark triad construct will hesitate to perform CWBs in organizations where the policies against it are clear and practical, as well as having the reputation of being applied when needed. Hegarty and Sims (1979) reported that a clear organizational policy had a deterrent influence on unethical behavior. Their results suggested that a clearly stated and communicated organizational policy can be useful and effective in guiding employee ethical behavior. An organizational environment where policies about unwanted behaviors are available and applied is not a preferable one for dark triad personalities because it increases the probability that they will be exposed and punished.

A similar logic applies to organizational policies as a moderator in the relationship between perceived accountability and CWBs. As mentioned previously, perceptions of high levels of accountability are likely to indicate that self-interested behavior is controlled and may lead to preventive action by the organization. Those who both score higher in the dark triad construct and perceive low accountability and who operate in a setting with no or unclear policies regarding CWBs would be more inclined to perform CWBs because they believe that the environment is safe for such actions and the probability of their being caught and punished is sufficiently low. According to Fine et al. (2010), employees who perceive that they are unlikely to be caught or that they would be dealt with leniently if caught are more likely to engage in CWBs. This is definitely relevant for dark triad personalities. Conversely, organizations with clearly defined, consistent, and severe anti-theft policies, for example, have lower theft rates. Those with low perceived accountability, operating in organizations with clear policies regarding CWBs, hesitate much more to perform CWBs because there is a higher probability that they will find themselves in a situation where they will be traced and punished.

Proposition 7: The positive relationship between perceived organizational politics and CWBs is weaker among those operating in organizations with strict policies regarding CWBs than among those working in organizations with no or vague policies regarding CWBs.

Proposition 8: The negative relationship between perceived accountability and CWBs is weaker among those working in organizations with strict organizational policies regarding CWBs than those operating in organizations with no or vague organizational policies regarding CWBs.

Organizational Culture or Climate as a Moderator

According to Schein (1992), organizational culture consists of a set of shared meanings, assumptions, values, and norms that guide employees' behavior via explicit structures and conventions. A concept similar to organizational culture is that of organizational climate, which refers to a set of attributes that can be perceived about a particular organization or its subsystems and that can be deduced from the way that the organization or its subsystems deal with their members and environment (Hellriegel & Slocum, 1974). According to Denison (1996) and Schneider, Ehrhart, and Macey (2013), there is a strong theoretical basis for integrating the two concepts rather than assuming that culture and climate are fundamentally different and non-overlapping systems. Therefore, the two concepts are treated here interchangeably based on the conceptual arguments already mentioned and the empirical findings mentioned by Kaptein (2011), which showed that the two concepts are not fundamentally different.

As discussed by Vardi (2001), just as there is a climate for leadership, a climate for power, a climate for motivation, or a climate for creativity, there is also a climate for CWBs. According to Treviño, Butterfield, and McCabe (1998), "ethical climate" can be defined as the perceptions of managers and employees about what constitutes unethical and ethical behavior in the organization. Likewise, ethical culture can be defined as the perception about the conditions that are in place in the organization for complying or not with what constitutes unethical and ethical behavior. According to Pinto, Leana, and Pil (2008), an ethical culture does not indicate whether or not an organization is corrupt. That is, it could promote either ethical or unethical behavior. As stated by Sims (1992), organizations vary in the ethical climate they establish for their members. The ethical tone or climate is established at the top. What top management do, and the culture they create and reinforce, has a profound influence on the way lower level employees act and the way the organization as a whole is managed when facing ethical dilemmas.

Undoubtedly, ethical standards are undermined when managers and supervisors communicate contradictory or inconsistent signals to subordinates. Behavior that is consistent with the organization's ethical standards reinforces the notion of compliance with these standards (Kaptein, 2011). According to Campbell and Göritz (2014), corrupt organizational culture aims to ensure employees' support of corruption. Therefore, corrupt organizational culture needs to address the work-related values and norms of work groups, including the organizations' expectations regarding employees' corruption. Sometimes corrupt organizations install and communicate ethical values to their employees by means of a code of conduct. In defiance of this code of conduct, corrupt organizations provide contradictory information to their employees, implying "We follow ethical values, but in fact, we do not care." When employees work in such an ambiguous environment, they need guidelines that change their perception to one that supports corrupt behavior. Therefore, the corrupt organizational culture emphasizes the message "we do not care" while building a framework that camouflages.

How is organizational culture related to CWBs? In a culture where the values and norms are heavily directed toward deviation, organizational misbehavior will become the norm (Vardi & Wiener, 1992). Pilch and Turska (2015) demonstrated this relationship in the context of bullying. According to them, in some cultures, bullying and aggression may be considered an effective means of achieving goals. If management concentrates on outcomes, disregarding the means by which they are achieved, if the results of the achieved outcomes are evaluated without considering the toll on the organization members, and if competition and combat are valued, bullying will be tolerated to the point that the organizational culture will allow certain forms of bullying. Pilch and Turska (2015) cited Aquino and Lamertz (2004), who described two types of cultural norms supporting bullying. Organizational culture may support aggressive behaviors if they are thought to be functional for motivating employees and if disrespectful behaviors and those harming others are tolerated and organizational standards support incivility and rude behavior. Ford and Richardson (1994) concluded, based on a review of empirical studies, that the more ethical the climate and culture of an organization is, the more ethical an individual employee's beliefs and decision behavior will be. In another study, Vardi (2001) found a negative relationship between organizational climate and CWBs.

Interaction Between Organizational Culture or Climate and Perceived Organizational Politics and Accountability

The model in Figure 6.1 contends that organizational culture or climate moderates the relationship between POPs and accountability and CWBs. The relationship between POPs and CWBs is weaker for those scoring high in the dark triad construct who operate in organizations with a culture that opposes ethical violations as well as CWBs. According to Riley (1983), a lack of rules regarding the means by which the firm's goals are achieved is generally reflected in its culture, allowing the culture to be more political. However, a culture that strongly supports ethical values and behaviors narrows the scope of unethical conduct. A strong ethical organizational culture that opposes CWBs introduces integrity and morality into the organization's decision-making processes. This, in turn, narrows the scope of politics in terms of affecting decisions in the organization. A clear ethical culture creates a very unfriendly setting for those scoring high in the dark triad construct. It is more than reasonable to predict that they would prefer to operate in an organizational setting with a vague organizational culture regarding CWBs. An organizational culture with a strong climate against unethical conduct is not a preferable one for the dark triad personalities because it increases the probability that their behavior, which contradicts the dominant culture, will be revealed and punished.

A similar logic applies to organizational culture or climate as a moderator in the relationship between perceived accountability and CWBs. As mentioned previously, perceptions of high levels of accountability are likely to indicate that self-interested behavior is controlled and may lead to preventive action by the organization. Individuals in different cultures are educated to understand the unique expectations that exist at different levels in the social system, the strength of these expectations, and the consequences for deviations from these expectations. Thus, as individuals are enculturated through socialization into a particular sociocultural context, they develop cognitive maps of how various individuals, groups, and organizations are answerable or accountable to one another (Gelfand, Lim, & Raver, 2004). Those who score higher in the dark triad construct, perceive low accountability, and operate in a setting with a vague or unethical culture that does not clearly condemn CWBs are more inclined to perform CWBs because they believe that the environment is safe and even supportive of such actions, and the probability of their being detected and criticized is sufficiently low. Conversely, those with low perceived accountability, who operate in organizations with a clear anti-CWB culture, are much more hesitant to perform CWBs because there is a much higher probability that they will find themselves in a situation where they will be traced and condemned.

> Proposition 9: *The positive relationship between perceived organizational politics and CWBs is weaker among those who operate in organizations with an ethical culture or climate that opposes CWBs than among those who are working in organizations with an organizational culture that supports CWBs.*
>
> Proposition 10: *The negative relationship between perceived accountability and CWBs is weaker among those who are working in organizations with strong pro ethical culture or climate that opposes CWBs than among those who are operating in organizations with an organizational culture that supports CWBs.*

In conclusion, Cohen's (2016) model attempts to enhance the understanding of the relationship between the dark triad and CWBs by proposing a framework that suggests that the relationship between dark triad personalities and CWBs is mediated and moderated by variables that, based on the person–organization fit theory, represent a friendly or unfriendly environment for the dark triad traits (Vardi, 2001). The model proposed by Cohen is comprehensive because it views the relationship between the dark triad and CWBs as complex and indirect. However, its derived propositions constitute only a preliminary step in exploring this issue. More empirical work is needed that will examine the model as a whole or partially.

Such an attempt was made by Cohen and Shoval (2018) and is presented in Figure 6.2. As can be seen, the model examines the relationship of both

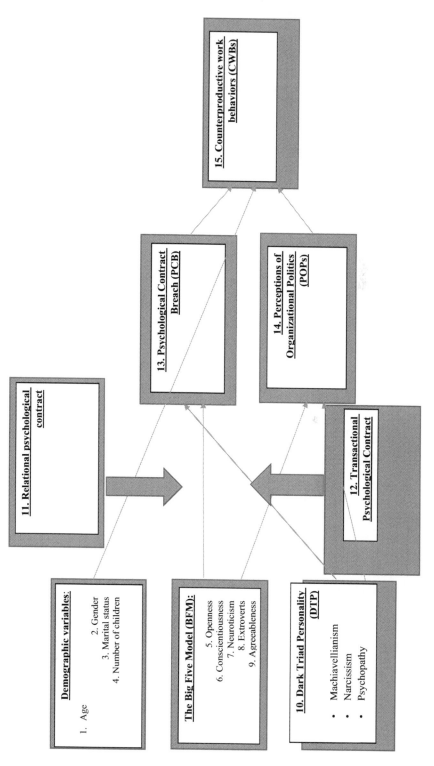

Figure 6.2 Research model
From Cohen & Shoval, 2018.

the Five-Factor Model (FFM) and the dark triad and CWBs. It should be noted, however, that the dark triad personalities were combined into one scale representing all constructs as one dimension. As can be seen in the research model (Figure 6.2), the direct relationship between the FFM and the dark triad and CWB is expected to differ, depending on the moderators and mediators suggested in the model. The research model suggests that two types of psychological contracts, relational and transactional, moderate the relationship between the personality variables and the two mediators, psychological contract breach and perceptions of politics. The main hypotheses and findings of this model are presented in the following section.

Psychological Contracts as Moderators

According to Hui, Lee, and Rousseau (2004), it is important to understand the nature and forms of psychological contracts and to examine the impact of these forms of contract on organizationally relevant outcomes. The actual nature of a psychological contract can send important messages, triggering particular employee responses (Hui et al., 2004). Transactional contracts are characterized by the limited involvement of the parties and emphasize specific, short-term monetary obligations. The identity of the parties is irrelevant. In contrast, a relational contract focuses on open-ended relationships, involving considerable investments on part of both employees (company-specific skills, long-term career development) and employers (extensive training). Such investments involve a high degree of mutual interdependence and barriers to exit (Rousseau, 1995).

Each position on the continuum of psychological contracts, with transactional contracts and relational contracts at the opposite poles, has correspondent types of behavior (Minjina, 2011). Thus, antisocial behaviors such as CWBs are associated with transactional contracts and relational contracts are associated with prosocial behaviors, such as OCB. When employees believe their employer is honor bound to fulfill a broad range of obligations (as in the form of relational contract), they may be more inclined to develop a stronger psychological attachment to the organization (Hui et al., 2004). This type of psychological contract implies that individuals fully internalize company values and link their identities with the organization. As a result, one can expect that the relationship between personality variables and the two mediators (psychological contract breach and perceptions of politics) are weaker for employees with a high relational psychological contract and stronger for those with a low relational psychological contract.

However, when employees believe their employer's obligation to them consists only of a short-term economic exchange (as in the form of transactional contract), they may be less likely to develop loyalty and a long-term relationship with the organization (Millward & Hopkins, 1998; Jensen, Opland, & Ryan, 2010). Under a transactional contract, an individual's identity is said to be derived from his or her unique skills and competencies, those on which the exchange relationship itself is based. For transactional-oriented employees, the organization is simply the place where they do their work. They seek immediate rewards from the employment situation, such as pay and credentials (Millward and Hopkins, 1998; Jensen et al., 2010), and invest little emotional attachment or commitment in the organization. This theory suggests that the relationship between personal variables and psychological contract breach and perceptions of politics is stronger for those with a high transactional contract and weaker for those with a low transactional contract.

> *Hypothesis 1a: The relational psychological contract moderates the relationship between personal variables and the two mediators (psychological contract breach and perceptions of politics). The relationship is weaker for those with a highly relational contract and stronger for those with a lower relational contract.*
>
> *Hypothesis 1b: The transactional psychological contract moderates the relationship between personal variables and the two mediators (psychological contract breach and perceptions of politics). The relationship is stronger for those with a highly transactional contract and weaker for those with a lower transactional contract.*

Perceptions of Organizational Politics as a Mediator

The role of perceptions of politics as a mediator in the relationship between a dark triad personality and CWB was strongly emphasized by Cohen's (2016) model. The rationale for POPs as a mediator was presented at length in the previous section and therefore will not be repeated here. Cohen and Shoval, however, examined the FFM in addition to the dark triad traits as independent variables. The rationale for this mediation relationship is presented in the following.

As already mentioned, the FFM represents positive personality traits (Youli & Chao, 2015). Employees with higher levels of each of the FFM traits tend to perceive their work environment (perceptions of politics and psychological contract breach) more positively than those with lower levels of the FFM traits, specifically, those with higher levels of the dark triad personality traits. A highly political environment is not necessarily the setting where employees higher in FFM traits feel comfortable. Employees with higher levels of the FFM traits perceive their environment as friendlier and are less inclined and less qualified to detect the negative aspects of the political environment in which they operate. This kind of rationale leads one to expect a negative relationship between each of the FFM traits and perceptions of politics. An environment that they perceive as highly political does not present opportunities for those high in the FFM traits because they are not in fact interested in the contextual cues of high levels of politics, signaling that engaging in CWB paves the way to success. For those high in FFM traits, political environments do not indicate that person-targeted CWB may lead to resource acquisition and career success. Because of their positive nature, they are less aware and interested in clues and opportunities for performing more CWBs in order to achieve their goals. Thus,

> *Hypothesis 1a: Perceptions of politics mediate the relationship between the dark triad personality and CWB. This relationship is positive, and the relationship between perceived politics and CWB is also positive.*
> *Hypothesis 1b: Perceptions of politics mediate the relationship between the FFM and CWB. The relationship between the FFM and perceptions of politics is negative, and the relationship between perceptions of politics and CWB is also negative.*

Psychological Contract Breach as a Mediator

The quality of the relationship between employees and their organization is based on the principle of reciprocity (Coyle-Shapiro & Kessler, 2003). That is, employees are likely to behave toward the organization in ways that they perceive as appropriate to compensate for the manner in which the organization has behaved toward them. Psychological contract breach reduces the employees' motivation to fulfill in-role responsibilities and increases their motivation to perform more CWBs in reaction to the unfairness of the contract breach, as they perceive it, caused by the organization. The belief that the organization breached the psychological contract is then translated into a behavior that inhibits employees' contributions to their organization (Chao, Cheung, & Wu, 2011). High levels of perceived psychological contract breach may increase employees' willingness to be involved in CWB. The feeling of being unfairly treated is a primary motivator of revenge (Furnham & Siegel, 2012), resulting in high levels of CWB.

That individual differences shape employees' perception of psychological contract breaches and sequential work behavior is supported both by theory and empirical findings (Shih & Chuang, 2013; Zagenczyk et al., 2013). Researchers have acknowledged that the norm of reciprocity, central to the psychological contract and other social exchange relationships, should be modified to take into account the role of individual differences (Orvis, Dudley, & Cortina, 2008). Furthermore, the role of personality in shaping responses to psychological contract breaches seems obvious.

That psychological contract-related perceptions are more a function of automatic than of deliberate mental processing suggests that personality traits, being intrinsic and elemental in nature, play a part in shaping such perceptions (Ho, Weingart, & Rousseau, 2004). It has been argued that dark triad personalities, by their nature, are looking for opportunities to engage in CWB to achieve their goals, and psychological contract breach provides them with a good additional internal motivation to do so. Individuals high in Machiavellianism, for example, are usually pragmatic, emotionally detached, and task—as opposed to person—oriented. Therefore, they are less likely to give organizations "the benefit of the doubt" regarding the reasons for which a psychological contract breach has occurred. Given that employees' beliefs about why a psychological contract breach has occurred exacerbate (or mitigate) their responses to the breach, this may suggest that highly Machiavellian employees respond more negatively to a psychological contract breach than less Machiavellian employees (Zagenczyk et al., 2013).

Research has shown that the FFM is also related to types of psychological contracts (Liao-Troth, 2005; Raja, Johns, & Ntalianis, 2004) and psychological contract breach (Ho et al., 2004). According to Ho et al. (2004), neuroticism captures the extent to which an individual is vulnerable to stress, which is important in perceiving the occurrence of a breach as a stress-inducing event. Anxious individuals have a greater tendency to pay attention to the negative aspects of the situation, thereby experiencing stronger reactions and greater sensitivity to negative events. Ho et al. found that indeed people who are high in neuroticism do not only focus on the more negative aspects of a broken promise but are also more strongly and negatively affected by these events.

Agreeableness refers to an individual's preference for interpersonal interactions. Agreeable people value their interpersonal relationships and are characterized as being more motivated to maintain positive relations with others. People who are high in agreeableness exhibit better emotional self-regulation. Ho et al. found in their study that in the event of a psychological contract breach, agreeable people do not experience a strong negative emotive response as do less agreeable people.

Following this theory and these findings, the expected relationship is different for those higher in the FFM traits than for dark triad personalities. As mentioned previously, these employees exhibit positive personality traits (Youli & Chao, 2015) and hesitate for a long time before interpreting an interaction with the organization as a psychological contract breach. The higher their level of FFM traits, the less they tend to perceive events as constituting a psychological contract breach. As a result, with a lower motivation to engage in CWB, the relationship between psychological contract breach and CWB ranges from non-existent to the opposite, as for those with high levels of dark triad personality traits. Thus,

Hypothesis 2a: Psychological contract breach mediates the relationship between the dark triad personality and CWB. This relationship is positive, and the relationship between perceptions of politics and CWB is also positive.

Hypothesis 2b: Psychological contract breach mediates the relationship between the Big Five Model (BFM) and CWB. The relationship between the FFM and perceptions of politics is negative, and the relationship between perceptions of politics and CWB is also negative.

The model proposed by Cohen and Shoval was examined in a sample of secular Israeli teachers working in secular Jewish schools. Questionnaires were distributed to 500 teachers in 19 public high schools located across Israel, and a total of 328 usable questionnaires were returned, a response rate of 68%.

The findings of their study showed that the dark triad personality is strongly related to CWB. The findings showed a strong positive relationship between the two as well as a strong effect of the dark triad personality when moderators and mediators were also examined. This finding provides important support for Cohen's (2016) contention that the dark triad personality construct is an important but somewhat overlooked correlate of CWB and should be researched more intensively. There is a logical fit between negative personality traits (dark triad personality) and negative behavior (CWB) (Cohen, 2016), and therefore it can be expected that the two constructs will be related, as demonstrated in Cohen and Shoval's (2018) study, as well as by others (Schneider et al., 2013). This finding strongly supports Youli and Chao's (2015) suggestion that research on dark personality traits, in particular those of the dark triad personalities, should be strengthened.

Another important contribution of Cohen and Shoval's study was the finding that the dark triad personality has an incremental contribution in addition to the contribution of the FFM traits. The findings showed that some of the FFM traits (conscientiousness, agreeableness, and emotional stability) were related consistently to CWB, and some (openness and extroversion) were not. The dark triad personality, however, had a significant and consistent relationship with CWB. The relationships were negative for the FFM and positive for the dark triad personality. The FFM is criticized because it does not fully summarize the existing personality traits, particularly antisocial personality traits, and too much attention to this positive personality model may limit personality research (Youli & Chao, 2015).

According to Youli and Chao (2015), it is feasible and important to compare positive and dark personality clusters in the empirical field of organizational behavior. The role of positive and negative personality traits should be equally important; therefore, future research should focus more on dark personality clusters to expand the personality theory. More specifically, Youli and Chao (2015) contended that a potential problem of the FFM is that the positive language description of its components leads to its being used mainly to describe positive personality traits. Thus, it does not adequately describe the dark side of personalities. The authors argued that presenting reality in this light leaves ample room for research on dark personality traits. The dark triad construct breaks the theoretical frame of the FFM personalities and makes personality theory more rigorous and complete. The findings of Cohen and Shoval's study also provide support for Guenole's (2014) suggestion that dark triad traits show incremental validity for the prediction of important work outcomes (Schneider et al., 2013); therefore, this line of research seems very promising. Cohen and

Shoval contended that future research indeed should further examine the relationship between the FFM and the dark triad personality with CWB in other settings and cultures to provide additional data regarding this important link.

Another contribution of Cohen and Shoval's study is related to the two moderators and the two mediators examined in their design. The findings showed some effect of the moderators on the relationship between the personality variables and the two mediators (perceptions of politics and psychological contract breach) and a stronger mediation effect. This finding supports Youli and Chao's (2015) contention that it is necessary to explore situational factors in depth. According to them, individual behaviors result from the interaction between environmental pressure and individual intrinsic qualities. People display different behaviors under different circumstances in an effort to meet the needs of their environment. Youli and Chao further contended that environmental factors can explain differences in stability and consistency when the FFM and dark triad personality are used to predict outcome variables. This argument was strongly supported by Cohen and Shoval's study for CWB as the outcome variable.

Moreover, all possible moderator and mediation effects were significant for the dark triad personality, while only some of the FFM traits were affected by the moderators and mediators. Of the FFM traits, agreeableness was strongly affected by the moderators and the mediators. Some of Cohen and Shoval's findings are similar to those of Ho et al. (2004), who found that agreeableness and emotional stability were related to psychological contract breach in the direction expected in their study. The only difference is that Ho et al. did not find any other significant relationship, while Cohen and Shoval's study found that conscientiousness was negatively related to psychological contract breach. Research has largely neglected the role of "dark" personality traits in the breach—outcomes relationship even though employees with such traits may be more inclined to retaliate through negative attitudes or behaviors in response to perceived mistreatment (Zagenczyk et al., 2013). According to Cohen and Shoval, future research should further examine the relationship between the BFM and psychological contract breach and perceptions of politics because of the importance of this relationship (Ho et al., 2004).

However, the strong effect of the moderators and mediators on the dark triad personality provides strong support for Youli and Chao's (2015) argument that the dark triad personality is more significantly influenced than others by environmental factors. As argued by Cohen (2016), because dark triad personalities are always looking for an environment perceived as friendly in terms of enabling them to achieve their goals, they are more inclined and more qualified to detect the political opportunities in every setting in which they operate. Being more sensitive than others to the contextual cues of their setting and the political opportunities this setting provides, they are more capable of reading and understanding them (Cohen, 2016).

The findings strongly support the importance of environmental factors, particularly perceptions of politics, in the relationship between the dark triad personality and work outcomes, CWB in this case.

The study of Cohen and Shoval (2018) and its findings are valuable and add to our understanding of one of the most important work behaviors, CWB, as well as one of the interesting and somewhat overlooked personality determinants, namely, the dark triad traits. There is definitely a need for many more studies to validate some of the findings of their study, particularly in settings other than that examined. Such studies would enable a better evaluation of the role of the dark triad in committing CWB.

References

Ammeter, A. P., Douglas, C., Ferris, G. R., & Goka, H. (2004). A social relationship conceptualization of trust and accountability in organizations. *Human Resource Management Review, 14*(1), 47–65.

Aquino, K., & Lamertz, K. (2004). A relational model of workplace victimization: Social roles and patterns of victimizations in dyadic relationships. *Journal of Applied Psychology, 89*(6), 1023–1034.

Babiak, P. (1995). When psychopaths go to work: A case study of an industrial psychopath. *Applied Psychology, 44*(2), 171–188.

Babiak, P. (2000). Psychopathic manipulation at work. In C. B. Gacono (Ed.), *The Clinical and Forensic Assessment of Psychopathy: A Practitioner's Guide* (pp. 287–312). Mahwah, NJ: Lawrence Erlbaum Associates, Inc.

Bellizzi, J. A., & Hasty, R. W. (2001). The effects of a stated organizational policy on inconsistent disciplinary action based on salesperson gender and weight. *Journal of Personal Selling & Sales Management, 21*(3), 189–198.

Best, J. (2012). Bureaucratic ambiguity. *Economy and Society, 41*(1), 84–106.

Boddy, C. R. (2010a). Corporate psychopaths and organizational type. *Journal of Public Affairs, 10*(4), 300–312.

Campbell, J. L., & Göritz, A. S. (2014). Culture corrupts! A qualitative study of organizational culture in corrupt organizations. *Journal of Business Ethics, 120*(3), 291–311.

Campbell, W. K., Hoffman, B. J., Campbell, S. M., & Marchisio, G. (2011). Narcissism in organizational contexts. *Human Resource Management Review, 21*(4), 268–284.

Chao, J. M., Cheung, F. Y., & Wu, A. M. (2011). Psychological contract breach and counterproductive workplace behaviors: Testing moderating effect of attribution style and power distance. *The International Journal of Human Resource Management, 22*(4), 763–777.

Cialdini, R. B., & Trost, M. R. (1998). Social influence: Social norms, conformity, and compliance. In D. T. Gilbert, S. T. Fiske, & G. Lindzey (Eds.), *The Handbook of Social Psychology* (4th ed., Vol. 2, pp. 151–192). Boston: McGraw-Hill.

Cicala, J. E., Bush, A. J., Sherrell, D. L., & Deitz, G. D. (2014). Does transparency influence the ethical behavior of salespeople? *Journal of Business Research, 67*(9), 1787–1795.

Cohen, A. (2015). *Fairness in the Workplace: A Global Perspective.* New York, NY: Palgrave McMillan.

Cohen, A. (2016). Are they among us? A conceptual framework of the relationship between the dark triad personality and counterproductive work behaviors (CWBs). *Human Resource Management Review, 26*(1), 69–85.

Cohen, A., & Shoval, L. (2018). *The dark triad personality and the Big Five model in their relationship to counterproductive work behaviors*. Manuscript submitted for publication.

Coyle-Shapiro, J. A. M., & Kessler, I. (2003). The employment relationship in the UK public sector: A psychological contract perspective. *Journal of Public Administration Research and Theory, 13,* 213–230.

Denison, D. R. (1996). What is the difference between organizational culture and organizational climate? A native's point of view on a decade of paradigm wars. *Academy of Management Review, 21*(3), 619–654.

Ehrhart, M. G., & Naumann, S. E. (2004). Organizational citizenship behavior in work groups: A group norms approach. *Journal of Applied Psychology, 89*(6), 960–974.

Ellis, S., Caridi, O., Lipshitz, R., & Popper, M. (1999). Perceived error criticality and organizational learning: An empirical investigation. *Knowledge and Process Management, 6*(3), 166–175.

Ferris, G. R., Kolodinsky, R. W., Hochwarter, W. A., & Frink, D. D. (2001). *Conceptualization, Measurement, and Validation of the Political Skill Construct.* Paper presented at the Academy of Management, 61st Annual National Meeting, Washington, DC.

Ferris, G. R., Treadway, D. C., Kolodinsky, R. W., Hochwarter, W. A., Kacmar, C. J., Douglas, C., & Frink, D. D. (2005). Development and validation of the political skill inventory. *Journal of Management, 31*(1), 126–152.

Ferris, G. R., Treadway, D. C., Perrewé, P. L., Brouer, R. L., Douglas, C., & Lux, S. (2007). Political skill in organizations. *Journal of Management, 33*(3), 290–320.

Ferry, L., & Eckersley, P. (2015). Accountability and transparency: A nuanced response to Etzioni. *Public Administration Review, 75*(1), 11–12.

Fine, S., Horowitz, I., Weigler, H., & Basis, L. (2010). Is good character good enough? The effects of situational variables on the relationship between integrity and counterproductive work behaviors. *Human Resource Management Review, 20*(1), 73–84.

Ford, R. C., & Richardson, W. D. (1994). Ethical decision making: A review of the empirical literature. *Journal of Business Ethics, 43,* 205–211.

Frink, D. D., & Klimoski, R. J. (1998). Toward a theory of accountability in organizations and human resource management. In G. R. Ferris (Ed.), *Research in Personnel and Human Resources Management* (Vol. 16, pp. 1–51). Greenwich, CT: JAI Press.

Furnham, A., & Siegel, E. (2012). Reactions to organizational injustice: Counter work behaviors and the insider threat. In E. Kals & J. Maes (Eds.), *Justice and Conflicts* (pp. 199–217). New York: Springer.

Gelfand, M. J., Lim, B. C., & Raver, J. L. (2004). Culture and accountability in organizations: Variations in forms of social control across cultures. *Human Resource Management Review, 14*(1), 135–160.

Grijalva, E., & Harms, P. D. (2014). Narcissism: An integrative synthesis and dominance complementarity model. *The Academy of Management Perspectives, 28*(2), 108–127.

Grimmelikhuijsen, S. G., & Welch, E. W. (2012). Developing and testing a theoretical framework for computer-mediated transparency of local governments. *Public Administration Review, 72*(4), 562–571.

Gruber, J. E. (1998). The impact of male work environments and organizational policies on women's experiences of sexual harassment. *Gender & Society, 12*(3), 301–320.

Guenole, N. (2014). Maladaptive personality at work: Exploring the darkness. *Industrial and Organizational Psychology, 7*(1), 85–97.

Harms, P. D., & Spain, M. S. (2015). Beyond the bright side: Dark personality at work. *Applied Psychology: An International Review, 64*(1), 15–24.

Harrison, A., Summers, J., & Mennecke, B. (2016). The effects of the dark triad on unethical behavior. *Journal of Business Ethics*, 1–25.

Harvey, P., Martinko, M. J., & Gardner, W. L. (2006). Promoting authentic behavior in organizations: An attributional perspective. *Journal of Leadership & Organizational Studies, 12*(3), 1–11.

Hegarty, W. H., & Sims, H. P. (1979). Organizational philosophy, policies, and objectives related to unethical decision behavior: A laboratory experiment. *Journal of Applied Psychology, 64*(3), 331–338.

Hellriegel, D., & Slocum, J. W. (1974). Organizational climate: Measures, research and contingencies. *Academy of Management Journal, 17*(2), 255–280.

Ho, V. T., Weingart, L. R., & Rousseau, D. M. (2004). Responses to broken promises: Does personality matter? *Journal of Vocational Behavior, 65*(2), 276–293.

Hochwarter, W. A., Parker Ellen III, B., & Ferris, G. R. (2014). Examining the interactive effects of accountability, politics, and voice. *Career Development International, 19*(4), 358–380.

Hochwarter, W. A., Perrewé, P. L., Hall, A. T., & Ferris, G. R. (2005). Negative affectivity as a moderator of the form and magnitude of the relationship between felt accountability and job tension. *Journal of Organizational Behavior, 26*(5), 517–534.

Hogan, R., & Fico, J. M. (2011). Leadership. In W. K. Campbell & J. D. Miller (Eds.), *The Handbook of Narcissism and Narcissistic Personality Disorder: Theoretical Approaches, Empirical Findings, and Treatments* (pp. 393–402). New York: Wiley.

Horne, C. (2012). Transparency: A concept analysis. *Nursing Science Quarterly, 25*(4), 326–331.

Hui, C., Lee, C., & Rousseau, D. M. (2004). Psychological contract and organizational citizenship behavior in China: Investigating generalizability and instrumentality. *Journal of Applied Psychology, 89*(2), 311–321.

Jensen, J. M., Opland, R. A., & Ryan, A. M. (2010). Psychological contracts and counterproductive work behaviors: Employee responses to transactional and relational breach. *Journal of Business and Psychology, 25*(4), 555–568.

Johns, G. (1999). A multi-level theory of self-serving behavior in and by organizations. In R. I. Sutton & B. M. Staw (Eds.), *Research in Organizational Behavior 21* (pp. 1–38). New York: Elsevier Science/JAI Press.

Kaiser, R. B., & Hogan, R. (2006). The dark side of discretion: Research report. Available at: www.hoganassessments.com/_hoganweb/documents/dark%20 side%20of%20discretion.pdf (accessed 11 December 2015), Tulsa, OK: Hogan Assessment Center.

Kaptein, M. (2008). Developing and testing a measure for the ethical culture of organizations: The corporate ethical virtues model. *Journal of Organizational Behavior, 29*(7), 923–947.

Kaptein, M. (2011). Understanding unethical behavior by unraveling ethical culture. *Human Relations, 64*(6), 843–869.

Kimura, T. (2013). The moderating effects of political skill and leader—member exchange on the relationship between organizational politics and affective commitment. *Journal of Business Ethics, 116*(3), 587–599.

Kruger, J., & Dunning, D. (1999). Unskilled and unaware of it: How difficulties in recognizing one's own incompetence lead to inflated self-assessments. *Journal of Personality and Social Psychology, 77*, 1121–1134.

Liao-Troth, M. A. (2005). Are they here for the long haul? The effects of functional motives and personality factors on the psychological contracts of volunteers. *Nonprofit and Voluntary Sector Quarterly, 34*(4), 510–530.

Luo, Y. (2005). An organizational perspective of corruption. *Management and Organization Review*, 1(1), 119–154.

Martin, L. E., Brock, M. E., Buckley, M. R., & Ketchen, D. J. (2010). Time banditry: Examining the purloining of time in organizations. *Human Resource Management Review*, 20(1), 26–34.

Michel, J. S., Newness, K., & Duniewicz, K. (2016). How abusive supervision affects workplace deviance: A moderated-mediation examination of aggressiveness and work-related negative affect. *Journal of Business and Psychology*, 31(1), 1–22.

Millward, L. J., & Hopkins, L. J. (1998). Psychological contracts, organizational and job commitment. *Journal of Applied Social Psychology*, 28(16), 1530–1556.

Minjina, B. (2011). Counterproductive work behaviors and their relationship with the psychological contract: Study on the sleep during the night security shift. *Romanian Journal of Psychology*, 1(1), 19–30.

Nelson, E., & Hogan, R. (2009). Coaching on the dark side. *International Coaching Psychology Review*, 4(1), 9–21.

Nübold, A., Bader, J., Bozin, N., Depala, R., Eidast, H., Johannessen, E. A., & Prinz, G. (2017). Developing a taxonomy of dark triad triggers at work: A grounded theory study protocol. *Frontiers in Psychology*, 8, 1–10.

O'Boyle Jr., E. H., Forsyth, D. R., Banks, G. C., & McDaniel, M. A. (2012). A meta-analysis of the dark triad and work behavior: A social exchange perspective. *Journal of Applied Psychology*, 97(3), 557–579.

O'Boyle, E. H., Forsyth, D., Banks, G. C., & Story, P. A. (2013). A meta-analytic review of the dark triad—intelligence connection. *Journal of Research in Personality*, 47(6), 789–794.

Orvis, K. A., Dudley, N. M., & Cortina, J. M. (2008). Conscientiousness and reactions to psychological contract breach: A longitudinal field study. *Journal of Applied Psychology*, 93(5), 1183–1193.

Padilla, A., Hogan, R., & Kaiser, R. B. (2007). The toxic triangle: Destructive leaders, susceptible followers, and conducive environments. *The Leadership Quarterly*, 18(3), 176–194.

Palmer, J. C., Komarraju, M., Carter, M. Z., & Karau, S. J. (2017). Angel on one shoulder: Can perceived organizational support moderate the relationship between the dark triad traits and counterproductive work behavior? *Personality and Individual Differences*, 110, 31–37.

Parilla, P. F., Hollinger, R. C., & Clark, J. P. (1988). Organizational control of deviant behavior: The case of employee theft. *Social Science Quarterly*, 69(2), 261–280.

Peterson, D. K. (2002). Deviant workplace behavior and the organization's ethical climate. *Journal of Business and Psychology*, 17(1), 47–61.

Pilch, I., & Turska, E. (2015). Relationships between Machiavellianism, organizational culture, and workplace bullying: Emotional abuse from the target's and the perpetrator's perspective. *Journal of Business Ethics*, 128(1), 83–93.

Pinto, J., Leana, C. R., & Pil, F. K. (2008). Corrupt organizations or organizations of corrupt individuals? Two types of organization-level corruption. *Academy of Management Review*, 33(3), 685–709.

Raja, U., Johns, G., & Ntalianis, F. (2004). The impact of personality on psychological contracts. *Academy of Management Journal*, 47(3), 350–367.

Riley, P. (1983). A structurationist account of political culture. *Administrative Science Quarterly*, 414–437.

Rosen, C. C., & Levy, P. E. (2013). Stresses, swaps, and skill: An investigation of the psychological dynamics that relate work politics to employee performance. *Human Performance*, 26(1), 44–65.

Rousseau, D. (1995). *Psychological Contracts in Organizations: Understanding Written and Unwritten Agreements*. Thousand Oaks, CA: Sage Publications, Inc.

Rubin, R. S., Dierdorff, E. C., & Bachrach, D. G. (2013). Boundaries of citizenship behavior: Curvilinearity and context in the citizenship and task performance relationship. *Personnel Psychology, 66*(2), 377–406.

Salin, D. (2003). Ways of explaining workplace bullying: A review of enabling, motivating and precipitating structures and processes in the work environment. *Human Relations, 56*(10), 1213–1232.

Schein, E. H. (1992). *Organizational Culture and Leadership* (2nd ed.). San Francisco: Jossey-Bass.

Schneider, B. (1987). The people make the place. *Personnel Psychology, 40*(3), 437–453.

Schneider, B., Ehrhart, M. G., & Macey, W. H. (2013). Organizational climate and culture. *Annual Review of Psychology, 64*, 361–388.

Schyns, B. (2015). Dark personality in the workplace: Introduction to the special issue. *Applied Psychology: An International Review, 64*(1), 1–14.

Shih, C. T., & Chuang, C. H. (2013). Individual differences, psychological contract breach, and organizational citizenship behavior: A moderated mediation study. *Asia Pacific Journal of Management, 30*(1), 191–210.

Sims, R. R. (1992). The challenge of ethical behavior in organizations. *Journal of Business Ethics, 11*(7), 505–513.

Smith, S. F., & Lilienfeld, S. O. (2013). Psychopathy in the workplace: The knowns and unknowns. *Aggression and Violent Behavior, 18*, 204–218.

Smithikrai, C. (2008). Moderating effect of situational strength on the relationship between personality traits and counterproductive work behavior. *Asian Journal of Social Psychology, 11*, 253–263.

Spain, S. M., Harms, P., & LeBreton, J. M. (2014). The dark side of personality at work. *Journal of Organizational Behavior, 35*(Supplement 1), S41–S60.

Spector, P. E. (2011). The relationship of personality to counterproductive work behavior (CWB): An integration of perspectives. *Human Resource Management Review, 21*(4), 342–352.

Steinert, S. W., Lishner, D. A., Vitacco, M. J., & Hong, P. Y. (2017). Conceptualizing successful psychopathy: An elaboration of the moderated-expression model. *Aggression and Violent Behavior, 36*, 44–51.

Tetlock, P. E. (1992). The impact of accountability on judgment and choice: Toward a social contingency model. *Advances in Experimental Social Psychology, 25*, 331–376.

Treadway, D. C., Ferris, G. R., Duke, A. B., Adams, G. L., & Thatcher, J. B. (2007). The moderating role of subordinate political skill on supervisors' impressions of subordinate ingratiation and ratings of subordinate interpersonal facilitation. *Journal of Applied Psychology, 92*(3), 848–855.

Treadway, D. C., Shaughnessy, B. A., Breland, J. W., Yang, J., & Reeves, M. (2013). Political skill and the job performance of bullies. *Journal of Managerial Psychology, 28*(3), 273–289.

Treviño, L. K., Butterfield, K. D., & McCabe, D. L. (1998). The ethical context in organizations: Influences on employee attitudes and behaviors. *Business Ethics Quarterly, 8*(3), 447–476.

Turilli, M., & Floridi, L. (2009). The ethics of information transparency. *Ethics and Information Technology, 11*(2), 105–112.

Vardi, Y. (2001). The effects of organizational and ethical climates on misconduct at work. *Journal of Business Ethics, 29*(4), 325–337.

Vardi, Y., & Wiener, Y. (1992). *Organizational Misbehavior (OMB): Toward a Motivational Model*. Paper presented at the Annual Meeting of Management, Miami Beach, FL.

Wallace, A. S. (2015). *Save Yourself: The Role of Narcissism and Political Skill in the Relationship between Ego Threat and Performance-Related Outcomes* (Doctoral dissertation). State University of New York at Buffalo.

Walton, M. (2007). Leadership toxicity—an inevitable affliction of organizations. *Organizations and People, 14*(1), 19–27.

Weber, M. (1947). *The Theory of Social and Economic Organization.* New York: Free Press.

Witt, L. A., & Spector, P. E. (2012). Personality and reactions to organizational politics. In G. R. Ferris & D. C. Treadway (Eds.), *Politics in Organizations: Theory and Research Considerations* (pp. 555–588). New York: Routledge.

Yang, J., & Diefendorff, J. M. (2009). The relations of daily counterproductive workplace behavior with emotions, situational antecedents, and personality moderators: A diary study in Hong Kong. *Personnel Psychology, 62*(2), 259–295.

Youli, H., & Chao, L. (2015). A comparative study between the dark triad of personality and the Big Five. *Canadian Social Science, 11*(1), 93–98.

Zagenczyk, T. J., Cruz, K. S., Woodard, A. M., Walker, J. C., Few, W. T., Kiazad, K., & Raja, M. (2013). The moderating effect of Machiavellianism on the psychological contract breach: Organizational identification/disidentification relationships. *Journal of Business and Psychology, 28*(3), 287–299.

Zuboff, S. (1988). *In the Age of the Smart Machine: The Future of Work and Power.* New York: Basic Books.

7 Can They Be Spotted?
Tools for Detecting
Dark Triad Personalities

It has been advocated that managers should be screened to find those who are immoral, dysfunctional, psychopathic, and bullying so that organizations, employees, and society can be shielded from their destructive behavior (Boddy, 2011). Individuals who have subclinical psychopathic personality tendencies have personality profiles similar to those having a clinical psychopathic personality but of a lower level. According to leading psychologists and some management theorists, many agency problems involving corporate scandals and failures could be prevented if corporations screened employees for psychopathy (Boddy, 2016). Organizations may be interested in identifying the 5% to 10% of the population with subclinical psychopathic personality tendencies who are most likely to be functioning in a work setting.

However, organizations encounter practical difficulties in preventing the recruitment of psychopaths, as well as Machiavellians and narcissists, using conventional selection tools because dark triad characteristics coexist with well-developed social skills. Moreover, psychopaths in the business community, for example, are not easily detected because they may appear as ideal leaders, concealing their dark side with poise and charm. Thus, dark-side tendencies are extremely difficult to detect in an interview; in fact, the characteristics of psychopathy typically come across as positive attributes in the short term. Interviews, for example, are brief and take place within a short time frame, which may not permit sufficient time for the darker sides of these individuals to be revealed (Kaiser & Hogan, 2006). Dark triad personalities are particularly clever at avoiding discovery by power figures in the organization. They shrewdly manipulate upward information and impressions. Thus, senior managers cannot easily and promptly discover their insidious behavior (Delbecq, 2001). The fact that these people are hired should not be a surprise, nor that these individuals are not detected and then summarily dismissed (Jonason, Slomski, & Partyka, 2012b).

Because of the growing awareness of the destruction that dark personalities can cause to an organization and its employees, an increasing number of researchers have emphasized in recent years the need to detect them in order to prevent their recruitment by the organization. Perry (2015), for example, contended that a university should be careful to select non–dark triad leaders. The entitlement beliefs that breed dark triad leadership practices feed on themselves. Seeing their position on unit displays or in the size of their car, office, or salary makes dark triad personalities think that their circle of power should be even bigger. People with dark triad personalities are usually so self-confident that they do not think they need to change their behavior or seek help. Thus, according to Perry, preventing their appointment would be preferable to investing wasted effort in curing or changing them. This argument can be generalized to any kind of organization.

A suggestion for screening dark triad personalities was advanced by Boddy (2016), who explicitly recommended that public agencies adopt psychopathy testing of candidates and apply subclinical psychopathy assessments in the case of promotions of leaders. Brain scanning should be used in contested cases. Boddy warns that "untrained personnel, directors, and managers who interview and review psychopaths in the workplace are easily duped by their charm, likeableness, and apparent sincerity" (Boddy, 2016, p. 262). Judge and LePine (2007) argued that organizations are well advised to select those who score high on bright traits and low on dark traits. However, they mentioned that even bright traits have dark effects under certain circumstances. Thus, the staff recruitment model becomes more complicated when the "side effects" of bright and dark traits have to be taken into account. Fennimore and Sementelli (2016) emphasized the need for rigorous selection procedures, combined with high levels of transparency and accountability, to limit the activities of subclinical psychopaths—and by extension, other dark personalities—in public agencies (Hanson & Baker, 2017).

However, several problems arise in the application of screening tests. Although screening for the dark side of personality can provide incremental knowledge about employees, the role such traits play in personnel selection is questionable (Spain, Harms, & LeBreton, 2014). First, it is unlikely that individuals who have high levels of these traits will respond honestly on the self-report assessments used in selection situations. Second, it is not always clear that such assessments are compliant with the Americans with Disabilities Act (ADA) (Wu & Lebreton, 2011) or with laws and regulations in other countries. Having said that, the questions and issues discussed in this chapter are as follows. Can organizations detect dark triad personalities and prevent their recruitment? What methods and tools are available to detect them, and what are their characteristic features? The chapter first presents the main existing personality tests that can be used to detect dark triad personalities. The specific tests for each of the dark triad personalities are presented followed by other possible methods, such as interviews and some possible innovative tools.

Personality Tests

Employment screening hosts a variety of tests for psychopathy, the dark triad personalities, and other forms of personality disturbance. However, dark personality screening is not yet widely used in leader selection and promotion processes (Hanson & Baker, 2017). Several personality tests were developed to detect dark personalities, the more conventional of which are presented in the following sections. As mentioned, the tests for each dark triad personality will be presented separately.

Personality Tests for Assessing Narcissism

Guenole (2014) suggested that the *Diagnostic and Statistical Manual of Mental Disorders (DSM)* is a solution for studying the maladaptive personality within the trait framework. The *DSM* is a comprehensive classification of officially recognized psychiatric disorders, published by the American Psychiatric Association for use by mental health professionals to ensure uniformity of diagnosis. The *DSM* describes symptoms and does not discuss the causes of the disorders. The *DSM* has passed through many revisions, the latest being the *DSM-5* (fifth edition) model, which was issued in 2013. The initial *DSM* trait model proposed was derived from and comprises six domain level traits (Skodol et al., 2011, p. 37): negative emotionality, detachment, antagonism, disinhibition, compulsivity, and psychoticism. Subsequent research supported a five-trait domain structure, in which compulsivity is seen as the opposite pole of disinhibition.

The new *DSM-5* model is revolutionary in the sense that it breaks down widely used dimensions of personality disorders into subdimensions to understand better the comorbidity of different disorders and enable effective treatment (Krueger et al., 2011). Narcissistic personality disorder (NPD) in the *DSM-IV* (fourth edition) and in Section II of the *DSM-5* is described as "a pervasive pattern of grandiosity (in fantasy or behavior), need for admiration, and lack of empathy...," indicated by five or more of the following: (a) a grandiose sense of self-importance, (b) preoccupation with fantasies of unlimited success, power, brilliance, beauty, or ideal love, (c) beliefs of being special and unique, (d) requirements of excessive admiration, (e) a sense of entitlement; (f) interpersonal exploitativeness, (g) lack of empathy, (h) envy of others, and (i) arrogant and haughty behaviors or attitudes (Skodol, Bender, & Morey, 2014). Miller, Gentile, Wilson, and Campbell (2013) found that the *DSM-5* trait model, as assessed by the Personality Inventory for *DSM-5* (PID5), appears capable of capturing a substantial portion of the variance associated with both grandiose and vulnerable narcissism. Their study also showed that traits from the domains of negative affectivity (e.g., depression, emotional lability, anxiousness) and detachment (e.g., withdrawal, anhedonia) are highly correlated with vulnerable narcissism but not with grandiose narcissism. It should be mentioned that researchers noted some problems involved in using the *DSM-IV* and the *DSM-5* for diagnosing narcissism (Skodol et al., 2014). This probably encouraged the development of other and alternative tools.

Campbell, Hoffman, Campbell, and Marchisio (2011) mentioned that the significant majority of research studies on narcissism in social-personality psychology applies the *narcissistic personality inventory* (NPI; Raskin & Terry, 1988). The NPI is a self-report, 40-item forced choice measure with items such as "If I ruled the world it would be a much better place," "I think I am a special person," and "I like to look at myself in the mirror." The NPI is a sound psychometric instrument, but it is also characterized by a very unstable factor structure. It is considered a measure of grandiose narcissism, but it is also relatively long and thus inefficient to administer. Gentile et al. (2013) contended that with a length of 40 items, this measure may not be ideal in settings in which time or participant attention may limit the types of measures to be used.

Gentile et al. (2013) cited Ames, Rose, and Anderson (2006), who, in response, created the NPI-16, which provides a shorter, unidimensional measure of the construct. Ames et al. contended that their shorter scale is a valid means of capturing narcissism in situations when the use of a longer measure would be impractical. Using their samples, Gentile et al. examined the reliability and validity of the NPI-16 in conjunction with another new short measure of narcissism, the NPI-13, which provides both a total score and three subscale scores. Their findings showed that both the NPI-13 and NPI-16 appear to be promising brief measures of grandiose narcissism. Their empirical evidence suggested that both measures are comparable with the NPI 40-items in terms of convergent and discriminant validity, while demonstrating adequate overall reliability. The two NPI brief forms save time without affecting the validity of the scale scores. Furthermore, in addition to its truncated length, the NPI-13 exhibits a relatively clear factor structure that suggests it can be useful in a more fine-grained assessment of narcissism. Gentile et al. also concluded that the NPI-13 might be more advantageous because of the availability of the three subscales in addition to a total score. This feature allows researchers to continue to test the manner in which these narcissism traits converge and diverge in regard to their relations with other central features of the nomological network of narcissism.

Miller, Lynam, and Campbell (2016) found that the NPI appears to be a good measure of the *DSM-IV* and *DSM-5* NPD. In addition, the NPI, which has quickly become one of the most frequently used measures of narcissism, has tenuous ties with widely accepted conceptualizations of NPD and grandiose narcissism. Although the NPI may in fact be more pathological in nature, as some have argued, this pathology stems less from its ability to assess traits considered central to the grandiose narcissism of NPD and more from its assessment of a much wider variety of pathological traits, many of which have little to no empirical or theoretical link to narcissism (e.g., submissiveness).

Concurrently, Miller and Campbell (2011) mentioned several limitations of the NPI, including (1) significant negative relations with psychological distress and certain forms of impairment, (2) positive relations with self-esteem and well-being, (3) questionable convergent validity, (4) inconsistent factor structure, and (5) divergent relations manifested by the NPI sub-scales. Nevertheless, Miller and Campbell contended that despite its limitations, the NPI has manifested quite substantial evidence of construct validity in the large number of studies conducted on this scale. They suggested that the field should refrain from referring to NPI scales as measuring normal or non-pathological narcissism because there is nothing inherently normal or non-pathological about high scores on this scale. They concluded that, overall, the nomological network associated with NPI narcissism is largely consistent with the construct of grandiose narcissism as conceived by researchers, clinicians, and the extant empirical data.

Hogan and Fico (2011) suggested another good way to assess narcissism by using the Bold scale of the Hogan Development Survey (HDS; Hogan & Hogan, 2009). The HDS was developed to predict (poor) managerial performance. Hogan and Fico (2011) collected HDS data for more than 1 million working adults and found that the construct validity of the Bold scale is well established. The scale has 14 items organized in three components: (1) Entitlement: "In time people will realize how important I am"; (2) Excessive Confidence: "People often sense my power"; and (3) Fantasized Talent: "If I were in charge I could get this country moving again." Hogan and Fico (2011) argued that those scoring high on the Bold scale are somewhat overbearing and self-promoting and focus on getting ahead at the expense of getting along. They mentioned that the scale is uncorrelated with neuroticism, which means that a person scoring high on Bold can have a low, average, or high score on neuroticism. They suggested that persons with high scores on Bold and low scores on neuroticism are pompous and self-important, but persons with high scores on both Bold and neuroticism are arrogant, hypersensitive, volatile, and abusive.

According to Campbell et al. (2011), for those interested in a more clinically grounded assessment, self-report measures are also available. These narcissism assessments are typically part of larger scales, and include the Personality Disorders Questionnaire (PDQ-IV; Hyler, 1994), the Dimensional Assessment of Personality Pathology (DAPP-BQ; Livesley, 2006), and the Millon Clinical Multiaxial Inventory-III (MCMI-III; Millon, 1997). Of the clinical measures, the MMCI, SCID-II (The Structured Clinical Interview for DSM-IV Axis I Disorders), and NEO(Neuroticism-Extraversion-Openness Inventory) profile assess more clearly grandiose narcissism. Other self-report measures for assessing grandiose narcissism include the narcissism subscale of the California Psychological Inventory (CPI; Gough & Bradley, 1996; Wink & Gough, 1990). The narcissism index of the CPI includes 49 true/false items that assess authority, inflated self-views, and attention seeking. Vulnerable narcissism is also open to self-report. Other common measures include the Hypersensitive Narcissism Scale (HSNS; Wink & Gough, 1990) and the newer Pathological Narcissism Inventory (PNI; Pincus et al., 2009).

Personality Tests for Assessing Psychopathy

A number of measures exist to determine the level of psychopathy, including the Psychopathic Personality Inventory, Personality Diagnostic Questionnaire, Hare's Psychopathy Checklist, and others (Boddy, 2011). The more established measures are presented here.

According to Ruchensky, Edens, Donnellan, and Witt (2017), among the self-report measures of psychopathic traits, the Psychopathic Personality Inventory (PPI; Lilienfeld & Andrews, 1996) and its revision, the Psychopathic Personality Inventory-Revised (PPI-R; Lilienfeld & Widows, 2005), are the most widely researched. Ruchensky et al. (2017) related that in developing the PPI, Lilienfeld and Andrews (1996) reviewed the literature to create items measuring a broad array of putative psychopathic traits, cutting across several theoretical models. This scale is a 187-item self-report questionnaire that assesses personality traits relevant to psychopathy and de-emphasizes criminal conduct (Kastner, Sellbom, & Lilienfeld, 2012). Over several rounds of analysis, they ultimately identified eight subscales, which were later factor analyzed. The results suggested that they could be used to operationalize two relatively orthogonal higher-order dimensions, labeled fearless dominance and self-centered impulsivity.

Not long after the initial publication of the PPI, a short form (PPI—SF) was developed to expedite the assessment of psychopathic traits in research contexts in which the long form might prove problematic. This short form is consisting of 56 items derived from the original version (Kastner et al., 2012). Numerous investigations supported this short form as a useful and valid measure of psychopathic traits and a viable alternative to the original PPI (Ruchensky et al., 2017). Some, however, reported that the PPI full-length version showed more evidence of construct validity than did the short form (Kastner et al., 2012). Other researchers, such as Lilienfeld and Widows (2005), made a number of revisions to the original PPI in an attempt to increase its clinical utility (e.g., by lowering the required reading level) while retaining its basic psychometric properties. No short forms of this new and still rather lengthy (154-item) scale existed until recently, when Eisenbarth, Lilienfeld, and Yarkoni (2015) developed a 40-item abbreviated version (the PPI-R-40) with the goal of making it more suitable for assessment in contexts with significant time constraints. According to Ruchensky et al. (2017), their study showed that the shortened subscales were strongly correlated with the original subscales (Eisenbarth et al., 2015). The PPI-R is considered a validated instrument for capturing subclinical levels of these tendencies. It is also a useful assessment tool for individuals in workplace settings. Also importantly, the use of the PPI-R and other subclinical inventories to capture psychopathic personality tendencies would be defensible under the ADA, but the use of clinically oriented inventories would likely violate the ADA (Schutte et al., 2015).

Hare (1980, 1999) developed the Psychopathy Checklist (PCL) based on clinical work with psychopaths in incarcerated populations. The original PCL consists of 22 personality and behavioral items, scored on a 3-point scale, which are completed on the basis of an interview and file information (Hare, 1980). The test aggregates Cleckley's (1941/1988) diagnostic criteria on four domains and assigns scores of 0, 1, or 2 for 20 observed traits. The maximum score is 40 (psychopath); 30 is the cutoff score for threshold psychopathy (for non-psychopaths, the average score is 4). Based on the clinical conception of psychopathy best typified by Cleckley, the PCL has proven to be a reliable and valid instrument for the assessment of psychopathy in male criminal populations (Harpur, Hakstian, & Hare, 1988).

Harpur, Hare, and Hakstian (1989) identified two factors of the PCL. The items in Factor 1 are concerned with impressions and inferences about interpersonal processes and are typically scored using both file information and impressions formed during the interview. This factor reflects the psychopath's verbal and interpersonal style. For many of these items, a high score results from differences between the inmate's presentation of himself in the interview and the documented evidence subsequently obtained from his file. Factor 2 describes behaviors indicative of a chronically unstable and antisocial lifestyle. In light of the reported results, Harpur et al. (1989) considered this factor a measure of social deviance. The items that define the factor depend predominantly on identifying the occurrence of specific behaviors, most often using the inmate's file. The behavioral emphasis in this factor resembles the criteria for antisocial personality disorder (ASPD) listed in the third edition of the *DSM* (DSM-III; American Psychiatric Association [APA], 1980).

Later, Hare (1991) proposed a revised version of the PCL, the PCL-R, which is a 20-item scale scored from interview and file information. This measure differs from the PCL in several ways. Two PCL items, previous diagnosis as a psychopath or a similar disorder and drug or alcohol use not being the direct cause of the inmate's antisocial behavior, have been omitted because they had relatively low correlations with the total score and were difficult to score. The scoring of some items became more stringent, requiring more extreme instances of deviant behavior for a score of 2. For a few items, the scoring criteria were somewhat modified (Hare et al., 1990). This scale is considered a widely used instrument for the assessment of psychopathy (Mathieu, Neumann, Babiak, & Hare, 2015). Although the PCL-R measures a unitary construct, confirmatory factor analyses of very large data sets (Neumann, Hare, & Newman, 2007; Neumann, Hare, & Pardini, 2015) support a superordinate model in which psychopathy is underpinned by four correlated factors or dimensions, labeled interpersonal (glibness/superficial charm, grandiose sense of self-worth, pathological lying, conning/manipulative), affective (lack of remorse or guilt, shallow affect, callousness/lack of empathy, failure to accept responsibility for actions), lifestyle (need for stimulation/proneness to boredom, parasitic lifestyle, lack of realistic long-term goals, impulsivity, irresponsibility), and antisocial (poor behavioral controls, early behavior problems, juvenile delinquency, revocation of conditional release, criminal versatility).

According to Mathieu et al. (2015), the Hare four-factor model of psychopathy, which is based on the PCL-R and its derivatives, has been validated in many studies, settings, and countries. However, they contended that because the PCL-R relies on the expertise of the assessor, typically a psychologist or psychiatrist, it is rarely used in organizational research. For business research, traditional paper-and-pencil instruments, based either on self-report or observer ratings, are much easier to implement. As a self-report measure of psychopathy, the Hare Self Report Psychopathy Scale (the SRP-III) and its revision (the SRP-4) include items that are derived, conceptually and empirically, from the PCL-R and that have the same four-factor structure as the PCL-R. According to Mathieu, Neumann, Hare, and Babiak (2014), the standard measures of adult psychopathy are the PCL-R and its derivative, the Psychopathy Checklist: Screening Version (see Hare & Neumann, 2009).

It should be noted that for clinical and applied purposes, only those with appropriate professional qualifications can administer the PCL and PCL-R, making them unsuitable for use by human resources (HR) personnel. Furthermore, one of the major difficulties in conducting research on corporate psychopathy is the absence of a validated instrument adapted to business settings (Babiak, Neumann, & Hare, 2010). This led Babiak and Hare (2006, 2014) to develop the Business Scan 360 (B-Scan 360), an instrument for rating psychopathy-related features in corporate and organizational settings. The B-Scan 360 was modeled on a structural model of the PCL-R (Neumann et al., 2007), which, as mentioned earlier, defines psychopathy as a multifaceted construct comprising four dimensions: interpersonal, affective, lifestyle, and antisocial. These first-order factors are significantly interrelated, suggesting that they are indicators of a second-order superordinate psychopathy factor (Newman, MacCoon, Vaughn, & Sadeh, 2005; Neumann et al., 2007). By means of exploratory and confirmatory factor analyses of a pool of potential B-Scan 360 items, Mathieu, Hare, Jones, Babiak, and Neumann (2013) derived a reliable 20-item, four-factor model that is consistent with the PCL-R structural model. They labeled the four factors manipulative/unethical, callous/insensitive, unreliable/unfocused, and intimidating/aggressive. A confirmatory factor analysis conducted on the B-Scan 360 items replicated this four-factor structure (Mathieu et al., 2014; Mathieu et al., 2015)

Mathieu et al.'s (2015) study, based on 491 civic employees and 116 employees of a branch of a large financial company, showed that the B-Scan 360 performed very well. Nevertheless, their results provide support for their assumptions that subordinates are capable of providing credible evaluations of manager behaviors, attitudes, and judgments related to psychopathic personality traits. Mathieu et al. (2015) concluded that their results provide good support for the generalizability of the B-Scan 360 four-factor model for corporate psychopathy. Although it still requires considerable research, Mathieu et al. concluded that the B-Scan 360 is an important tool for understanding how psychopathic individuals enter organizations, operate within them, and in some cases attain high-level leadership positions. To date, the B-Scan 360 is the only instrument specifically designed to assess psychopathy in corporate settings. (Henning, Wygant, & Barnes, 2014).

Mathieu and Babiak (2016a) further developed an assessment instrument that the business community finds acceptable by using business-appropriate items that can easily blend into pre-existing organizational measurement systems yet still provide psychopathy researchers with a valid tool to assess corporate psychopathy as conceptualized by Babiak and Hare (2006). The instrument, called the B-Scan Self, was also designed with an eye toward its possible inclusion, together with its sister instrument, the B-Scan (expert rater), in management development programs. To these ends, the researchers developed and selected items consistent with the Hare Four-Factor Model of Psychopathy as operationalized in the PCL-R. To assure that all the items reflect actual business behavior and tap into valid psychopathic traits and characteristics, they were reviewed by psychopathy experts and business executives and only those items deemed relevant to psychopathy and to the problems that businesses face were retained. Ultimately, behaviors, attitudes, and judgments reflecting 15 of the 20 PCL-R facets (loaded onto four factors) were identified and retained as the initial pool of items for the B-Scan Self. Mathieu and Babiak's (2016a) findings showed that the B-Scan Self, composed of 15 facets and four factors, performed well when subjected to tests of concurrent validity, its four factors demonstrating good parallels with the four SRP-III factors. Their findings also showed that the B-Scan Self, as is the case with the PCL-R and its other derivatives, is better represented by a four-factor model solution.

Mathieu and Babiak (2016a) argued that this method is innovative because the B-Scan is the only instrument that addresses psychopathic traits as exhibited in workplace misbehavior. Although other self-report psychopathy measures exist, they could not be used in business settings because of the nature of their items (some explicitly ask about previous mischief, sexual history, stealing, and substance abuse). These specific items would be highly problematic from a legal standpoint for both employee selection or promotion processes. According to them, the B-Scan Self items tap into observable business behaviors to measure corporate psychopathy. The items are not as "direct" as other self-report psychopathy measures; rather, they sometimes relate to the individual's personality and sometimes to the way the individual views or behaves in the business world.

According to Henning et al. (2014), the *DSM-5* trait conceptualization of ASPD has the capability to capture psychopathy better than the previous *DSM* versions, primarily because of the emphasis on the dimensional personality traits that define the disorder. The *DSM-5* ASPD criteria require the presence of a series of personality traits reflecting facets of antagonism and disinhibition. These traits cover a wider range of the psychopathy construct than the *DSM-IV* criteria. Moreover, FFM variations of these traits have already been found to be effective in capturing psychopathy. In addition, impairment in both self and interpersonal functioning is required. The *DSM-5* Section III diagnosis of ASPD includes a Psychopathy Specifier, which comprises additional evidence of low levels of *anxiousness* (negative affectivity domain) and *withdrawal* (detachment domain) and high levels of *attention seeking* (antagonism domain). These additional traits reflect a socially persuasive interpersonal style and higher levels of immunity to stress, which is consistent with the fearless-dominance or boldness qualities of psychopathy. Consequently, the *DSM-5* ASPD trait model should be useful for capturing psychopathy in the workplace as conceptualized by the B-Scan 360, although this needs to be established empirically.

Another management research tool for identifying the presence of corporate psychopaths in organizations is the Psychopathy Measure–Management Research Version (PM-MRV) (Boddy, 2011). The idea behind this measure was to develop one that is uncontaminated by antisocial behavior. This tool is based on the essential elements of commonly used psychopathy measures, and it has been shown to have good levels of statistical reliability, internal and external validity, and face validity when used in management research (Boddy, 2009). Later, version 2 of this measure, the PM-MRV2, a 10-item measure relying on reports by others, was advanced (Boddy, Miles, Sanyal, & Hartog, 2015; Fennimore & Sementelli, 2016). This measure of psychopathy is recommended for use in management research. As mentioned by Boddy (2016), based on Boddy, Ladyshewsky, and Galvin (2010), the elements of the PM-MRV 2 are as follows: (1) superficial charm and apparent intelligence; (2) untruthfulness and insincerity; (3) a cheating personality; (4) total egocentricity; (5) lack of remorse about how their actions harm other employees; (6) emotional shallowness; (7) unresponsiveness to personal interactions; (8) refusal to take responsibility for their own actions; (9) calmness, poise, and apparent rationality; and (10) lack of self-blame and self-insight about their own behavior. According to Boddy (2016), this measure can be applied to available archival material and documents or published accounts such as biographies to re-assess the personalities of businesspeople to determine whether they could be "qualified" as corporate psychopaths.

A note regarding most of these tools is in place here. Psychiatric diagnosis is not a typical competency of industrial-organization psychologists. Thus, while these constructs are relevant to workplace assessments, the practice of psychiatric diagnosis should not be undertaken without appropriate training or consultation with a qualified clinical psychologist. It should also be noted that while currently limited attempts are being made to detect psychopathy in the workplace for selection purposes, some studies contain scales that were developed for the evaluation of the supervisors' level of psychopathy by their employees (Mathieu et al., 2014). There is a need for continued effort in this direction, but already HR management has been offered some tools that would enable potential psychopaths to be screened.

Personality Tests for Assessing Machiavellianism

Corral and Calvete (2000) cited Christie (1970a), who postulated that the tendency to accept Machiavelli's beliefs about the world and human nature is a measurable individual differential variable and proposed a three-dimensional structure for the Machiavellianism construct. The first dimension refers to the use of manipulative tactics in interpersonal relationships; the second dimension consists of a cynical view of human nature as weak, cowardly, and susceptible to social pressures; and the third dimension is described as disregard for conventional morality. Christie went on to develop instruments to measure Machiavellianism, which included several phases (Christie, 1970b), resulting in two different versions of the Machiavellianism scale. The Mach-IV scale (Christie & Geis, 1970) comprises 20 items, from an original pool of 71. These items were selected by counterbalancing the wording of the items, content variety, and discriminatory power. Of these 20 items, 10 refer to Machiavellianism and 10 to non-Machiavellianism. The items are presented in a standard six-category Likert format with half of the items reversed. The lowest possible Machiavellianism score is 40, and the highest is 160 (Williams, Hazleton, & Renshaw, 1975). The construct validity of the Mach-IV scale was supported by studies (e.g., Gurtman, 1992).

The dimensionality of the Mach-IV scale has been examined in several studies and various factor structures have been found, opening the entire construct of Machiavellianism to criticism. When Christie (1970b) developed the Mach-IV scale, he classified the items into the three categories mentioned earlier: interpersonal tactics, cynical view of human nature, and disregard for conventional morality. The last category contains the fewest items because "Machiavelli was less concerned with abstractions and ethical judgements than with pragmatic advice" (Christie, 1970b, p. 14). In fact, the Mach-IV scale has only two items in this category, one of which (item 19) has been dropped in studies because of poor psychometric properties. In consequence, several studies show "disregard for conventional morality" as the least reliable subscale of Mach-IV, with the most complex factor loadings. The other two factors, tactics and views, are in general supported by various studies, although masked by the tendency of positively and negatively worded items to load on separate factors (Corral & Calvete, 2000). Corral and Calvete cited Fehr, Samson, and Paulhus (1992), who, after a

a higher order latent variable that shapes these characteristics. Specifically, because these dimensions were viewed as manifestations of Machiavellianism that are likely to be highly correlated and share similar relationships with antecedents and consequences, they thought that a latent variable structure would be a better fit than an aggregate variable model. Their scale (Dahling et al., 2009), the Machiavellian Personality Scale (MPS), includes 16 items of which 5 represent amoral manipulation, 5 distrust of others, 3 desire for status, and 3 desire for control. Their results indicate that the hierarchical four-factor structure is supported, consistent with their theory. Furthermore, their validation results demonstrate that their new measure of Machiavellianism is similar to but distinct from related variables (several dimensions of political skill, and narcissism) and differs from conceptually discriminant variables. They concluded that the MPS shows considerable promise for use in future research and applied settings.

In short, while there are scales for measuring Machiavellianism, further conceptual and methodological work is needed to design a more valid and stable scale in terms of its dimensionality.

Integrative Measures for the Dark Triad

Recently, the development of new measures that assess all three dark triad constructs simultaneously and efficiently has gained increased attention (Maples, Lamkin, & Miller, 2014). As has been shown, most research on the dark triad used separate assessment measures for each of the dark triad constructs, which together require sometimes more than 120 items. Concerns have been raised that such an assessment battery could result in fatigue for participants and hinder participation under the circumstances of limited incentives or time. Jonason and Webster (2010) argued that there is a growing trend in psychological assessment to create concise measures of core personality traits. These concise measures are appealing because they take less time to complete than the more protracted personality inventories by eliminating redundancy, thus reducing participant fatigue.

In response to these criticisms, the 27-item Short Dark Triad (SD3; Jones & Paulhus, 2014) and the 12-item Dirty Dozen (DD) (Jonason & Webster, 2010) were created. The SD3 scale of Jones and Paulhus (2014) was developed based on a literature review. Jones and Paulhus generated items, subjected them to a variety of analyses, and found three clear dimensions for each component of the dark personality triad. Each dimension was composed of nine items. Jones and Paulhus findings suggest that the SD3 scale achieves an optimal compromise between instrument brevity and respectable reliability and validity. Using a variety of approaches, they showed that the SD3 subscales provide useful proxies for the established dark triad measures they are intended to replace. Jones and Paulhus confirmed that the three subscales fall in the theoretically appropriate circumplex locations and provided full coverage of the classic constructs. Their findings demonstrated external validity by showing that the SD3 scales predicts corresponding informant ratings. Hence, the dark triad constructs are not only artifacts of self-report variance. According to Jones and Paulhus, the SD3 questionnaire has already drawn support from other research groups.

Jonason and Webster (2010) developed and validated a concise measure of the dark triad that includes 12 items, 4 for each of its dimensions. Their findings demonstrated that the scales have reasonable psychometric properties and showed acceptable convergent and discriminant validity with the other measures they examined and proved to be reliable over time and across a number of tests. According to them, the short 12-item version of the dark triad measure will not only reduce participant fatigue, but will also allow all the three constructs to be measured using the same response scale format. The DD scale was validated, for example, in an Italian sample (Schimmenti et al., 2017).

A study that compared the two scales (Maples et al., 2014) found that both the DD and SD3 proved to be efficient measures because both represent significant time savings compared with the time sum of the longer measures often used in this research. Given the evidence that scores from the SD3 demonstrate stronger convergent and incremental validity, it appears that this brief measure of the dark triad navigates more effectively the tension between precision and efficiency. Maples et al. (2014) noted, however, that it takes less than 9 minutes to assess the dark triad using the longer, more established instruments, which is also relatively brief and efficient. They advocated that individuals use the longer dark triad instruments except in cases when time is truly of the essence; in these cases, the SD3 scales yield effect sizes that are more consistent with the established dark triad scales.

Limitations of Personality Tests

As much as there is a demand for further developed personality tests for screening dark triad personalities, we cannot ignore the complexity of these tools in terms of practically applying them in organizations. Guenole (2014) raised five important reasons for the hesitation of organizations to apply personality tests for detecting and probably rejecting applicants who would score high on the dark triad scales. The first is the concern that the use of maladaptive inventories might infringe rights protected by law (Wu & Lebreton, 2011). According to Schutte et al. (2015), from a legal standpoint, it is important to note that (at least in the US) it is illegal for organizations to discriminate against workers on the basis of a disability. A psychopathic personality, however, has never been classified as a disability (cf. the *DSM-5*). Nonetheless, the use of personality inventories to identify individuals with clinical levels of psychopathic personality traits would be considered a violation of the ADA of 1990 (amended in 2008) because the survey would be considered a pre-employment medical screening. Therefore, it is critical that organizations that wish to screen for these tendencies during the hiring process utilize an appropriate instrument for doing so because some psychopathic personality inventories have been purposed and validated as clinical screening tools (e.g., the Psychopathy Checklist—Revised; Hare, 1991, 2003). Therefore, whereas the use of subclinical inventories to capture psychopathic personality tendencies would be defensible under the ADA, the use of clinically oriented inventories would be likely to violate the ADA.

It should be noted in this regard that Wu and Lebreton (2011) advanced two reasons why screening for the dark triad is unlikely to violate the ADA. First, the individuals of the type discussed here have elevated levels of the dark triad traits but are perfectly capable of leading normal lives, including securing and maintaining employment, maintaining relationships, and so on. There is no reason to believe that these individuals are clinically impaired in their ability to perform the essential functions of the job for which they were hired. What in fact happens with these individuals is that they move beyond the essential job functions (i.e., core task behaviors) to engage in extra-role behaviors that are detrimental to the organization, such as CWBs. Second, Wu and Lebreton (2011) contended that most of the assessment devices developed to diagnose dark triad personalities have been developed for use with normal populations. They do not assess anything approaching a clinical personality disorder or anything that might represent a pre-employment clinical or medical examination and therefore do not violate any aspect of the ADA. Guenole (2014) also contended, based on a thorough review, that maladaptive inventories are work related and legally defensible.

The second reason for the hesitation of organizations to apply personality tests is social responsibility, which concerns inadvertent and unnecessary exclusion of candidates with mental health problems from the workplace. Guenole (2014) argued that the biggest threat to the spirit of the ADA is not the individual's access to employment opportunities, but his or her fair treatment when employed. The third reason raised by Guenole (2014) is the belief that any model of personality pathology is redundant if measures of the FFM are already used in assessment and would therefore have no incremental validity. If researchers and practitioners believe that the incremental validity of the FFM is marginal, adding another maladaptive FFM is unlikely to be very helpful. However, recent studies, according to Guenole, have indicated that dark triad traits show incremental validity for predicting important work outcomes, and therefore this line of work seems to be very promising. The fourth concern is that personality tests show low validity in general and are not predictive of performance. Guenole (2014) argued that, while results are mixed, it seems that validities emerging for the maladaptive personality model would be considered useful by a substantial proportion of academic and practitioner readers. The fifth reason is a concern that individuals may fake their responses in screening tests. This is too much of a fear for maladaptive inventories. Guenole contended in that regard that there is little that can be done to deal with faking other than using social desirability scales, spotting the faking post hoc with statistical analyses, or using forced choice response options in the measurement instrument. The latter solution is the preferable one.

In short, organizations that consider using personality tests for screening dark triad personalities should take into account the complexities mentioned earlier.

Selection Interviews

Many organizations use selection interviews for hiring employees. In light of the quite modest predictive validities of selection interviews, these tools are disastrous in terms of screening dark triad personalities. According to Boddy (2016), the increasingly rapid turnover of senior managers and the speed with which they are replaced using "shallow" recruitment processes means that the charismatic individual tends to overshadow the less charismatic in interview selection processes. Those with "dark charisma" are most impressive because they are happy to lie about their past achievements and so appear to have the competencies, values, and employee engagement abilities that characterize effective leadership. They appear to be the type of leader who can ruthlessly deliver the increasingly ambitious targets demanded of management in the public sector. In reality, corporate psychopaths have none of these competencies, values, or abilities; they are incompetent, selfish rather than selfless, and do not value other employees, who, therefore, subsequently disengage from the organization or even undermine it (Boddy, 2016). This represents a potential area of concern for HR branches such as recruitment, selection, and promotion (Campbell et al., 2011).

Campbell et al. (2011) cited Paulhus, Westlake, and Calvez (2010), who focused directly on personnel selection in an interview context and found that narcissism positively predicted interviewer evaluations. A key mechanism seems to be verbal quantity. That is, narcissists talk a good deal in interviews, and this gives them an air of competence. This finding is joined by the findings that these individuals tend to be more positively evaluated by trained assessors in assessment center exercises (Brunell et al., 2008). Psychopaths are adept at image management and can deceive trained and experienced psychologists (Boddy, 2016). Therefore, personnel directors and managers untrained in psychopathy who interview and review psychopaths in the workplace are easily duped by the charm, likeableness, and apparent sincerity of the corporate psychopath because they are too impressed with the psychopath's seeming expertise, energy, creativity, and leadership qualities to consider the negative reports by those at the same level or at a level below the psychopath (Boddy, 2016).

It appears that HR functions are vulnerable to the recruitment and selection of narcissists (Brunell et al., 2008). To combat this problem, recruiters, interviewers, and assessors should be trained to be on the lookout for behaviors indicative of the dark triad personalities (Brunell et al., 2008). More specifically, in the recruitment stage, interviewers should be wary of smooth-talking and charming extroverts who say all the right things and seem to be ideal candidates. References from their ex-bosses, as well as from their peers and their subordinates, can illuminate their true nature (Boddy, 2006).

Other Methods for Detecting Dark Triad Personalities

Because of the complexities and difficulties inherent in the more traditional tools as methods for screening for dark triad personalities, some researchers advocate more innovative and even challenging methods. According to Boddy (2016), screening for corporate psychopaths may be undertaken by looking for psychopathic traits in leadership candidates, such as emotional unresponsiveness and a lack of caring for other people. Screening can be achieved by asking the employees who report to them to apply psychopathy measures to managers. Employees could rate their current manager on psychopathic traits, and typically, high-scoring managers will also be found to be highly dysfunctional in other areas of their responsibilities. Self-report psychopathy measures could also be used for screening purposes, in which managers report on their own traits and behavior.

In contested cases, brain scans could be used to triangulate results so that the results of other measures can be confirmed or refuted. The psychopathic brain is characterized by a lack of emotional response in line with the psychopath's callous indifference to other people. According to Boddy (2016), psychology researchers have even suggested that brain scans should be the decisive measure to determine an individual's level of psychopathy. Alternatively, recruiting people who demonstrably do care for and value others would achieve the same objective in that it would eliminate psychopaths from the selection process.

Another interesting means of detecting dark triad personalities was advanced by Spain et al. (2014), who suggested reports by knowledgeable others could be used for this purpose. According to them, when it comes to a normal personality, other people may be particularly good sources of information. In the dark personality realm, peer nominations are an effective means of avoiding the problems typically found with self-report measures in the prediction of real-world behavior. If the dark personality is of interest, reports from knowledgeable others should be considered because those who are exposed to individuals with dark personalities are more than capable of reporting their patterns of destructiveness. However, it is worth noting that knowledgeable others still do not have access to the individual's inner thoughts, and this could make the accurate assessment of the dark side more difficult.

According to Furnham and Crump (2016), one means of finding whether a person is a subclinical psychopath lies in his or her biography. It may be possible to detect early signs of delinquency, such as evidenced by brushes with the law, in an individual from the age of adolescence onward, and a string of people may line up to testify, quite willingly, about the way they were lied to, cheated, and "conned" by a particular individual they trusted. Babiak and Hare (2006) also emphasized the need to review résumés thoroughly, verify all stated facts through references and background checks, and ensure that the interviewers are indeed highly qualified. For senior positions, executive recruiters experienced in screening for personality traits could be asked to flag suspect candidates. Succession planning and internal management development would allow agencies to groom leaders internally under close, intensive, and long-term supervision (Hanson & Baker, 2017).

According to Hanson and Baker (2017), servant leadership might offer public agencies a protocol for culling toxic, destructive, or dark leader prospects by increasing their capability to identify constructive leaders, those who are pro-organization and pro-employee, as conceived in the destructive leader model. In Boddy's (2016) words, "Recruiting of people who demonstrably do care for and value others would achieve the same objective [as psychopathy screening] in eliminating psychopaths from the selection process" (p. 266). Increasing the overall rate of constructive leadership might also translate into greater trust in government. As the term "servant" implies, a servant leader invests his or her personal ambition in prosocial agency, service, and stewardship. Servant leaders create conditions that enhance followers' well-being and functioning and thereby facilitate the realization of a shared vision; servant leaders trust followers to do what is necessary for the organization.

Campbell et al. (2011) contended that if narcissistic individuals are recruited into an organization, a comprehensive performance evaluation system might aid in preventing their continued advancement. In terms of assessment, it is advisable to focus on ethical, interpersonal, and various citizenship-oriented behaviors. A clear picture is beginning to emerge that narcissism primarily impedes organizational functioning through its association with increased unethical behavior and decreased organizational citizenship behaviors. Likewise, gathering multiple perspectives on performance (supervisor, peer, and subordinate), in addition to objective metrics, is important for identifying narcissistic employees. If you find that you have a narcissistic employee, there is no sure fire mechanism for reducing his or her narcissism. In the laboratory, increasing the sense of connection to others seems to mitigate some of the narcissist's more destructive behaviors. Another option is to find an area in an organizational setting where the narcissistic employee can excel. Narcissistic individuals, for example, do well in situations that require public performance or short-term relationships. Placing a narcissistic individual in a role that fits his or her talents could be a win/win situation for both the organization and employee (Campbell et al., 2011).

In conclusion, screening for psychopaths in public leadership positions may have beneficial results that are of significant consequence at multiple levels. Other employees may be spared distress and career derailment, organizations may be spared reduced performance, fraud, and financial collapse, and societies may benefit from increased levels of corporate social responsibility, increased concern for the vulnerable, and more sustainable economic growth. More studies that will develop more valid tools for detecting dark triad traits are valuable and needed.

References

American Psychiatric Association Diagnostic and Statistical Manual of Mental Disorders. (1980). *American Psychiatric Association* (4th ed., text revision). Washington, DC.

Ames, D. R., Rose, P., & Anderson, C. P. (2006). The NPI-16 as a short measure of narcissism. *Journal of Research in Personality, 40*(4), 440–450.

Babiak, P., & Hare, R. D. (2006). *Snakes in Suits: When Psychopaths Go to Work*. New York: Regan Books.

Babiak, P., & Hare, R. D. (2014). *The B-Scan 360 Manual*. In preparation.

Babiak, P., Neumann, C. S., & Hare, R. D. (2010). Corporate psychopathy: Talking the walk. *Behavioral Sciences & the Law, 28*(2), 174–193.

Boddy, C. R. (2006). The dark side of management decisions: Organizational psychopaths. *Management Decision, 44*, 1461–1475.

Boddy, C. R. (2009). *Corporate Psychopaths in Australian Workplaces: Their Influence on Organizational Outcomes*. Perth, Western Australia: Curtin University of Technology.

Boddy, C. R. (2011). *Corporate Psychopaths: Organizational Destroyers*. London: Palgrave MacMillan.

Boddy, C. R. (2016). Psychopathy screening for public leadership. *International Journal of Public Leadership, 12*(4), 254–274.

Boddy, C. R., Ladyshewsky, R., & Galvin, P. G. (2010). The influence of corporate psychopaths on corporate social responsibility and organizational commitment to employees. *Journal of Business Ethics, 97*(1), 1–19.

Boddy, C., Miles, D., Sanyal, C., & Hartog, M. (2015). Extreme managers, extreme workplaces: Capitalism, organizations and corporate psychopaths. *Organization, 22*(4), 530–551.

Brunell, A. B., Gentry, W. A., Campbell, W. K., Hoffman, B. J., Kuhnert, K. W., & DeMarree, K. G. (2008). Leader emergence: The case of the narcissistic leader. *Personality and Social Psychology Bulletin, 34*(12), 1663–1676.

Campbell, W. K., Hoffman, B. J., Campbell, S. M., & Marchisio, G. (2011). Narcissism in organizational contexts. *Human Resource Management Review, 21*(4), 268–284.

Christie, R. (1970a). Why Machiavelli? In R. Christie & F. L. Geis (Eds.), *Studies in Machiavellianism* (pp. 1–9). New York: Academic Press.

Christie, R. (1970b). Scale construction. In R. Christie & F. L. Geis (Eds.), *Studies in Machiavellianism* (pp. 10–34). New York: Academic Press.

Christie, R., & Geis, F. L. (1970). *Studies in Machiavellianism*. New York, NY: Academic Press.

Cleckley, H. (1941/1988). *The Mask of Sanity (5th ed.), Private Printing for Educational Use by Emily Cleckley 1988* (Formerly first published by C. V. Mosley Co. in 1941). Georgia: Augusta.

Corral, S., & Calvete, E. (2000). Machiavellianism: Dimensionality of the Mach IV and its relation to self-monitoring in a Spanish sample. *The Spanish Journal of Psychology, 3*(1), 3–13.

Dahling, J. J., Whitaker, B. G., & Levy, P. E. (2009). The development and validation of a new Machiavellianism scale. *Journal of Management, 35*(2), 219–257.

Delbecq, A. L. (2001). "Evil" manifested in destructive individual behavior: A senior leadership challenge. *Journal of Management Inquiry, 10*(3), 221–226.

Eisenbarth, H., Lilienfeld, S. O., & Yarkoni, T. (2015). Using a genetic algorithm to abbreviate the Psychopathic Personality Inventory-Revised (PPI-R). *Psychological Assessment, 27*(1), 194–202.

Fehr, B., Samson, D., & Paulhus, D. L. (1992). The construct of Machiavellianism: Twenty years later. In C. D. Spielberger & J. N. Butcher (Eds.), *Advances in Personality Assessment* (Vol. 9, pp. 77–116). Hillsdale, NJ: Lawrence Erlbaum Associates.

Fennimore, A., & Sementelli, A. (2016). Public entrepreneurship and sub-clinical psychopaths: A conceptual frame and implications. *International Journal of Public Sector Management, 29*(6), 612–634.

Furnham, A., & Crump, J. (2016). A Big Five facet analysis of a psychopath: The validity of the HDS mischievous scale of sub-clinical psychopathy. *Scandinavian Journal of Psychology, 57*, 117–121.

Gentile, B., Miller, J. D., Hoffman, B. J., Reidy, D. E., Zeichner, A., & Campbell, W. K. (2013). A test of two brief measures of grandiose narcissism: The Narcissistic Personality Inventory-13 and the Narcissistic Personality Inventory-16. *Psychological Assessment, 25*(4), 1120–1136.

Gough, H. G., & Bradley, P. (1996). *California Personality Inventory Manual.* Palo Alto, CA: Consulting Psychologists.

Grace, D., & Jackson, M. (2014). Reflections on the misrepresentation of Machiavelli in management: The mysterious case of the MACH IV personality construct. *Philosophy of Management, 13*(3), 51–72.

Guenole, N. (2014). Maladaptive personality at work: Exploring the darkness. *Industrial and Organizational Psychology, 7*(1), 85–97.

Gurtman, M. B. (1992). Trust, distrust, and interpersonal problems: A circumflex analysis. *Journal of Personality and Social Psychology, 62*(6), 989–1002.

Hanson, L., & Baker, D. L. (2017). "Corporate psychopaths" in public agencies? *Journal of Public Management & Social Policy, 24*(1), 21–41.

Hare, R. D. (1980). The assessment of psychopathy in criminal populations. *Personality and Individual Differences, 1*, 111–119.

Hare, R. D. (1991). *The Hare Psychopathy Checklist Revised.* New York, NY: Multi-Health Systems Inc.

Hare, R. D. (1999). *Without Conscience: The Disturbing World of the Psychopaths among Us.* New York, NY: Guilford Press.

Hare, R. D. (2003). *The Psychopathy Checklist: Revised.* Toronto, ON, Toronto, Canada: Multi-Health Systems Inc.

Hare, R. D., Harpur, T. J., Hakstian, A. R., Forth, A. E., Hart, S. D., & Newman, J. P. (1990). The revised psychopathy checklist: Reliability and factor structure. *Psychological Assessment: A Journal of Consulting and Clinical Psychology, 2*(3), 338.

Hare, R. D., & Neumann, C. S. (2009). Psychopathy and its measurement. In P. Corr & G. Matthews (Eds.), *Cambridge Handbook of Personality Psychology* (pp. 660–686). Cambridge: Cambridge University Press.

Harpur, T. J., Hakstian, A. R., & Hare, R. D. (1988). Factor structure of the psychopathy checklist. *Journal of Consulting and Clinical Psychology, 56*(5), 741–747.

Harpur, T. J., Hare, R. D., & Hakstian, A. R. (1989). Two-factor conceptualization of psychopathy: Construct validity and assessment implications. *Psychological Assessment: A Journal of Consulting and Clinical Psychology, 1*(1), 6–17.

Henning, J. B., Wygant, D. B., & Barnes, P. W. (2014). Mapping the darkness and finding the light: DSM-5 and assessment of the "corporate psychopath." *Industrial and Organizational Psychology*, 7(1), 144–148.

Hogan, R., & Fico, J. M. (2011). Leadership. In W. K. Campbell & J. D. Miller (Eds.), *The Handbook of Narcissism and Narcissistic Personality Disorder: Theoretical Approaches, Empirical Findings, and Treatments* (pp. 393–402). New York: Wiley.

Hogan, R., & Hogan, J. (2009). *Hogan Development Survey Manual* (2nd ed.). Tulsa, OK: Hogan Assessment Systems.

Hunter, J. E., Gerbing, D. W., & Boster, F. J. (1982). Machiavellian beliefs and personality: Construct invalidity of the Machiavellianism dimension. *Journal of Personality and Social Psychology*, 43(6), 1293–1305.

Hyler, S. E. (1994). *PDQ-4+ Personality Questionnaire*. New York: Author.

Jonason, P. K., Slomski, S., & Partyka, J. (2012b). The dark triad at work: How toxic employees get their way. *Personality and Individual Differences*, 52(3), 449–453.

Jonason, P. K., & Webster, G. D. (2010). The dirty dozen: A concise measure of the dark triad. *Psychological Assessment*, 22(2), 420–432.

Jones, D. N., & Paulhus, D. L. (2014). Introducing the short dark triad (SD3): A brief measure of dark personality traits. *Assessment*, 21(1), 28–41.

Judge, T. A., & LePine, J. A. (2007). The bright and dark sides of personality: Implications for personnel selection and team configuration. In J. Langan-Fox, C. Cooper, & R. Klimoski (Eds.), *Research Companion to the Dysfunctional Workplace: Management Challenges and Symptoms* (pp. 332–355). Cheltenham, England: Elgar.

Kaiser, R. B., & Hogan, R. (2006). The dark side of discretion: Research report. Available at: www.hoganassessments.com/_hoganweb/documents/dark%20 side%20of%20discretion.pdf (accessed 11 December 2015), Tulsa, OK: Hogan Assessment Center.

Kastner, R. M., Sellbom, M., & Lilienfeld, S. O. (2012). A comparison of the psychometric properties of the Psychopathic Personality Inventory full-length and short-form versions. *Psychological Assessment*, 24(1), 261–267.

Krueger, R. F., Eaton, N. R., Derringer, J., Markon, K. E., Watson, D., & Skodol, A. E. (2011). Personality in DSM-5: Helping delineate personality disorder content and framing the metastructure. *Journal of Personality Assessment*, 93(4), 325–331.

Lilienfeld, S. O., & Andrews, B. P. (1996). Development and preliminary validation of a self-report measure of psychopathic personality traits in noncriminal populations. *Journal of Personality Assessment*, 66, 488–524.

Lilienfeld, S. O., & Widows, M. R. (2005). *Psychopathic Personality Inventory-Revised: Professional Manual*. Lutz, FL: PAR, Inc.

Livesley, W. J. (2006). The Dimensional Assessment of Personality Pathology (DAPP) approach to personality disorder. In S. Strack (Ed.), *Differentiating Normal and Abnormal Personality* (2nd ed., pp. 401–425). New York: Springer Publishing Company.

Maples, J. L., Lamkin, J., & Miller, J. D. (2014). A test of two brief measures of the dark triad: The dirty dozen and short dark triad. *Psychological Assessment*, 26(1), 326–331.

Mathieu, C., & Babiak, P. (2016a). Validating the B-Scan Self: A self-report measure of psychopathy in the workplace. *International Journal of Selection and Assessment*, 24(3), 272–284.

Mathieu, C., Hare, R. D., Jones, D. N., Babiak, P., & Neumann, C. S. (2013). Factor structure of the B-Scan 360: A measure of corporate psychopathy. *Psychological Assessment*, 25, 288–293.

Mathieu, C., Neumann, C., Babiak, P., & Hare, R. D. (2015). Corporate psychopathy and the full-range leadership model. *Assessment, 22*(3), 267–278.

Mathieu, C., Neumann, C. S., Hare, R. D., & Babiak, P. (2014). A dark side of leadership: Corporate psychopathy and its influence on employee well-being and job satisfaction. *Personality and Individual Differences, 59*, 83–88.

Miller, J. D., & Campbell, W. K. (2011). Addressing criticisms of the Narcissistic Personality Inventory (NPI). In W. K. Campbell & J. D. Miller (Eds.), *The Handbook of Narcissism and Narcissistic Personality Disorder: Theoretical Approaches, Empirical Findings, and Treatments* (pp. 146–152). Hoboken, NJ: Wiley.

Miller, J. D., Gentile, B., Wilson, L., & Campbell, W. K. (2013). Grandiose and vulnerable narcissism and the DSM-5 pathological personality trait model. *Journal of Personality Assessment, 95*(3), 284–290.

Miller, J. D., Lynam, D. R., & Campbell, W. K. (2016). Measures of narcissism and their relations to DSM-5 pathological traits: A critical reappraisal. *Assessment, 23*(1), 3–9.

Millon, T. (1997). *Millon Clinical Multiaxial Inventory-III* (Manual 2nd ed.). Bloomington, MN: Pearson Assessments.

Neumann, C. S., Hare, R. D., & Newman, J. P. (2007). The super-ordinate nature of the psychopathy checklist-revised. *Journal of Personality Disorders, 21*(2), 102–117.

Neumann, C. S., Hare, R. D., & Pardini, D. A. (2015). Antisociality and the construct of psychopathy: Data from across the globe. *Journal of Personality, 83*(6), 678–692.

Newman, J. P., MacCoon, D. G., Vaughn, L. J., & Sadeh, N. (2005). Validating a distinction between primary and secondary psychopathy with measures of Gray's BIS and BAS constructs. *Journal of Abnormal Psychology, 114*(2), 319.

Paulhus, D. L., Westlake, B. G., & Calvez, S. S. (2010). *Why Self-Enhancers Flourish in Job Interviews: Unpacking Their Responsiveness and Effectiveness*. Unpublished manuscript. University of British Columbia.

Perry, C. (2015). The "dark traits" of sociopathic leaders: Could they be a threat to universities? *Australian Universities' Review, 57*(1), 17–24.

Pincus, A. L., Ansell, E. B., Pimentel, C. A., Cain, N. M., Wright, A. G., & Levy, K. N. (2009). Initial construction and validation of the Pathological Narcissism Inventory. *Psychological Assessment, 21*(3), 365–379.

Raskin, R., & Terry, H. (1988). A principal-components analysis of the Narcissistic Personality Inventory and further evidence of its construct validity. *Journal of Personality and Social Psychology, 54*(5), 890–902.

Rauthmann, J. F. (2013). Investigating the MACH-IV with item response theory and proposing the trimmed MACH. *Journal of Personality Assessment, 95*(4), 388–397.

Ruchensky, J. R., Edens, J. F., Donnellan, M. B., & Witt, E. A. (2017). Examining the reliability and validity of an abbreviated Psychopathic Personality Inventory-Revised (PPI-R) in four samples. *Psychological Assessment, 29*(2), 238–244.

Schimmenti, A., Jonason, P. K., Passanisi, A., La Marca, L., Di Dio, N., & Gervasi, A. M. (2017). Exploring the dark side of personality: Emotional awareness, empathy, and the dark triad traits in an Italian sample. *Current Psychology*, 1–10.

Schutte, N., Blickle, G., Frieder, R. E., Wihler, A., Schnitzler, F., Heupel, J., & Zettler, I. (2015). The role of interpersonal influence in counterbalancing psychopathic personality trait facets at work. *Journal of Management*, in press.

Skodol, A. E., Bender, D. S., & Morey, L. C. (2014). Narcissistic personality disorder in DSM-5. *Personality Disorders: Theory, Research, and Treatment, 5*(4), 422–427.

Skodol, A. E., Bender, D. S., Morey, L. C., Clark, L. A., Oldham, J. M., Alarcon, R. D., Krueger, R. F., Verheul, R., Bell, C. C., & Siever, L. J. (2011). Personality disorder types proposed for DSM-5. *Journal of Personality Disorders, 25*(2), 136–169.

Spain, S. M., Harms, P., & LeBreton, J. M. (2014). The dark side of personality at work. *Journal of Organizational Behavior, 35*(Supplement 1), S41–S60.

Williams, M. L., Hazleton, V., & Renshaw, S. (1975). The measurement of Machiavellianism: A factor analytic and correlational study of MACH-IV and MACH-V. *Communications Monographs, 42*(2), 151–159.

Wink, P., & Gough, H. G. (1990). New narcissism scales for the California Psychological Inventory and MMPI. *Journal of Personality Assessment, 54*(3–4), 446–462.

Wu, J., & Lebreton, J. M. (2011). Reconsidering the dispositional basis of counterproductive work behavior: The role of aberrant personality. *Personnel Psychology, 64*(3), 593–626.

8 The Dark Triad and Leadership

Leadership is an important area of management research because leaders are known to be able to change organizations according to their own personalities and preferences. This includes changing the moral fabric of the organization by setting an example and exerting influence (Boddy, 2011). Leaders have the power and authority to change an organization in ways that may be either beneficial or detrimental to its long-term success. Leaders influence the tone of an organization and have to be honest, act with integrity, and be trustworthy in order to succeed in their capacity. Concern regarding the unethical and criminal behavior of business leaders has increased in recent years, energizing interest in this dark side of leadership. Incompetent leaders can cause serious damage to any organization. It is therefore important to distinguish between managers who are simply ineffective or incompetent and managers who are malevolent (Spain, Harms, & LeBreton, 2014; Furtner, Maran, & Rauthmann, 2017). The results of explorations of the reasons for managerial failure helped revitalize interest in the role of personality in leadership (Kaiser, LeBreton, & Hogan, 2015). The interest of this book is in destructive leaders, a topic that has received increased attention because of the realization that although leaders may fail or derail an organization for a variety of reasons, many fail because of personal rather than structural or economic reasons.

Researchers have suggested that some of these business leaders may in fact display psychopathic behaviors that are associated with immense personal, social, and economic costs. However, despite these claims, to date, little empirical research has been conducted on the linkage between psychopathic traits and leadership behavior (Westerlaken & Woods, 2013; Furtner et al., 2017). According to Herbst (2014), behavioral leadership characteristics associated with the dark side include "petty tyranny," "toxic leadership," "destructive leadership," "bad leadership," "leadership derailment," "aversive leadership," and "evil leadership." Toxic leadership is significant because such leaders put their self-interest before the organizational interest and in so doing cause severe harm to employees and organizations (Boddy, 2016a). Toxic (dark, dysfunctional, psychopathic) leadership is particularly destructive, whether at the organizational or departmental level, and therefore is worth investigating.

Destructive or toxic leadership has long been associated with aversive personality traits (Hanson & Baker, 2017). It is recognized that the personalities of leaders can affect their performance in management roles. Very often the cause of their failure is an overriding personality defect or character flaw that prevents them from building a cohesive team and alienates them from their subordinates (Herbst, 2014). Some leaders may have one or several personality disorders that make their leadership toxic to the organization and to those who work around them (Boddy, 2011). Indeed, with the recent global financial crisis, management researchers are increasingly interested in investigating the aspects of dark leadership in an attempt to explain the current financial and organizational turmoil around the world. Thus, the study of leaders with personality disorders should be of interest to management researchers because broad knowledge about the different existing types of toxic leadership is lacking (Boddy, 2011).

As mentioned in previous chapters, the dark side of personality in the workplace has received renewed attention, mainly over the past two decades, with much of the literature suggesting narcissism (and then more recently, psychopathy) is the dark triad personality most implicated in leadership (Khoo & Burch, 2008). There is evidence that dark triad personalities are likely to be attracted to positions of influence and thus might be slightly overrepresented in leadership and top management positions (Schyns, 2015). Schyns and Schilling (2013) found in their meta-analysis a quite strong relationship between counterproductive work behaviors (CWBs) and destructive leadership, lending support to the notion that it is necessary to examine the relationship between the dark triad personalities and leadership. The mounting evidence of personality disorders found among leaders has been noted and reported as a phenomenon that warrants additional assessment and consideration (Hogan & Hogan, 2001; Boddy, 2016a). The emergent literature on corporate psychopaths provides a powerful framework for investigating corporate leadership in view of the corporate scandals reported in the media. The subject of psychopathic leadership is also worth examining in terms of its possible contribution to understanding leadership in general and toxic leadership in particular. Additionally, understanding toxic and bad leadership may help to illuminate, in contrast, our understanding of good and ethical leadership. However, with a few exceptions, the research of toxic leadership has been neglected (Boddy, 2016a, 2016b).

Another reason for the need for more research on this topic is the spread of destructive leadership. Hogan (2007) wrote that, based on the results from all the organizational climate surveys conducted over a year and on the research at the Center for Creative Leadership, the base rate for incompetent managers is 65% to 75%. That is, between 65% and 75% of existing managers are alienating their staff. Herbst (2014) cited Virkler (2005), who estimated that 10% to 13% of the US population—more than 30 million people—have personality disorders. The conventional wisdom in the occupational psychology community in the 1980s was that the base rate for managerial incompetence was 3% to 5%. This estimate was self-serving and designed to flatter potential clients (Hogan, 2007). Hogan mentioned three points concerning this estimate. First, whatever the precise number may be, it is considerably larger than it needs to be. Second, the popular press reports evidence every day to support the claim that incompetent management is widespread. Three, the number of incompetent managers today is not higher than it was 30 to 50 years ago; there is simply more awareness of the problem than in the past.

To sum up, the argument advanced in this book is that a large part of leadership ineffectiveness can be attributed to the destructive personalities of managers. Indeed, personality disorders were cited by Hogan (2007) as one of the reasons for managerial incompetence, leading to recommendations that more research focus on dark personalities to better understand leadership and leader derailment (Hogan & Hogan, 2001; Spain et al., 2014). This chapter is focused on the "dark side" of leadership, as it both negatively affects the organization and harms its employees. What are the effects of such leaders on the organization and its employees? What theories have been developed to characterize and explain these leaders? What are the main characteristics and outcomes of leaders from each of the dark triad components? What can we learn from research on toxic leadership? These and other issues regarding destructive leadership are reviewed in this chapter.

Destructive Leadership

While the dominant approaches to leadership in the workplace focus on positive theories of leadership, the approach of this book takes us in the opposite direction, namely, to the dark side of leadership. This dark side, in terms of its manifested outcome, is termed in this book "destructive leadership. What exactly does the term 'destructive leadership,' attributed in many occasions to the dark triad traits, mean?" Researchers have proposed several definitions and descriptions of destructive leadership. Hanson and Baker (2017) cited the definition of destructive leadership of Einarsen, Aasland, and Skogstad (2007, p. 208). According to this definition, destructive leadership is the "systematic and repeated behavior by a leader, supervisor or manager that violates the legitimate interest of the organization by undermining and/or sabotaging the organization's goals, tasks, resources, and effectiveness and/or the motivation, well-being or job-satisfaction of subordinates." Herbst (2014) cited Higgs (2009), who found four themes related to dark-side behaviors, namely, the abuse of power, inflicting damage on others, excessive exercise of control, and rule breaking to satisfy personal needs. According to Herbst (2014), these leaders are perceived by their subordinates as untrustworthy, overly ambitious, and disingenuous.

Padilla, Hogan, and Kaiser (2007) described destructive leadership in terms of five features: (1) Destructive leadership is not entirely destructive; there are both good and bad results in most leadership situations. (2) The process of destructive leadership involves dominance, coercion, and manipulation rather than influence, persuasion, and commitment. (3) The process of destructive leadership has a selfish orientation; it is focused more on the needs of the leader than on those of the larger social group. (4) The effects of destructive leadership are outcomes that compromise the quality of life for employees and detract from the organization's main purposes. (5) Destructive organizational outcomes are not exclusively the result of destructive leaders but are also the product of susceptible followers and conducive environments (Padilla et al., 2007).

Destructive leadership can be viewed as a process, and scholars focusing on process, that is, on what destructive leaders do, emphasize behavior. This approach emphasizes dark traits that are associated with alienation and betrayal or behaviors such as manipulation, intimidation, coercion, and one-way communication. From this viewpoint, destructive leadership is something leaders do, independent of the outcomes of their behavior. The definition of destructive leadership as a process assumes that a leader's bad intentions are an essential component of his or her destructiveness. It also assumes that certain behaviors are inherently destructive (Padilla et al., 2007). Either way, destructive leadership results in undesirable behavior and outcomes.

Some of these adverse outcomes were mentioned by Babiak and Hare (2006), who described common leadership failures, or "red flags," that could be manifestations of corporate psychopathy. These include a person's difficulty forming a team and sharing ideas and credit with others, disparate treatment of staff, deceptiveness, immodesty, inability to accept blame, acting unpredictably and impulsively, and acting aggressively. Similarly, Leslie and Van Velsor (1996) described four aspects of leader behaviors that lead to career "derailment": poor interpersonal skills (i.e., being arrogant, cold, insensitive, and overly ambitious), inability to get work done (i.e., betraying trust, not following through), inability to build a team, and inability to make an effective transition following promotion. These features are similar to those suggested by Babiak and Hare (2006) to be indicative of corporate psychopathy. Regardless of their exact nature and style, such psychopath-like bosses have a significant impact on employees' mood, psychological well-being, and job performance (Spector, 1997).

Another aspect of the possible outcomes of destructive leadership was advanced by Myung and Choi (2017), who argued that the stronger a leader's dark side in an organization, the more are his or her unethical management practices increased and the higher the stress experienced by others. They further contended that the dark triad is negatively coupled with the level of perception of and concern for corporate social responsibility. The ethics of top management operates as an essential driver of corporate civil responsibility. The dark triad may not recognize corporate social responsibility as a critical issue and may have little concern for solving social and environmental problems.

Careful reading of the literature shows that destructive leadership has not been extensively researched (Padilla et al., 2007) and has not been given the importance or attention it deserves (Boddy, 2016a). Recently, researchers recommended expanding the leadership domain to include undesirable dispositions, variously described as counterproductive, subclinical, and dysfunctional, that collectively are referred to as the dark side. Kaiser et al. (2015) cited Harms, Spain, and Hannah (2011, p. 508), who noted that the nature of the dark side appears "far more complex than originally thought" and suggested that "there is a great deal of research to be done" to understand how it affects leadership. According to them, studies of the dark side may lead to a better understanding of leadership by complementing the traditional positive emphasis on the subject. This is particularly true because research across a number of domains shows that negative information, experiences, and people have a stronger effect than positive ones, suggesting that "bad is stronger than good" is a sound psychological principle.

Dark Triad Traits and Leadership

Concerning the roots of destructive leadership, according to Herbst (2014), the childhood background of a person has a significant influence on determining how the leader's dark side will develop, as well as how she or he will deal with it. A person's childhood traumatic experiences determine the extent to which he or she will be controlled by the dark side of his or her personality. The combined effect of unmet needs and traumatic experiences, which threatens the satisfaction of certain needs, as well as emotional debts, result in the development of the dark personality. As we mature toward adulthood, our dark side begins to develop quietly, only to surface at some future date, often after leadership has been achieved. Dark-side tendencies typically coexist with well-developed social skills that mask or compensate for them in the short term. With time, however, dark-side tendencies erode trust and undermine relationships (Herbst, 2014).

Recent reviews of the leadership literature have demonstrated that considerable interest in the trait approach to leadership remains, but the vast majority of this research has focused on variants of the FFM traits (Kaiser et al., 2015; Spain et al., 2014). Employees with high levels of FFM are less deviant and delinquent than employees with low levels (Kim & Cohen, 2015). With the exception of a few discussions on charisma, social scientists have avoided the dark side of leadership for many years. In recent years however, there is a growing interest on the subject and as a result a growing research.

Hogan and Hogan (2001, 2009) proposed that the personality disorders described in the fourth edition of the *Diagnostic and Statistical Manual of Mental Disorders* (*DSM-IV*; American Psychiatric Association, 1994) provide a taxonomy of the most important causes of managerial failure. Personality disorders are not forms of mental illness; they are dysfunctional interpersonal dispositions that (1) coexist with talent, ambition, and good social skills and (2) prevent people from completing the essential task of leadership: building a team. These dysfunctional dispositions are the dark side of personality. More specifically, Boddy (2011) provided a summary definition of the three personality disorders that leaders may possess. Corporate psychopaths are white-collar psychopaths who can present themselves as extroverted and charismatic leaders, charm their way into organizations, and strategically manipulate their way to top leadership positions. Typically conscienceless, they dispose of colleagues and patrons when these people are no longer needed. Machiavellians are corporate schemers who ascend the organizational hierarchy through adroit and calculated political maneuvering, ruthless exploitation of others, and dedicated self-promotion. Narcissists are people who are so in love with their own abilities and so convinced of their own superiority that they are able to persuade others of this as well and rise accordingly in organizations. Unlike psychopaths, who are indifferent to their surroundings, they want to be liked by those around them.

In a very interesting study, Wisse and Sleebos (2016) examined specifically how a supervisor's dark triad personality and position of power were related to employees' perceptions of abusive supervision. They examined 225 teams in various organizations and found a positive relationship between a supervisor's Machiavellianism and employees' ratings of abusive supervision. They also found that this relationship was stronger when the supervisors perceived themselves as being in a position of power. A somewhat unexpected finding was that a supervisor's narcissism and psychopathy were not significantly related to abusive supervision in the team. While the researchers contended that they did not expect narcissism to be related to abusive supervision per se, they did expect psychopathy, just like Machiavellianism, to be related to it, particularly in the case where the individual holds a position of power. The main explanation Wisse and Sleebos provided for this finding is that whereas a substantial component of Machiavellianism is the environment they share with others, psychopathy can largely be explained by genetic factors and factors other than their shared environment. This suggests that Machiavellians may have adjusted to their environment more and may have acquired their Machiavellianism over time, while psychopaths are less adaptable. Machiavellians, therefore, may be more sensitive to external cues than psychopaths.

In the following sections, a separate review of the leadership characteristics of each of the dark triad personalities is presented.

Narcissism and Leadership

The subject of narcissism lies at the heart of leadership because some degree of narcissism is a prerequisite for climbing the corporate ladder (Herbst, 2014). Therefore, there is more theory and research on the relationship between leadership and narcissism than the other two dark personalities The literature on narcissism and leadership revolves mainly around one important question: Is it good or bad for a leader to be a narcissist? The question has been phrased in many different ways, ranging from whether certain narcissistic traits are positive leadership characteristics while others are negative, to whether narcissism is necessary to provide the drive and vision needed to attain a leadership position, to whether all narcissistic leaders are ultimately doomed to fail (Rosenthal & Pittinsky, 2006). Yet despite the growing body of literature focusing on the relationship between narcissism and leadership, no consensus has been reached regarding the impact of narcissism on leadership (Grijalva, Harms, Newman, Gaddis, & Fraley, 2015). The following section covers some of this debate.

According to Campbell, Hoffman, Campbell, and Marchisio (2011), the link between narcissism and leadership has long been recognized, with early psychological research of narcissism linking narcissism and leadership (Freud, 1931/1950). It is common to identify narcissism at the top of organizations. Campbell et al. (2011) cited Kets de Vries and Miller's (1984) quotation that:

> Narcissistic personalities ... are frequently encountered in top management positions. Indeed, it is only to be expected that many narcissistic people, with their need for power, prestige, and glamour, eventually end up seeking leadership positions. Their sense of drama, their ability to manipulate others, their knack for establishing quick, superficial relationships serve them as well (p. 32).

Indeed, narcissists are likely to be perceived by others as self-confident and outgoing, two characteristics that occupy a prominent place in the perception of effective leadership. Grijalva and Harms (2014) claimed, based on their literature review, that narcissists' desire for status and power results in their holding more leadership roles, partly because they self-nominate themselves for available leadership positions.

Narcissism is correlated with destructive leadership. In extreme cases, "malignant narcissism" is associated with hyper aggressiveness and sadistic, exploitative personal relationships. Narcissistic leaders are self-absorbed and attention seeking and ignore others' viewpoints or welfare. They often claim special knowledge or privilege and demand unquestioning obedience, their sense of entitlement often leads to self-serving abuse of power, and their leadership style is typically autocratic (Padilla et al., 2007). However, the relationship between narcissism and leadership is less clear cut than its relationship with CWB (Grijalva & Harms, 2014) because narcissism is likely to be moderated by an unidentified set of variables, causing a complex relationship with leadership that is neither wholly positive nor completely negative. The results of past studies are inconsistent regarding narcissism's relationship with leadership effectiveness or how well narcissists perform in leadership roles (Grijalva & Harms, 2014). As seen in the following sections, theories and findings suggest that in some situations, narcissistic leaders can be beneficial for the organization and its employees, and in other situations, they can be destructive.

Theories for the Relationship Between Narcissism and (Destructive) Leadership

Sedikides and Campbell (2017) proposed a process model of narcissism, the Energy Clash Model, which clarifies some of the negative effects of narcissists on organizations. The model borrows and adapts a phase or state physics metaphor to conceptualize narcissism as a force that enters or emerges in a stable system (i.e., the organization) in the form of a leader, destabilizes it, and then stabilizes it at a different state or is expelled. The model consists of three time-contingent phases: perturbation, conflict, and resolution. According to this metaphor, the narcissistic leader enters the organization as a force, causing instability (perturbation). Armed with boldness and resilience, the leader smashes barriers, tears down old structures, and erects new ones, thus infusing the organization with excitement, optimism, and purpose, albeit with some initial concomitant doubt. Organizational awareness and alertness ensue, culminating in conflict. Antipathy and dissatisfaction with the leader grow as a result of conflict between the three domains of organizational life.

The leader's antagonism, contempt, and mistreatment of employees blemish the organizational climate, thus breeding mistrust, suspicion, and disrespect. Second, the leader's financial decisions are risk prone, engendering few, if any, organizational benefits. Third, the leader's ethical decisions are substandard, creating organizational embarrassment. Next, narcissistic energy clashes with organizational energy, eventually re-stabilizing the system (i.e., organization) at a different state, either through the exit of the narcissistic leader or the accommodation of the leader by the organization (resolution) (Sedikides & Campbell, 2017). Much depends on the extent of the success of the specific accommodation tactics (i.e., introducing micro-interventions, initiating personal development through coaching, strengthening the leader-employee fit, implementing systemic checks and balances via accountability, instituting synergistic leadership, and increasing leader organization identification). Sedikides and Campbell (2017) concluded that if narcissism as a force remains directionless, it may ultimately be self-serving or nihilistic; however, if it is directed appropriately and constructively, it may confer favorable organizational (and perhaps societal) change in the long run.

Hogan and Fico (2011) contended that to understand how narcissism interacts with leadership, it is important to recall the distinction between emergent and effective leadership. They argued that whereas narcissism promotes emergence—and little else—modesty impedes emergence and promotes subsequent success. Narcissists specialize in self-promotion and are usually the first to speak in a group of strangers; thus, leaderless group discussions are a good milieu for identifying narcissists. Hogan and Fico (2011) raised the question why, given the risks that narcissistic leadership brings to the organization, narcissists often emerge as leaders and in the short run at least as successful ones. They suggested that when private companies lack leaders who are confident, decisive, and willing to take initiative, they will not prosper. Therefore, confidence and eagerness to drive toward goals, combined with the ability to communicate a compelling vision, are needed for success in competitive industries. Hogan and Fico (2011) also cited Paulhus' (1998) study, showing that in their sample in the early stages of group formation, narcissists were seen as agreeable, well-adjusted, and competent; in the later stages, however, they received negative performance ratings from the other members, although their self-evaluations remained high.

Sankowsky (1995) focused on one special kind of power and its abuse by narcissist leaders, labeling it "symbolic status." It refers to a psychological phenomenon: the tendency for followers to tacitly regard leaders as parental figures (i.e., to mentally construct their relationship with leaders in child–parent terms), a tendency that becomes pronounced in the presence of charismatic leaders. The term "symbolic status" has its origins in a concept known in psychoanalytic circles as *transference*. This occurs when clients "symbolize" their therapists as parents. According to Sankowsky, the parallels between the leader–follower relationship and the therapist–client relationship were explored by various management theorists, indicating that transference is a phenomenon that exists in both relationships. This means that followers tend to be strongly motivated to gain the leader's personal approval and are highly affected by the leader's actions and beliefs. Followers are susceptible to the way a leader communicates, particularly with respect to philosophies or visions, interpretations of shared events, and proposed courses of action. The motivation and vulnerability described go beyond the present-based "normal" reactions to a leader. The power of symbolic status, rooted in powerful, unconscious drives, enhances leaders' potential to fundamentally alter their followers' perceptions, emotions, and thoughts. Abuse of this power can insidiously and significantly undermine their psychological well-being. A narcissistic leader tends to abuse symbolic status. When a leader is both charismatic and narcissistic, he or she is likely to *successfully* abuse the power of symbolic status, that is, to induce followers to buy into abusive behaviors.

negligible Furthermore, narcissism was not related to supervisor or subordinate ratings of effectiveness. These findings suggest that narcissism is associated with the dark side of charismatic leadership. The narcissistic-charismatic leader establishes a parental relationship with his or her "chosen" followers. These followers are motivated to seek the approval of their leader because they perceive him or her as a parental figure; thus, the leader's shortcomings are often ignored by the "chosen" followers. The tendency of narcissists to surround themselves with unquestioning followers may further lend support to this relationship (Blair et al., 2008).

Campbell et al. (2011) cited the study of Allen et al. (2009), who found that narcissistic entitlement in protégés was not related to seeking or attracting a mentor but predicted a shorter duration relationship with the mentor. Likewise, narcissistic entitlement in protégés was associated with protégé reports of less career support, less psychosocial support, and overall more negative mentoring experiences. It appears that the follower's narcissism affects the behavior of leaders, a finding that could have key implications for the development of leader member exchange. In summary, narcissism had a long-term (but not short-term) negative effect on mentoring.

Positive Outcomes of Narcissist Leaders

Although narcissism has a very negative connotation, it is important to realize that every leader needs a certain degree of narcissism to be able to function effectively (Herbst, 2014). Therefore, it might not be surprising that Grijalva et al.'s (2015) meta-analysis results did not support the predicted negative association between narcissism and leader effectiveness, and in fact, no linear association was found between them. However, there was one exception to this generalization: the relationship between narcissism and leadership effectiveness was significant when leadership effectiveness ratings were based on self-reports. These self-report findings offer further evidence that narcissists will self-enhance their own leadership achievements. More interestingly, Grijalva et al. (2015) found that the narcissism–leadership effectiveness relationship was curvilinear (an inverted U shape), that is, leaders were more effective when they had moderate levels of narcissism instead of very high or very low levels. They contended, based on the findings, that narcissism is neither wholly beneficial nor deleterious but is most effective in moderation.

The air of supreme confidence and dominance that constitutes the hallmarks of narcissism is in some cases exactly what inspires a group of followers. Moreover, there are clearly situations that call for the kind of great vision and dramatic action that are likely to be spurred by a narcissistic leader but are not, however, implemented (Herbst, 2014). Despite their image of independence, they are highly dependent on their followers for the admiration and affirmation that they desperately seek. This explains their sensitivity to criticism because it is contrary to their desire for affirmation and the recognition of their greatness, as well as their inherent lack of listening skills (Rosenthal & Pittinsky, 2006). Narcissists are especially gifted in attracting followers, and more often than not, they do so through language. Narcissists believe that words can move mountains and that inspiring speeches can change people. Narcissistic leaders are often skillful orators, and this is one of the talents that makes them so charismatic. Indeed, anyone who has seen narcissists perform can attest to their personal magnetism and their ability to stir enthusiasm among audiences. Yet this charismatic gift is more of a two-way affair than most people would think because, as mentioned earlier, narcissists need affirmation and preferably adulation from their admirers (Maccoby, 2000).

Narcissism may be healthy at one end of the continuum or destructive or pathological at the other end. It is therefore important to discriminate between reactive and constructive narcissism. Constructive narcissism characterizes leaders who grew up in a stable, supportive environment; have a positive self-regard; and are in general pleasant people. These people are assertive and goal oriented and not completely self-centered (Herbst, 2014). According to Herbst (2014), narcissist leaders are often good orators and know how to use symbol manipulation and strong imagery. Furthermore, they believe that they can only rely on themselves to gratify their needs and as a result project an image of independence and are highly exploitative. In contrast, reactive narcissists have experienced a considerable trauma in their lives. Because of their own lack of empathic experiences, they typically lack empathy and are often unable to experience how others feel. As a result, they are left with a legacy of feelings of deprivation, insecurity, and inadequacy in adulthood. Thus, they may develop a sense of entitlement as a means of overcoming their feelings of inadequacy and insecurity (Herbst, 2014). Theory and findings do suggest that there are positive outcomes of narcissist leaders. However, in many cases, the strengths of narcissists are conditioned on the specific environment in which they operate.

There are two major strengths of productive narcissists that make them ideal leaders for our times: They are visionaries, and they can inspire great numbers of followers. Productive narcissists are "not only risk takers willing to get the job done but also charmers who can convert the masses with their rhetoric" (Maccoby, 2000, p. 70) to help shape our "public and personal agendas" (Maccoby, 2000, p. 69). As visionaries, narcissistic leaders always see the big picture and tend to leave the analyzing and minutiae to others. When they do not like the rules, they ignore or even change them. Their visions are grand ones because they are inspired by a personal need to achieve power and glory and to leave a legacy behind them. And through these grand visions, coupled with great charisma, they gain devoted followers. In turn, the followers fulfill the narcissistic leaders' need for admiration, further bolstering their confidence and conviction in their visions (Maccoby, 2000).

with them. Psychopathic leadership entails engaging in publicly bullying people. Furthermore, it involves employing manipulative actions, such as presenting a false, cooperative persona to the upper management (Boddy & Taplin, 2016). According to Westerlaken and Woods (2013), it is the psychopaths' charismatic interpersonal skills, which quite possibly assist them in being hired in the first place, that also enable them to manage impressions and continue in their roles despite their poor performance. Other psychopathic traits such as manipulation and deceitfulness may be mistaken for typical transformational leadership behaviors, such as influence, persuasion, and visionary and strategic thinking. Conversely, psychopathic traits may parallel transactional and passive leadership behaviors. Boddy (2011) characterized psychopathic leadership as being fundamentally unfair and archetypally abusive. Psychopaths enjoy hurting people because it amuses them; furthermore, they use humiliation to cause confusion, chaos, and fear to hide their other activities. They also ruthlessly manipulate and unfairly abuse others, without conscience, to further their own aims and objectives.

The manipulation of others for their own ends constitutes the biggest part of the daily organizational existence of psychopathic leaders (Herbst, 2014). These leaders are masters of conning and manipulation, which leads people to perceive them as having strong persuasion and leadership skills. Herbst (2014) mentioned two important features of psychopathic leaders, namely, the extensive use of impression management techniques and the use of secrecy. In corporate settings, psychopathically motivated behavior is very often confused with genuine leadership talent. For example, the psychopathic leaders' charming demeanor and grandiose talk can easily be mistaken for charismatic leadership and self-confidence. Furthermore, the psychopaths' emotional deficiency or their inability to experience normal human emotions and extreme lack of conscience can be mistaken for other executive skills, especially the ability to make difficult decisions, to keep their emotions in check, and to remain cool under pressure. Herbst (2014) argued that, similar to great leaders, psychopaths are also risk takers who often put themselves and others in harm's way, a behavior that is accentuated by their impulsivity and thrill seeking. This could also easily be mistaken for high energy, action orientation, courage, and the ability to multitask, all of which are important characteristics of leaders.

The results of two studies that examined the relationship between psychopathic tendencies and leadership styles support the notion that the style of psychopaths as leaders is problematic. Westerlaken and Woods (2013) found that participants who self-identified themselves as displaying traits associated with psychopathy (e.g., callous disregard, lack of empathy, or poor behavioral control) were less likely to enact transformational leadership behaviors such as inspiring or satisfying others' needs for self-worth or self-actualization through mentoring and guidance strategies. In practical terms, Westerlaken and Woods suggested that employers may need to pay closer attention to managers who exhibit more passive leadership behaviors. The positive relationship between passive leadership behaviors, which are said to be ineffective, and psychopathy, which is associated with adverse personal, social, and economic costs, may indicate the potential of individuals who display higher levels of psychopathy and passive leadership behaviors to cause significant damage to organizations and their employees in terms of economic and emotional costs. Thus, instead of testing for psychopathy, which is inherently difficult given the legal and ethical implications, transformational, transactional, and passive leadership traits could be assessed and the results used as a starting point for identifying potentially damaging leaders.

Similar findings were reported by Mathieu, Neumann, Babiak, and Hare (2015), who examined in their two-sample study the relationship between employees' ratings of their supervisor on the B-Scan 360 and their ratings of the same supervisor on the Full-Range Leadership model. Their results indicated that employees who rated their supervisor high on the B-Scan 360 (high psychopathy) also rated the same supervisor as high in laissez-faire leadership style and low on both transactional and transformational leadership styles. In fact, the B-Scan 360 total score and all the B-Scan factors were significantly related to all the subscales of the Full-Range Leadership model. Mathieu et al. (2015) also found that the B-Scan 360 factors (manipulative/unethical, callous/insensitive, unreliable/unfocused, and intimidating/aggressive) were all strongly and positively related to laissez-faire leadership, indicating that there could be psychopathy-related personality traits underneath the destructive aspects of laissez-faire leadership. The destructive nature of laissez-faire leadership implies that such leaders do not meet the needs and expectations of the subordinates, fail to protect employees in a risk-exposed environment, and withhold important information from employees.

The Effect of Psychopath Leaders on the Organization and Its Employees

Leaders who are psychopaths often create the illusion of being successful people. They present themselves as smooth, charming, polished extroverts who are in control of themselves and their environment. However, they are attracted to positions of leadership mainly because of the access to personal rewards and power that senior management positions involve. They definitely want to be leaders for their own, and only their own, advantages. The impact that psychopathic leaders can have on organizational outcomes is noteworthy (Boddy, 2011). When corporate psychopaths are present as managers in organizations, employees are significantly less likely to agree that the corporation does business in a way that shows commitment to employees or that they receive due recognition for doing a good job, their work is appreciated, and their efforts are appropriately rewarded. Boddy argued that malevolent leaders callously disregard the needs and wishes of others and are prepared to lie, bully, cheat, and ignore the welfare of others (Boddy, 2011).

Herbst (2014) listed the long-term organizational consequences of psychopathic leaders:

1. *Inability to form a team* because of their unwillingness and inability to collaborate with others, especially those they see as adversaries
2. *Inability to share* because they do not see others as equals and therefore do not see the need to share resources or credit with them
3. *Disparate treatment of others*
4. *Inability to tell the truth.* Pathological lying is a hallmark of psychopaths given that they do not experience any guilt when telling a lie.
5. *Inability to be modest.* Although both narcissists and Machiavellians tend to be immodest, it is the arrogance of the psychopath that stands out.
6. *Inability to accept blame and to take responsibility for their actions.* Psychopaths not only blame others but also create "evidence" to inculpate others, called active instrumental aggression.
7. *Inability to act predictably*
8. *Inability to react calmly during a crisis because of their lack of control of their behavior.* However, because psychopaths are able to moderate their behavior while in the presence of authority, this can go unnoticed for a considerable amount of time.
9. *Inability to act without aggression.* Despite their charming and engaging persona, psychopaths revert to overt bullying and are masters of manipulation, intimidation, and coercion.

Mathieu and Babiak (2016b) found that employees' ratings of psychopathic traits in supervisors predicted their ratings of abusive supervision. According to them, this finding suggests that the dark personality of psychopathy is an antecedent of abusive supervision and that abusive supervisory behaviors might be expressions of "covert" aggression in the workplace. It thus seems reasonable to suggest that one way psychopathic individuals express their aggression in the workplace is through abusive supervisory behaviors. Mathieu and Babiak (2016b) also found that supervisors' psychopathic traits are a good predictor of employees' intention to quit. Their results showed that psychopathic traits in supervisors influenced turnover intentions directly, while abusive supervision had only an indirect effect on turnover intentions through its influence on job satisfaction. Mathieu, Neumann, Hare, and Babiak (2014) found in their two samples a significant positive relationship between employees' ratings of psychopathy traits in their supervisors and the employees' self-reported psychological distress and job satisfaction. They also found that supervisors' B-Scan 360 scores most strongly predicted employee job satisfaction. Furthermore, for both samples, the findings showed that the B-Scan 360 variable had a significant negative association with the work–family conflict. That is, non-supportive supervision increases the work–family conflict.

Finally, it should be noted that despite the significant negative relationship between psychopathic leadership and work outcomes, according to a few reports, such leaders might have some positive impact. Mathieu et al. (2015) cited Babiak et al. (2010), who found in their sample of senior-level managers that high psychopathy scores of leaders were positively related to in-house ratings of creativity, good strategic thinking, and communication skills but negatively associated with ratings of being a team player, management skills, and overall accomplishments. According to Mathieu et al., these results suggest that similar to narcissism, psychopathy may be associated with leader emergence or "identification" but not with leader effectiveness. Naturally, more studies are needed to confirm whether sound positive outcomes exist when psychopaths are in leadership positions.

Machiavellians and Leadership

More research is definitely necessary on the relationship between Machiavellians and leadership. Most extant research is quite obsolete, and the target populations in most of the scarce studies on this issue comprised samples of students. For example, Drory and Gluskinos (1980), in an experiment among 84 male students in an introductory psychology course at an American university, found that high and low Machiavellian led groups did not differ in their productivity. The group leaders were also not described by their groups as acting differently. The high Machiavellian leaders proved to have a wider range of appropriate behaviors than the low Machiavellian leaders. They also found that the high Machiavellian leaders were consistently less concerned with the feelings of their group members. Is it possible to generalize from these findings to employees? Probably not much. This section covers the more updated and relevant, although quite limited, research.

In the relatively few existing research, the topic most investigated in relation to Machiavellian leadership is the extensive use of impression management to manipulate employees for personal gain (Belschak, Muhammad, & Den Hartog, 2016). Therefore, the link between Machiavellianism and abusive supervision seems rather obvious, given that those who tend to manipulate and exploit others in order to maximize their self-interests are characterized as Machiavellian. Individuals exhibiting high levels of Machiavellianism tend to resist social influence, endeavor to control their interpersonal interactions, and display a general lack of affect in their personal relationships. They also tend to be more persuasive, more motivated to lead, and more charismatic than those low in Machiavellianism (Kiazad, Restubog, Zagenczyk, Kiewitz, & Tang, 2010).

According to Belschak et al. (2016), Machiavellian leaders have been found to be adaptable to situations but detached from their employees' interpersonal concerns. Machiavellianism influences leadership behaviors, yielding a more directive style with less genuine interpersonal consideration (Dahling, Whitaker, & Levy, 2009). Machiavellian leaders are focused on organizational politics and seek to control employees. They are skilled at creating a desirable image and rely on deceptive strategies and lying in their social relationships. Their persuasive powers are such that they can influence others in ways that run counter to the organizational goals and to the individuals' own prosocial values. Machiavellians show a strong goal orientation and lack feelings of guilt and emotional concern regarding the means of achieving these goals, exerting pressure on their subordinates to meet their targets, regardless of the manner in which they do so. Similarly, Brown and Treviño (2006) contended that in contrast to ethical leaders, Machiavellian leaders are motivated to manipulate others in order to accomplish their own goals. They have little trust in people and in turn tend not to be trusted by others.

Drawing on the General Aggression Model (Anderson & Bushman, 2002) as a domain-specific framework to explain the direct link between Machiavellianism and abusive supervision, Kiazad et al., (2010) posited that certain traits predispose individuals to engage in aggressive behavior by influencing the accessibility of aggressive thoughts, which subsequently bias behavior toward aggression. Accordingly, they argued that Machiavellianism in supervisors increases their accessibility to aggressive thoughts and biases their behavior so that they exhibit more hostility toward others. As a result, supervisors with higher levels of Machiavellianism are more likely to behave in a manner that their subordinates construe and report as abusive. Their findings showed that supervisors' Machiavellianism was positively related to subordinates' perceptions of abusive supervision, even after controlling for their demographics.

Girodo (1998) found that of the interpersonal influence methods available to managers involved in administration, the Machiavellian style was the most often and the transformational style the least often used. The opposite was found for managers involved in training and in directing community-oriented activities. Given Machiavellian leaders' exploitative leadership nature and lack of interpersonal interests, it is not surprising that Gkorezis, Petridou, and Krouklidou (2015) found among employees working in a Greek private hospital that they play an important role in increasing emotional exhaustion. They also found that organizational cynicism partially mediated the relationship between leader Machiavellianism and employees' emotional exhaustion.

In an interesting study, the implications of a combination of a Machiavellian employee and a Machiavellian leader were investigated. Machiavellianism is a trait that, when found in both the leader and the employee, yields particularly negative outcomes, and the combination of a Machiavellian employee and a Machiavellian leader is likely to be toxic (Belschak et al., 2016). According to Belschak et al. (2016), Machiavellian followers are likely to exhibit a low trust level which, in turn, is associated with higher levels of stress and engaging in more CWB. This low trust level is exacerbated when they have a Machiavellian leader who acts with similar manipulativeness and whom they cannot control. Belschak et al. further proposed that Machiavellianism is a trait that, when appearing at a high level in both leader and employee, exacerbates negative effects, and a match of high-Machiavellian personalities between leader and employee is likely to form a toxic combination that is particularly disadvantageous for the employee. Instead of building a positive empowering relationship based on positive similarity, Machiavellian leaders with Machiavellian employees are likely to collide and interact in destructive ways because they are both trying to control and manipulate each other.

When they have a Machiavellian leader, Machiavellian employees' expectations of what they want (e.g., to be in control and have the freedom to act as they see fit) and what they receive from their leader (tight monitoring and a wary and distrusting leadership) may be too disparate for the development of a trusting or healthy relationship. Thus, for Machiavellian employees, trust is already a scarce resource. Therefore, Machiavellian employees trust Machiavellian leaders significantly less than non-Machiavellian leaders. Belschak et al.'s (2016) findings showed that the relationships with outcome variables were similar for Machiavellian leadership and Machiavellian employees: both a Machiavellian employee and leader were significantly correlated with employees' lack of trust and their engagement in CWB. They concluded that Machiavellianism can potentially have detrimental effects on employee attitudes and behavior regardless of the level at which it is present (employee or leader).

To conclude, based on what we know so far, psychopathic leaders can be disastrous to both the organization and its employees. They are the "darkest" dark triad trait in organization leadership (Furtner et al., 2017). Narcissist leaders have some positive aspects in their leadership style that in some situations can be beneficial to the organization but less so to the employees. More specifically, very low and very high levels of narcissism are hindering, whereby moderate narcissism is positively related to leadership effectiveness (Furtner et al., 2017). More research is needed on the relationship between Machiavellianism and leadership. Until now, research interest was directed mostly toward the relationship between narcissism and leadership and less toward the relationship between leadership and the two other dark personalities: Machiavellianism and psychopathy. Scholars are still uncertain about the exact nature of the relationship between Machiavellianism and leadership behaviors because few, if any, studies have explored this relationship (Kiazad et al., 2010). If we want to gain a better understanding of leadership in the context of the dark triad, we need more theories and studies on all dark personalities and particularly Machiavellians and psychopaths.

References

Allen, T. D., Johnson, H. A., Xu, X., Biga, A., Rodopman, O. B., & Ottinot, R. C. (2009). Mentoring and protégé narcissistic entitlement. *Journal of Career Development, 35*, 385–405.

American Psychiatric Association. (1994). *DSM-IV® Sourcebook* (Vol. 1). American Psychiatric Pub.

American Psychiatric Association (2000). *Diagnostic and statistical manual of mental disorders*, 4th ed. Washington, D.C.: American Psychiatric Association.

Anderson, C. A., & Bushman, B. J. (2002). Human aggression. *Annual Review of Psychology, 53*, 27–51.

Babiak, P., & Hare, R. D. (2006). *Snakes in Suits: When Psychopaths Go to Work.* New York: Regan Books.

Babiak, P., Neumann, C. S., & Hare, R. D. (2010). Corporate psychopathy: Talking the walk. *Behavioral Sciences & the Law, 28*(2), 174–193.

Belschak, F. D., Muhammad, R. S., & Den Hartog, D. N. (2016). Birds of a feather can butt heads: When Machiavellian employees work with Machiavellian leaders. *Journal of Business Ethics*, 1–14.

Blair, C. A., Helland, K., & Walton, B. (2017). Leaders behaving badly: The relationship between narcissism and unethical leadership. *Leadership & Organization Development Journal, 38*(2), 333–346.

Blair, C. A., Hoffman, B. J., & Helland, K. R. (2008). Narcissism in organizations: A multisource appraisal reflects different perspectives. *Human Performance, 21*(3), 254–276.

Boddy, C. R. (2011). *Corporate Psychopaths: Organizational Destroyers.* London: Palgrave MacMillan.

Boddy, C. R. (2016a). Unethical 20th century business leaders: Were some of them corporate psychopaths? The case of Robert Maxwell. *International Journal of Public Leadership, 12*(2), 76–93.

Boddy, C. R. (2016b). Psychopathy screening for public leadership. *International Journal of Public Leadership, 12*(4), 254–274.

Boddy, C. R., & Taplin, R. (2016). The influence of corporate psychopaths on job satisfaction and its determinants. *International Journal of Manpower, 37*(6), 965–988.

Braun, S., Aydin, N., Frey, D., & Peus, C. (2016). Leader narcissism predicts malicious envy and supervisor-targeted counterproductive work behavior: Evidence from field and experimental research. *Journal of Business Ethics*, 1–17.

Brown, M. E., & Treviño, L. K. (2006). Ethical leadership: A review and future directions. *The Leadership Quarterly, 17*(6), 595–616.

Brunell, A. B., Campbell, W. K., Smith, L., & Krusemark, E. A. (2004). *Why Do People Date Narcissists? A Narrative Study.* Poster presented at the Annual Meeting of the Society for Personality and Social Psychology, Austin, TX.

Brunell, A. B., Gentry, W. A., Campbell, W. K., Hoffman, B. J., Kuhnert, K. W., & DeMarree, K. G. (2008). Leader emergence: The case of the narcissistic leader. *Personality and Social Psychology Bulletin, 34*(12), 1663–1676.

Campbell, W. K., Hoffman, B. J., Campbell, S. M., & Marchisio, G. (2011). Narcissism in organizational contexts. *Human Resource Management Review, 21*(4), 268–284.

Chatterjee, A., & Hambrick, D. C. (2007). It's all about me: Narcissistic chief executive officers and their effects on company strategy and performance. *Administrative Science Quarterly, 52*(3), 351–386.

Dahling, J. J., Whitaker, B. G., & Levy, P. E. (2009). The development and validation of a new Machiavellianism scale. *Journal of Management, 35*(2), 219–257.

Drory, A., & Gluskinos, U. M. (1980). Machiavellianism and leadership. *Journal of Applied Psychology, 65*(1), 81.

Einarsen, S., Aasland, M. S., & Skogstad, A. (2007). Destructive leadership behaviour: A definition and conceptual model. *The Leadership Quarterly, 18*(3), 207–216.

Freud, S. (1931/1950). Libidinal types. In J. Strachey (Ed.), *The Standard Edition of the Complete Psychological Works of Sigmund Freud* (Vol. 21, pp. 217–220). London: Hogarth (Original work published in 1931).

Furtner, M. R., Maran, T., & Rauthmann, J. F. (2017). Dark leadership: The role of leaders' dark triad personality traits. In *Leader Development Deconstructed* (pp. 75–99). Cham: Springer.

Girodo, M. (1998). Machiavellian, bureaucratic, and transformational leadership styles in police managers: Preliminary findings of interpersonal ethics. *Perceptual and Motor Skills, 86*(2), 419–427.

Gkorezis, P., Petridou, E., & Krouklidou, T. (2015). The detrimental effect of Machiavellian leadership on employees' emotional exhaustion: Organizational cynicism as a mediator. *Europe's Journal of Psychology, 11*(4), 619–631.

Grijalva, E., & Harms, P. D. (2014). Narcissism: An integrative synthesis and dominance complementarity model. *The Academy of Management Perspectives, 28*(2), 108–127.

Grijalva, E., Harms, P. D., Newman, D. A., Gaddis, B. H., & Fraley, R. C. (2015). Narcissism and leadership: A meta-analytic review of linear and nonlinear relationships. *Personnel Psychology, 68*(1), 1–47.

Hanson, L., & Baker, D. L. (2017). "Corporate psychopaths" in public agencies? *Journal of Public Management & Social Policy, 24*(1), 21–41.

Harms, P. D., Spain, S., & Hannah, S. (2011). Leader development and the dark side of personality. *Leadership Quarterly, 22*, 495–509.

Herbst, T. (2014). *The Dark Side of Leadership: A Psycho-Spiritual Approach towards Understanding the Origins of Personality Dysfunctions: Derailment and the Restoration of Personality.* UK: Author House.

Higgs, M. (2009). The good, the bad and the ugly: Leadership and narcissism. *Journal of Change Management, 9*(2), 165–178.

Hogan, R. (2007). *Personality and the Fate of Organizations.* Hillsdale, NJ: Erlbaum.

Hogan, R., & Fico, J. M. (2011). Leadership. In W. K. Campbell & J. D. Miller (Eds.), *The Handbook of Narcissism and Narcissistic Personality Disorder: Theoretical Approaches, Empirical Findings, and Treatments* (pp. 393–402). New York: Wiley.

Hogan, R., & Hogan, J. (2001). Assessing leadership: A view from the dark side. *International Journal of Selection and Assessment, 9*(1–2), 40–51.

Hogan, R., & Hogan, J. (2009). *Hogan Development Survey Manual* (2nd ed.). Tulsa, OK: Hogan Assessment Systems.

Kaiser, R. B., LeBreton, J. M., & Hogan, J. (2015). The dark side of personality and extreme leader behavior. *Applied Psychology: An International Review, 64*(1), 55–92.

Kets de Vries, M., & Miller, D. (1984). *The Neurotic Behavior of Organizations.* San Francisco: Jossey-Bass.

Khoo, H. S., & Burch, G. S. J. (2008). The "dark side" of leadership personality and transformational leadership: An exploratory study. *Personality and Individual Differences, 44*(1), 86–97.

Kiazad, K., Restubog, S. L. D., Zagenczyk, T. J., Kiewitz, C., & Tang, R. L. (2010). In pursuit of power: The role of authoritarian leadership in the relationship between supervisors' Machiavellianism and subordinates' perceptions of abusive supervisory behavior. *Journal of Research in Personality, 44*(4), 512–519.

Kim, Y., & Cohen, T. R. (2015). Moral character and workplace deviance: Recent research and current trends. *Current Opinion in Psychology, 6*, 134–138.

Leslie, J. B., & Van Velsor, E. (1996). *A Look at Derailment Today.* Greensboro, NC: Center for Creative Leadership.

Maccoby, M. (2000). Narcissistic leaders: The incredible pros, the inevitable cons. *Harvard Business Review,* 69–77.

Mathieu, C., & Babiak, P. (2016b). Corporate psychopathy and abusive supervision: Their influence on employees' job satisfaction and turnover intentions. *Personality and Individual Differences, 91*, 102–106.

Mathieu, C., Neumann, C., Babiak, P., & Hare, R. D. (2015). Corporate psychopathy and the full-range leadership model. *Assessment, 22*(3), 267–278.

Mathieu, C., Neumann, C. S., Hare, R. D., & Babiak, P. (2014). A dark side of leadership: Corporate psychopathy and its influence on employee well-being and job satisfaction. *Personality and Individual Differences, 59*, 83–88.

Myung, J. K., & Choi, Y. H. (2017). The influences of leaders' dark triad trait on their perception of CSR. *Asian Journal of Sustainability and Social Responsibility,* 1–15.

Oltmanns, T. F., Friedman, J. N. W., Fiedler, E. R., & Turkheimer, E. (2003). Perceptions of people with personality disorders based on thin slices of behavior. *Journal of Research in Personality, 38*, 216–239.

Padilla, A., Hogan, R., & Kaiser, R. B. (2007). The toxic triangle: Destructive leaders, susceptible followers, and conducive environments. *The Leadership Quarterly, 18*(3), 176–194.

Paulhus, D. L. (1998). Interpersonal and intrapsychic adaptiveness of trait self-enhancement: A mixed blessing? *Journal of Personality and Social Psychology, 74*, 1197–1208.

Paunonen, S. V., Lönnqvist, J. E., Verkasalo, M., Leikas, S., & Nissinen, V. (2006). Narcissism and emergent leadership in military cadets. *The Leadership Quarterly, 17*(5), 475–486.

Rosenthal, S. A., & Pittinsky, T. L. (2006). Narcissistic leadership. *The Leadership Quarterly, 17*(6), 617–633.

Sankowsky, D. (1995). The charismatic leader as narcissist: Understanding the abuse of power. *Organizational Dynamics, 23*, 57–71.

Schyns, B. (2015). Dark personality in the workplace: Introduction to the special issue. *Applied Psychology: An International Review, 64*(1), 1–14.

Schyns, B., & Schilling, J. (2013). How bad are the effects of bad leaders? A meta-analysis of destructive leadership and its outcomes. *The Leadership Quarterly, 24*(1), 138–158.

Sedikides, C., & Campbell, W. K. (2017). Narcissistic force meets systemic resistance: The energy clash model. *Perspectives on Psychological Science, 12*(3), 400–421.

Spain, S. M., Harms, P., & LeBreton, J. M. (2014). The dark side of personality at work. *Journal of Organizational Behavior, 35*(Supplement 1), S41–S60.

Spector, P. E. (1997). *Job Satisfaction: Application, Assessment, Causes, and Consequences.* Thousand Oaks, CA: Sage Publications, Inc.

Virkler, H. A. (2005). Personality disorders. In T. Clinton, Archibald D. Hart et al. (Eds.), *Caring for People God's Way: Personal and Emotional Issues, Addictions, Grief, and Trauma* (pp. 221–247). Nashville: Thomas Nelson.

Westerlaken, K. M., & Woods, P. R. (2013). The relationship between psychopathy and the full range leadership model. *Personality and Individual Differences*, *54*(1), 41–46.

Wisse, B., Barelds, D. P., & Rietzschel, E. F. (2015). How innovative is your employee? The role of employee and supervisor dark triad personality traits in supervisor perceptions of employee innovative behavior. *Personality and Individual Differences*, *82*, 158–162.

Wisse, B., & Sleebos, E. (2016). When the dark ones gain power: Perceived position power strengthens the effect of supervisor Machiavellianism on abusive supervision in work teams. *Personality and Individual Differences*, *99*, 122–126.

9   The Victims of the Dark Triad

One of the most severe organizational dangers is workplace victimization (Solas, 2015). The propensity toward this type of abuse in government organizations, as well as in private ones, is most disturbing because of its bearing on the fate of ever increasing numbers of organizations and personnel. Workplace victimization is a particularly poisonous strain of organizational malice. It includes bullying, harassment, "mobbing," and more (Solas, 2015). Bullying, for example, is a major barrier to organizational efficiency and productivity and a major cost to organizations and to economies as a whole (Boddy, 2011a, 2011b). One relatively unexplored aspect of the dark triad personalities is their victims, who are not chosen by accident. The implications of the dark triad's effect on them is detrimental from both the organizational and personal point of view, and therefore it is quite surprising that this issue has not received the attention it deserves.

Several important aspects of this subject may attract the attention of scholars and practitioners. Some of these are covered in this chapter based on the existing research. For example, what is the incidence of work victimization? How do dark triad personalities assess the vulnerability of their potential victims? How do dark triad personalities choose their victims? What are the clues that they look for before taking action? Are there any demographic and personal characteristics of the potential victims that are particularly attractive to dark triad personalities? Another aspect covered by this chapter is the implications for and reactions of the victims of dark triad persons' abuse. In this chapter, we attempt to answer some of these important questions that have not been discussed and examined sufficiently in the literature but have many undesirable implications for the organization and its employees who are victimized by dark triad personalities in their workplace.

Incidence of Work Victimization

The incidence of workplace victimization is relatively high and is costly to organizations. Solas (2015) maintained that annual reports for the past decade show that each year, between 15% and 19% of workers in the

Australian public sector were bullied or harassed by a supervisor (39%), or some other senior figure (40%). In 2011 to 2012, 28,659 government employees (17% of the public sector workforce) reported being subjected to harassment or bullying (Australian Public Service Commission [APSC], 2011, p. 62). According to Solas (2015), psychological injury resulting from interpersonal conflicts between peers and supervisors has contributed to the growth in compensable claims lodged by Australian government workers in recent years (Comcare, 2008). Over a third of all these claims are the result of bullying and harassment (around 25%) and exposure to workplace or occupational violence (10%) (Comcare, 2008, p. 8). Almost a third of the total payments in 2011 compensated claimants for psychological injury, at an average cost of AUD$ 205,000 per claim (Comcare, 2014). Boddy (2011b) stated that according to one UK report, bullying costs the UK economy £13.75 billion a year. Based on Boddy's (2011b) finding that 26% of all bullying is related to the presence of corporate psychopaths, this UK figure gives a rough estimate of the cost of bullying by corporate psychopaths: it costs the UK economy £3.575 billion a year, a substantial amount.

Linton and Power (2013) noted that the prevalence of bullying found in their study was high and similar to that observed in the studies mentioned earlier. They found that 37.5% of their participants reported being victimized once a week in the 6 months before their study, a figure that falls between the values of 46.8% for American and 24.1% for Finnish employees found by Lutgen-Sandvik, Tracy, and Alberts (2007) meeting the same frequency criteria. The finding that 17.4% of their participants reported perpetrating negative acts corresponds with the figure of 24% found by Lee and Brotheridge (2006). Their observation that bullies and victims made up 15.6% of the study sample corresponds with the figure of 20% reported by Lee and Brotheridge (2006), who measured bullies and victims simultaneously. In addition, Linton and Power (2013) mentioned that their finding that of the bullies and victims, 41.7% were victims and 89.7% were bullies corresponds with the figures of 50% victims and 83% bullies described by Lee and Brotheridge (2006).

These data are quite impressive and devastating. Considerably more data on work victimization exist in addition to those presented here. But what is the role of dark triad personalities in work victimization? This issue has rarely been discussed in research concerning the incidence of work victimization. Babiak and Hare (2006), for example, reported that in their study that around 29% of the corporate psychopaths they identified were also bullies. According to Boddy (2015), corporate psychopaths seem to be responsible for between a quarter and a third of all workplace bullying. The bullying experienced can be particularly vicious and involve multiple victims, occurring several times per week on a continuous basis. However, so far we have very few data on the incidence of employees' abuse by dark triad personalities, possibly because collecting data on the occurrence of work victimization by dark triad personalities is quite complicated. This is aggravated by the fact that diagnosing dark triad personalities in the workplace is itself a complicated issue both practically and legally, as discussed in Chapter 7.

One means of handling this issue was advanced by Boddy (2011b, 2014). In his studies, Boddy first asked the respondents to rate their managers on a psychopathic scale and then asked them about the incidence of work victimization they witnessed in their workplace or department. This made it possible for Boddy to determine whether there were more work victimization incidences among managers who were rated higher on the psychopathic scales by the target populations than among those who were rated lower. Boddy's findings are both interesting and troubling in the sense of the occurrence of this disturbing phenomenon. In his first study, Boddy (2011b) surveyed 346 Australian senior white-collar workers. His findings showed that where corporate psychopaths were not present, the average number of incidents of employees witnessing unfavorable treatment of others per year (bullying) at work was 9.0 (less than monthly), and it was 64.4 (more than weekly) when corporate psychopaths were present. This finding clearly showed that the presence of corporate psychopaths is strongly associated with the existence of bullying, which increases in their presence. When corporate psychopaths are present, supervisors are strongly perceived as being unfair to employees and uninterested in their feelings. Boddy (2011b) concluded that around 26% of bullying is accounted for by 1% of the employee population, those who are corporate psychopaths.

The second study (Boddy, 2014) was based on 304 senior (mainly managerial and professional) white-collar employees in Britain. The findings showed that where corporate psychopaths were not present, the average number of witnessed incidents of unfavorable treatment of others per year (bullying) at work was 13.2 (about once every 4 weeks), and it was 84.4 (about 1.6 times per week) when corporate psychopaths were present. Similar results were obtained for the other elements of conflict. For example, in organizations where corporate psychopaths were not present, the average number per year of incidents of conflicts at work was 8.9, and it was 59.7 when corporate psychopaths were present. This result shows that the presence of corporate psychopaths is strongly associated with the existence of conflict in an organization. The findings also showed that corporate psychopaths account for 35.2% of all bullying. Where no corporate psychopaths were present, 38.5% of the employees reported having witnessed unfavorable treatment of others (bullying) at work compared with the significantly greater figure of 97% for employees in organizations where corporate psychopaths were present. In other words, when corporate psychopaths are present, conflict and bullying occur more frequently and affect more employees than when they are not present. The findings also showed that there was no difference between women and men in the degree of negative reaction to the presence of managers who are corporate psychopaths.

Boddy's (2011b, 2014) conclusion that corporate psychopaths have large and significant impacts on conflict and bullying and on employees' affective well-being is not surprising; nor is their considerable and significant impact on counterproductive work behavior. However, much more research is needed to provide more established data on the role of dark triad personalities in work victimization. Despite the complexity of this issue, such data are essential for a more precise and comprehensive evaluation of the destructive consequences of dark personalities from the victims' point of view. Boddy (2011b, 2014) proposed a convenient method for collecting such data on these incidents, as well as suggesting how to apply this method to other settings to facilitate the collection of such valuable information.

The Impact of Work Victimization on the Victims and the Organization

A general categorization of the tactics used by the dark triad to exploit their employees is to divide them to soft tactics (e.g., ingratiation and reason) and hard tactics (e.g., assertiveness and direct manipulations). The primary distinction between these two types of tactics of influence lies in their forcefulness. Hard tactics are essentially tactics in which the user forces her or his will on another person. In contrast, soft tactics are designed to convince the target that it is in his or her best interest to engage in the advocated behavior (Jonason, Slomski, & Partyka, 2012b). Because of the exploitative nature shared by the dark triad personalities, it is not surprising that they adopt both soft and hard tactics but tend to use more hard than soft tactics. In addition, given that aggressiveness is attributed to psychopathy, dark triad personalities probably prefer hard tactics rather than soft tactics. Those high in the dark triad traits may also forge alliances to delegate their work to others. For instance, ingratiation, exchange of favors, and joking may create workplace friendships. These friendships could be later exploited to offload work obligations. Because the targets think that a friendship exists between them, they are less likely to detect the exploitation, thinking they are doing a favor for a friend (Jonason et al., 2012b).

Jonason et al. (2012b) concluded based on their study that the dark triad traits facilitate workplace influence through the use of forceful, aggressive, and ultimately hard tactics of social influence in the workplace. Employees working under psychopaths—and probably also under narcissists and Machiavellians—experience less instruction, less training, and less help from others. These employees also receive less recognition for doing a good job, less appreciation, and fewer rewards. They also experience a less friendly work environment, with poorer communication, and suffer more unfairness from their supervisor when psychopaths are present (Boddy, 2010a, 2010b).

According to Babiak (2000) employees who were victims of psychopaths reported a significantly greater number of negative emotional feelings than is normally encountered. The most frequently reported feelings were confusion mixed with disbelief and self-doubt over the changing relationship with the psychopath, namely from colleague to a victim. Many individuals reported feeling shame for being conned. Several who had their career derailed by the psychopath reported feelings of betrayal and humiliation; they expressed anger at the psychopath as well as frustration toward management for not seeing what was going on. Organizations are also victim of psychopaths as well victims of narcissists and Machiavellians. The destructive activities generated by the psychopaths lead to a breakdown in teamwork, a decline in department morale, and a general disintegration of the work unit (Babiak, 2000).

The following section covers the devastating impact on the victims and on the organization of the different tactics used by the dark triad personalities.

Bullying

Bullying is one of the more frequent strategies used by dark triad personalities against their victims. It is also one of the more researched misconducts of supervisors and managers. Linton and Power (2013) reported that Machiavellianism, narcissism, and psychopathy were ranked as the highest magnitude personality predictors of bullying others. Because the dark triad is associated with antisocial behavior, grandiosity, self-entitlement, manipulation, aggression, hostility, low empathy, interpersonal conflict, and cruelty, it is not surprising that these traits are so prominently linked with bullying others. Linton and Power (2013) also reported based on their study that psychoticism and Machiavellianism were also significant predictors of victimization and that the aggression measures were associated, as expected, with both bully and victim behavior. What is interesting and deserves future research is the finding that the sensation seeking subscale was significantly related to bullying others.

Bullying could perhaps be used by psychopaths in organizations as a tactic to humiliate subordinates. Such bullying may occur because many psychopaths enjoy and are stimulated by hurting others. As was found by Linton and Power (2013), dark triad personalities might bully their victims just for sensation-seeking purposes and not necessarily as a tactic for achieving their goals. This possibility is more than troubling in terms of the victims' experience and the personal consequences it incurs. Moreover, bullying may take place as a tactic to confuse and disorientate those who may be a threat to the psychopath's activities, which may otherwise be noticed by a normally functioning staff (Boddy, 2015).

The impact of bullying on the individual is upsetting. Bullying affects people's health and well-being to an alarming extent. Studies across many countries have indicated the existence of a relationship between bullying and depression, anxiety, aggression, insomnia, psychosomatic effects, and general physical and mental ill health (Vega & Comer, 2005). Those who are victimized by their bully counterparts readily find themselves systematically overlooked in workplace operations and excluded from social activities and from decisions and actions central to the day-to-day operations of their employing organizations (Dzurec, Kennison, & Gillen, 2017). Boddy (2015) wrote that there is some evidence that bullying influences the personalities of those within the abusive environment. Employees become less open and less agreeable. This implies that the negativity of the corporate psychopath, via the creation of an abusive and bullying atmosphere, spreads across employees, who become less helpful to each other as a result. Employees working for corporate psychopaths are disheartened, disillusioned, and dissatisfied (Boddy, 2015).

Bullying at work is also an extreme social stressor with threat potentials comparable to those inherent in other traumatic life events (Mikkelsen & Einarsen, 2002). Similar other victims of physical and emotional abuse, victims of bullying typically feel that the offender aims to harm them. Consequently, for most victims, this creates a strong sense of vulnerability, the effect of which is dramatically increased, as they constantly have to deal with the possibility of being subjected to additional infringements. When at work, the victims are subjected to a continuing, prolonged threat. For some victims, such a situation may create a profound, exaggerated, and perhaps unrealistic anxiety. Mikkelsen and Einarsen's (2002) study showed a high prevalence of symptomatology analogous with posttraumatic stress disorder among victims of bullying at work. Most victims exhibit moderate to severe symptoms. Furthermore, a large majority of the victims display a moderate or severe impairment in functioning in various important areas of their lives. These findings indicate that the detrimental effects of exposure to bullying at work may in many ways be compared to those of other traumatic life events. Many victims of bullying feel that, as a result of the bullying, their lives have permanently changed for the worse. When being bullied at their workplace, and sometimes even after the bullying has ceased, victims are subjected to threats to their personal, social, and professional identities and in some cases also to their financial and societal status (Mikkelsen & Einarsen, 2002).

The negative consequences of bullying are not only personal. The culture of bullying can spread in the organization through what can be termed counteraggressive bullying behaviors (Lee & Brotheridge, 2006). This behavior involves the displacement of frustrations and anger onto other individuals. This occurs as a result of the transfer of arousal from one event to another. For example, if a manager loudly insults a secretary, the secretary might, as in a ripple effect, insult another person, and so on. Bullying may also be a means of gaining social control by isolating targets for abuse, who, in turn, become abusive toward others. Such individuals may come to believe that they have a right to exercise such control, precisely because they suffered at the hands of others, and, according to Lee and Brotheridge's (2006) findings, when individuals perceive that established norms of acceptable behavior have been violated, abusive treatment may spiral into further acts of mistreatment.

Targets may experience negative emotions that fuel their need to abuse others. The threat to one's self-concept appears to be at the core of this process. Personal identity becomes so salient during interpersonal conflict that individuals engage in coercive behaviors in proportion to the extent that their identity has been threatened or attacked. Targets may thus mistreat others as a means of repairing an eroded sense of self or redressing the social injustices visited upon them (Lee & Brotheridge, 2006). The consequences of this counteraggressive bullying behavior on the organization and its employees are definitely devastating. The inevitable result is that many victims are also bullies (Linton and Power, 2013). In their study, Linton and Power (2013) found that bullies/victims score significantly higher than non-bullies/victims in Machiavellianism, narcissism, and psychopathy. In fact, sporadic observations suggest that bullies/victims may score higher on other bully-typifying traits, such as aggression. According to Linton and Power (2013), certain personality traits increase the likelihood that their possessors will become targets of bullying. These include factors such as general disagreeableness, cruelty, hostility, impulsiveness, and a disregard for social conventions, rules, and the feelings of others. All these may be among the features that elicit a bullying response from others. It is clear that, apart from the individual pathology of bully leaders, the combination thereof with the dark side of their followers can produce a stronger negative effect. The dark side present in the leader can itself produce serious personal and organizational outcomes, and, combined with the dark side of his or her followers, its impact can be devastating (Kets de Vries, 1989).

Other Forms of Victim's Abuse

In addition to bullying, dark triad personalities can use other tactics to harm their victims. Castille, Kuyumcu, and Bennett (2017) focused on how and why Machiavellians undermine their peers, presenting reasoning that is relevant also to the other two dimensions of the dark triad. Relying on the trait activation theory, they argued that organizational constraints motivate Machiavellians to view their coworkers as threats that have to be marginalized. Focusing or zooming in on the Machiavellians' perceptions of resource constraints, Castille et al. (2017) demonstrated that constraints motivate Machiavellians to increasingly undermine their coworkers, resulting in reduced production deviance. The presence of competition motivates Machiavellians to engage in social undermining. Therefore, it seems highly unlikely that Machiavellians would be an asset in work situations or occupations described by high levels of competition requirements. Furthermore, resource competition may promote a vicious cycle, in which undermined employees view their coworkers as unsupportive, leading a proportion of these individuals to continue to undermine others. By undermining their peers in a context that promotes competition, Machiavellians might achieve higher relative status while also harming organizational well-being. According to Castille et al. (2017), when Machiavellians perceived low resource constraints, they did not engage in social undermining and relatively were not counterproductive. The individual implications of social undermining are severe based on their study. Victims of social undermining experience poorer work attitudes, feel less able to voice concerns, are more likely to be absent from work, wish to leave their work setting, and work less effectively with others (Castille et al., 2017).

Intervention in career success is another tactic used by dark triad personalities against their victims (Volmer, Koch, & Göritz, 2016). A study by Volmer et al. among German employees found that leaders' Machiavellianism and psychopathy were unfavorable for their subordinates' career success and well-being. Leader Machiavellianism was negatively related to subordinates' objective career success (salary), and leader psychopathy was negatively related to subordinates' career satisfaction. Psychopaths, as well as Machiavellians, recklessly pursue their own goals and do not shy away from manipulating others. Psychopaths are likely to claim the credit for their subordinates' work or blame them for their own failures. Additionally, leader Machiavellianism was positively related to their subordinates' emotional exhaustion, and leader psychopathy was negatively related to their subordinates' job satisfaction.

Quite interestingly and somewhat unexpectedly, their study showed that subordinates who rated their leaders high in narcissism reported higher own objective career success in terms of salary and number of promotions. Thus, it seems that leaders' narcissism is beneficial for their subordinates' careers. According to Volmer et al., this may be because persons high in Machiavellianism and in psychopathy do not care for others and do not show empathy. They concluded that in comparison with narcissism, Machiavellianism and psychopathy form the "Malicious Two" and are more detrimental. As a result, organizations should pay attention to leaders' Machiavellianism and psychopathy because of their harmful effects.

To conclude, Boddy (2006) cited Clarke (2005), who, in his book *Working with Monsters*, describes the destructive effects organizational psychopaths can have on the interpersonal relationships, mental health, and self-image of the people working around them. According to Sankowsky (1995), psychopaths, Machiavellians, and narcissists may be unaware of their abuse; in blaming others, they are masking doubts about their own self-confidence and deceiving themselves about their role in any failure. Therefore, employers should be reminded that they have the duty to protect their workforce from harm. This should include providing protection from the effects of working with dark triad personalities (Boddy, 2006).

Characteristics of the Victims and the Dark Triad Offenders

Recently, however, some researchers have begun to take a different position, arguing that individual antecedent factors, such as the personality of the bullies and victims, may be involved as causes of bullying (Glasø, Matthiesen, Nielsen, & Einarsen, 2007) and probably other forms of work victimization. Glasø et al. (2007) cited Zapf and Einarsen (2003), who contended that no comprehensive model of workplace bullying would be satisfactory without also including the personality and individual factors of both perpetrators and victims and their contributory effects to the onset, escalation, and the consequences of the bullying process. Glasø et al. (2007) also cited Niedl (1995), who asserted that the probability of being the target of bullying increases if the person is unable to defend him- or herself or is trapped in a situation because of dependency factors. Such a dependent relationship may be of a psychological nature, influenced by the victim's self-esteem, personality, or cognitive capacity. Targets of workplace bullying seem to be submissive, anxious, and neurotic, lacking in social competence and self-esteem and characterized by behavioral patterns related to overachievement and conscientiousness (Glasø et al., 2007). The following section presents specific characteristics of the dark triad traits offenders and in particular those of the victims.

According to Herbst (2014), followers play a significant role in the manifestation of the dark side. The leader is not the source of all counterproductive behaviors; followers also participate in unhealthy influence processes. Followers are shown to be collaborators in the influence process, irrespective of the leadership model employed. If dysfunctional aspects of personality can affect leaders, they can affect followers as well. Herbst cited Kets de Vries (1989), who identified personality dispositions that have the potential to negatively impact the well-being of the leader–follower relationship at a relatively pathological level:

1. *The controlling disposition*: The controller is very similar to the authoritarian personality. Individuals characterized as this type often ultimately reach a leadership position, and followers are also often characterized as this type. They tend to see relationships in terms of superior–inferior and dominant–submissive, and their position in the hierarchy defines their behavior. Followers with this disposition are likely to submit to authority and can be very deferential and ingratiating when interacting with superiors.

2. *The histrionic disposition*: Histrionic individuals have a desperate need to be the focus of attention at all costs. They overreact to external stimuli, and their behavior is determined by other people's moods and desires. Similar to controllers, they also respond positively to people in authority and are highly impressionable. They provide unquestionable loyalty to transformational or charismatic leadership.

3. *The passive-aggressive disposition:* These individuals can appear acquiescent, which makes them difficult to confront. They are, however, poor followers because of their pessimism, resentment, and covert resistance. Their cordial and compliant behavior on the surface makes it difficult for the leader to realize their negative impact on performance.

4. *The dependent disposition:* People with this disposition take extreme measures to place themselves in dependent situations and are therefore extremely likely to be followers. Followers whose dependency needs have not been met are likely to form extremely intense and overpowering connections with a leader to fulfill these needs. Such followers may be willing to sacrifice anything, including reality, to satisfy their dependency needs or their need for direction. They avoid giving any objective or critical feedback to their leader even when he or she actively seeks it.

5. *The masochistic disposition:* People with this disposition encourage others to take advantage of them. They accept blame for things for which they are not responsible and find positive reinforcement in their misfortune. Similar to most of the other types, they are unlikely to offer critical, objective feedback to their leader.

Padilla, Hogan, and Kaiser (2007), more specifically, described several reasons why followers are motivated to work with a destructive leader. The first is that they hope to fulfill unmet basic needs. For example, poor people living in daily fear of losing their jobs are easier to control. Furthermore, destructive leaders can attract followers by offering them a sense of community and a group to which to belong. The second is a low core of self-evaluation. Persons with low self-esteem, low self-efficacy, and an external locus of control are susceptible to destructive leaders. Persons with low self-esteem and low self-efficacy are more likely to identify with a charismatic person because such leaders want to control and manipulate others, and these followers believe they deserve such treatment. Followers with an external locus of control do not see themselves as leaders, are easier to manipulate, and are attracted to others who seem powerful and willing to care for them. A low maturity level is another factor that causes followers to be attracted to a destructive leader. Psychological maturity is needed to oppose destructive authority. Psychologically immature individuals are more likely to conform to authority and to participate in destructive acts. Such followers lack a clear sense of self and adopt the values of charismatic leaders, which then enhances their self-esteem.

According to Zapf and Einarsen (2011), the development of bullying is dominated by three mechanisms of the victim's characteristics: (1) the exposed position of the victim, (2) social competence and self-esteem deficits, and (3) overachievement and conflict with group norms. Concerning the first mechanism, the exposed position of the victims, Zapf and Einarsen contended that people who are outsiders and who differ from the rest of the group incur the risk of getting in trouble with others and may even be forced into the role of the scapegoat. According to the social identity theory, being different may cause others to see a person as "one of them," not as "one of us," which may, under certain circumstances, lead to displaced aggression toward the person who seems to be the outsider. Zapf and Einarsen argued that outsiders have a weaker social network and therefore receive less social support. According to the labelling theory, deviant behavior may escalate when small peculiarities that are in themselves unimportant are used to label (as a mischief maker, moaner, failure, and so on) and socially exclude someone.

Concerning the second mechanism, social competence and self-esteem deficits, Zapf and Einarsen (2011) argued that some people are more vulnerable to bullying because they are low in self-assertiveness, unable to defend themselves, and unable to manage the inevitable conflicts constructively. Therefore, they are seen as natural victims of bullying. Individuals low in self-esteem, self-assertion, and social competencies but high in anxiety and depression may be bullied not just because they are defenseless and thus easy targets. Rather, because of their own behavior, the victims may actively create conflicts that may make them into the targets of aggression and harassment. Zapf and Einarsen contended that being socially incompetent, as well as nonassertive, may contribute to their rejection by colleagues and superiors and thus explain why some individuals may easily become a target of workplace bullying.

The third mechanism portrayed by Zapf and Einarsen (2011) is overachievement and conflict with group norms. According to this argument, victims of bullying are more conscientiousness and achievement oriented than their colleagues. They are also generally more bound, honest, punctual, and accurate. Such persons may be very annoying to others, which may contribute to frustration and aggressive outbursts in their colleagues. These victims may well be highly qualified and experienced workers; however, they may clash with the norms of the workgroup to which they belong because they often "know it better," tend to be legalistic, and insist on their own view, as well as having difficulties taking the perspective of others. By being overcritical, they may pose a constant threat to the self-esteem of their colleagues and superiors. According to Zapf and Einarsen, their being at odds with group norms may imply that these victims challenge low performance standards, informal rules, and privileges. In some cases, they may actually be the "good guys" from the employer's point of view. However, in practice, management is dependent more on the group than on the victim. Therefore, and because information about the conflict situation is likely to be biased in favor of the group, management tends to take the view of the group rather than that of the victim, thus leaving the victim in a hopeless position.

Mikkelsen and Einarsen (2002) contended that low self-worth is a consistent correlate of exposure to workplace bullying. They argued that comparisons of the basic assumptions of victims and non-victims of bullying show that victims consider themselves less worthy, others as less caring, and the world as less meaningful and just, indicating that exposure to bullying at work may indeed result in increased negative assumptions about self, other people, and the world. Mikkelsen and Einarsen (2002) mentioned that the low perceived self-worth reported by many victims of bullying might be related to a prolonged exposure to persistent and systematic attacks, which have gradually undermined their sense of self-assurance both personally and professionally. Consequently, whereas many victims state that prior to their victimization, they considered themselves assertive, independent, and self-efficacious, as a result of the bullying, they are often forced to reshape their self-image into one of weakness and helplessness. When this perceived low self-worth is generalized, they may ultimately feel unworthy and useless. In the most severe cases, this depressive, self-defeating state of mind may lead to suicide or attempts at such.

The results of empirical studies that examined the characteristics of the dark triad victims support in general the relationship between dark triad personalities and abusive leadership. The studies also showed some interesting findings regarding the victims' characteristics.

Chung and Charles (2016) investigated the characteristics of individuals who enable and abet people scoring high in the dark triad traits (e.g., through tolerating unpleasant behaviors, not challenging unethical conduct). They contended that individuals who score high in the dark triad traits may be able to identify individuals who are susceptible to social manipulation and are therefore less likely to challenge their behaviors. Their findings showed that high neuroticism and agreeableness scores were predictors of vulnerability. This is in accordance with the view that victims exhibit higher levels of distress and negativity, which in turn reinforce further victimization. Those higher in agreeableness are less likely to behave aggressively or retaliate. They are also more trusting of others and perceive others positively. Although agreeableness is linked to positive interpersonal relationships, their high levels of agreeableness may be one of the reasons some people fall victim to dark triad individuals because very agreeable people are more forgiving and tend to react to hostility in a more temperate manner.

In their study, Black, Woodworth, and Porter (2014) found that dark personalities were more likely to perceive targets as being disagreeable; as having low self-esteem; and as being highly neurotic, depressed, and anxious. Similar results were found for each of the individual subcomponents. For example, psychopathic observers generally perceived their targets as being less agreeable and highly neurotic, depressed, and anxious, Machiavellian observers perceived them as being more neurotic, anxious, and depressed, and narcissistic observers perceived them as low in openness to new experiences, conscientiousness, and extraversion and high in depression. It should be noted that the last two studies yielded contradictory results regarding agreeableness as a characteristic of victims.

Chung and Charles (2016) found, in addition, that victims of dark triad personalities had low extraversion levels. Introverts tend to be more isolated and less assertive and as a result more likely to be targeted. Their findings also showed that the group that scored high in vulnerability reported significantly lower conscientiousness scores. This is probably because those who are more conscientious are also more determined, making them more able to ward off potential threats offered by perpetrators. Furthermore, lower conscientiousness is associated with greater anger and negative effect in peer conflicts. People high in neuroticism and low in conscientiousness may have difficulty regulating their behavior in conflict situations. Chung and Charles concluded that people who are vulnerable to victimization should not be viewed as homogeneous and undifferentiated. There are different ways in which personality factors may be associated with vulnerability. Linton and Power (2013) showed in their unique study, conducted among 224 young Canadian students with prior work experience, that bullies and victims share a wide range of bully-typifying personality traits. They found that bullying was associated with Machiavellianism, narcissism, and psychopathy. More strikingly, the majority of bully-typifying traits (Machiavellianism, narcissism, and psychopathy) were associated with being a victim.

As can be seen from the studies presented, more studies that examine the victims' characteristics are needed, particularly in the work setting. It is difficult to generalize from studies conducted in other settings to that of the workplace.

Confronting the Predators (or Not?)

An interesting question also partially overlooked by research is: How do the victims of the dark triad personalities respond to abuse? It seems that there are three main reactions. The first is to join and cooperate with the offenders. The second is to confront and to attempt to beat them. The third is to leave the situation in order to avoid any contact with the offenders. Concerning the first reaction, Sankowsky (1995) contended that even when a leader conceals his or her blame in a failed venture, followers often not only go along with the leader but even try to assume still more guilt. They accept the leader's judgment and find fault with themselves ("I must have been inadequate"). Moreover, they bond even more strongly with a leader who also blames external agencies ("If the rest of the world is hostile, causing our difficulties, then whom else can we turn to?"). Not surprisingly, their psychological well-being is seriously affected by this.

Padilla et al. (2007) distinguish between two groups of followers: conformers and colluders. Whereas conformers comply with destructive leaders out of fear, colluders actively participate in the agenda of the destructive leader. Both types are motivated by self-interest, but their concerns are different: conformers try to minimize the consequences of not going along with the leader, while colluders seek personal gain through association with the destructive leader. The vulnerability of the conformers stems from unmet basic needs, negative self-evaluations, and psychological immaturity. In contrast, colluders are ambitious and selfish and share the worldviews of the destructive leader.

Padilla et al. (2007) discussed several reasons for cooperating with dark triad leaders. First, followers might collude with the dark personalities because although destructive leadership creates negative outcomes for organizations, some members might prosper from it. These are the individuals close to the leader and others who are willing to implement the destructive vision. People striving for status and those who sometimes engage in exploitative relations may be willing to follow coercive policies if doing so advances their personal agendas. Congruent values and beliefs were mentioned by Padilla et al. as the second reason. Individuals whose beliefs are consistent with those of the destructive leader are likely to commit to his or her cause. The closer the leader is to the follower's self-concept, the stronger the bond and the greater the motivation to follow. To complete the cycle, behaving in ways that are consistent with the leader's vision and the follower's self-concept boosts the follower's self-esteem and self-efficacy. The third reason for cooperating mentioned by Padilla et al. is unsocialized values. Individuals who endorse unsocialized values such as greed and selfishness are more likely to follow destructive leaders and engage in destructive behavior. Ambitious but under-socialized followers are likely to engage in destructive acts, especially if they are sanctioned or encouraged by the leader (Padilla et al., 2007).

The other option victims have is to confront and fight back against the dark triad personalities. This is not an easy option. Peers and subordinates might be frightened of the power of bad personalities and afraid of retribution if they enter into a struggle, and they often experience self-doubt when facing the unwavering certitude of this difficult opponent (Delbecq, 2001). Because of this self-doubt, the members of the peer group do not stand shoulder to shoulder to deal with the challenging and demoralizing behavior. For everyone, peers and executives alike, because the behavior lies outside the normative managerial protocols and expectations, there is a long period of denial that an exceptional behavior pattern is at play. Finally, however, the situation might deteriorate, and individuals might become so injured that a few would hesitantly ask the senior manager to intervene. When these initial individuals begin to report their concerns, their opponent often masks the issues under the cloak of being a protector of superordinate norms, such as higher quality standards. Not sure what to do and afraid of the damage that the aggressive evil player might do to their personal career, peers begin to retreat to self-protective behaviors. They might withdraw from full engagement in organizational tasks and experience work-related stress symptoms, which only increase their withdrawal and leave their opponent in control of the playing field (Delbecq, 2001).

In support of the contention that individuals may hesitate to confront dark triad personalities, as described earlier, Lee and Brotheridge (2006) found in their study that as self-doubt grew, psychological strain also became more intense. The conservation of resources theory suggests that if targets are unable to muster the necessary resources to meet the emotional demands of coping with bullying, they experience increased stress and strain. They argued, based on their findings, that self-doubt appears to bridge the link between bullying and emotional well-being. To the extent that the targets' sense of mastery and control are diminished as a result of bullying, as they inevitably are, feelings of helplessness and futility are likely to emerge.

However, there are definitely employees who fight back when they think they are being abused by dark triad leaders. One such profile is termed by Zapf and Einarsen (2011) "the provocative victim." There are victims who are constantly striking back and who may even start the conflict. When individuals perceive that norms of acceptable behaviors have been violated by aggressive behavior, they often feel the need to retaliate to reestablish justice; this action and reaction, in turn, may spiral into further aggression on both sides. Their need to retaliate is fueled by the need to protect themselves. These individuals are victims who display active bullying behavior and can be viewed as perpetrators and victims at the same time. They are characterized by a combination of both anxious and aggressive reaction patterns. Provocative victims may possess an "abrasive personality," which is characterized by insensitive and ruthless behaviors, especially when they are under social pressure. Revenge and retaliation may be motives for counteraggression. Victims may sometimes use aggression against their perpetrators in their fight for justice, but in doing so, they may only further escalate the conflict (Zapf and Einarsen, 2011).

According to Solas (2015), coworkers can take some practical courses of action in response to victimization without imposing further hardship on themselves. In simple terms, these are (1) knowing the enemy, (2) reframing the reality, (3) playing by the rules, and (4) ending the game. Most of these tactics are neither exhaustive nor mutually exclusive and can be undertaken with the investment of minimal time and effort. These are personalized, unobtrusive, and tailored responses designed to maximize maneuverability rather than use passive or aggressive defenses for self-preservation. An added advantage is that they provide the bases for more advanced strategies, such as media and political campaigns, whistleblowing, and industrial action. The first three measures guide intervention. The last one brings an end to victimization. A brief review of each of these courses of actions as described by Solas follows.

Knowing the Enemy: According to Solas (2015), it is critical to recognize that one has become the target of victimization, since it may be obscured by toxic behaviors considered "normal" in the organization. Once the fact of victimization has been established, it is important to reveal the identity of the victimizer. Psychopaths are not unthinking.

They are, however, a closed book. While their motives may be hidden, their behavior can be subjected to ethical and moral scrutiny, particularly since scruples are not taken seriously by psychopathic victimizers with little or no conscience. Labelling a behavior as victimizing allows the shame and guilt to be directed away from targets toward the perpetrators and at the same time helps the intended victims to maintain their sense of decency, dignity, and agency. It also serves to highlight for others who the victimizers are and what they are capable of doing.

Reframing Reality: People's impressions and expectations play an important part in constructing what counts as reality in organizations. Their views form the bases of official and unofficial accounts that can be used to "frame" a target's reputation. Psychopathic managers will always seek to discredit those they single out. It is important, therefore, to grasp how one is being framed by tapping as many sources of intelligence as possible. According to Solas (2015), it is imperative to canvas personal networks and monitor personnel files. Service records enable targets to discover who has written about them, and what. Knowledge of these details allows them to gather countermanding evidence that can be used in the preparation of official rejoinders and reviews. This evidence will prove invaluable for framing a positive self-image. It is possible for targets to reframe unchosen work personae. Advances in digital technology can make transfiguration an organizational reality. Nevertheless, as sophisticated as mass self-communication is, the power of informal channels, most notably, word of mouth and the office grapevine, to filter and disseminate news and information far and wide quickly, can be neither underestimated nor ignored (Solas, 2015).

Playing by the Rules: According to Solas (2015), the predators who cohabit workplaces continually scan the administrative horizon for possible means of turning the organization's rules and regulations against their targets. An understanding of them is therefore essential. Knowing how the organization's rules operate both for and against them empowers targets, especially given the profound sense of frustration that psychopaths typically experience from being caught up in rules and red tape. Connecting rules with their uses in practice puts targets in a strong position to outmaneuver their rule-bound tormentors.

Ending the Game: Evidence suggests that a predisposition to psychopathy is lifelong, and even if treatment is sought, outcomes are likely to be poor. If there is no need to stay, then prospective ex-targets are free to turn their attention toward the manner of their departure. The exit options include resigning in protest or simply walking away. Either way, the decision, and the emotional, psychological, and physical distance it brings, invites some level of reappraisal and reinvention. The change in circumstances affords an opportunity for introspection from a safe vantage point, and with it, the promise of gaining greater leverage. Although leaving does not guarantee that survivors will enter a more civilized organization, it does hasten the end of a potentially relentless pursuit, and brings with it the possibility of a new start with new energies (Solas, 2015).

Ending the game presents the third option not frequently discussed in the literature: leave the situation. Do not join dark personalities if it contradicts your values; do not confront them if you think that the personal costs might be too high. To protect oneself, sometimes the best option might be to move away from the situation' namely the abusive dark triad leader. This might include avoiding any contact with dark personalities. Can it be done? Gordon and Platek (2009) presented an interesting perspective of the victim's side in encounters with dark triad personalities. They argued that potential victims can sense when they encounter a psychopath and can consider avoiding such personalities in the workplace.

Another option involving leaving the situation is to move to another department in the organization, if a person thinks he or she will be safer there, or to another organization. Living side by side with dark triad personalities, whether one joins them or confronts them, might be very costly. Moving away from them might be sometimes the best option in terms of protecting one's career and health. More research on the frequency with which this option, as well as the others, is chosen and on the implications of such decisions on the individual and on the organization is definitely needed. There is a need for much more research on all aspects regarding the victims of the dark triad traits.

References

Australian Public Service Commission. (2011–2012). *State of the Service Report*. Canberra: APSC.

Babiak, P. (2000). Psychopathic manipulation at work. In C. B. Gacono (Ed.), *The Clinical and Forensic Assessment of Psychopathy: A Practitioner's Guide* (pp. 287–312). Mahwah, NJ: Lawrence Erlbaum Associates, Inc.

Babiak, P., & Hare, R. D. (2006). *Snakes in Suits: When Psychopaths Go to Work*. New York: Regan Books.

Black, P. J., Woodworth, M., & Porter, S. (2014). The big bad wolf? The relation between the dark triad and the interpersonal assessment of vulnerability. *Personality and Individual Differences, 67*, 52–56.

Boddy, C. R. (2006). The dark side of management decisions: Organizational psychopaths. *Management Decision, 44*, 1461–1475.

Boddy, C. R. (2010a). Corporate psychopaths and organizational type. *Journal of Public Affairs, 10*(4), 300–312.

Boddy, C. R. (2010b). *Corporate Psychopaths in Australian Workforce: Their Influence on Organizational Outcomes*. Perth: Curtin University of Technology.

Boddy, C. R. (2011a). *Corporate Psychopaths: Organizational Destroyers*. London: Palgrave MacMillan.

Boddy, C. R. (2011b). Corporate psychopaths, bullying and unfair supervision in the workplace. *Journal of Business Ethics, 100*(3), 367–379.

Boddy, C. R. (2014). Corporate psychopaths, conflict, employee affective well-being and counterproductive work behavior. *Journal of Business Ethics, 121*(1), 107–121.

Boddy, C. R. (2015). Organizational psychopaths: A ten-year update. *Management Decision, 53*(10), 2407–2432.

Castille, C. M., Kuyumcu, D., & Bennett, R. J. (2017). Prevailing to the peers' detriment: Organizational constraints motivate Machiavellians to undermine their peers. *Personality and Individual Differences, 104*, 29–36.

Chung, K. L., & Charles, K. (2016). Giving the benefit of the doubt: The role of vulnerability in the perception of dark triad behaviors. *Personality and Individual Differences, 101*, 208–213.

Clarke, J. (2005). *Working with Monsters: How to Identify and Protect Yourself from the Workplace Psychopath*. Sydney: Random House.

Comcare. (2008). *Working Well: An Organizational Approach to Preventing Psychological Injury*. Canberra: AGPS.

Comcare. (2014). Costs of psychological injury. Available at: www.comcare.gov.au/safety__and__prevention/health_and_safety_topics/psychological_injury/costs_of_psychological_injury

Delbecq, A. L. (2001). "Evil" manifested in destructive individual behavior: A senior leadership challenge. *Journal of Management Inquiry, 10*(3), 221–226.

Dzurec, L. C., Kennison, M., & Gillen, P. (2017). The incongruity of workplace bullying victimization and inclusive excellence. *Nursing Outlook, 56*(5), 588–596.

Glasø, L., Matthiesen, S. B., Nielsen, M. B., & Einarsen, S. (2007). Do targets of workplace bullying portray a general victim personality profile? *Scandinavian Journal of Psychology, 48*(4), 313–319.

Gordon, D. S., & Platek, S. M. (2009). Trustworthy? The brain knows: Implicit neural responses to faces that vary in dark triad personality characteristics and trustworthiness. *Journal of Social, Evolutionary, and Cultural Psychology, 3*(3), 182.

Herbst, T. (2014). *The Dark Side of Leadership: A Psycho-Spiritual Approach towards Understanding the Origins of Personality Dysfunctions: Derailment and the Restoration of Personality*. UK: Author House.

Jonason, P. K., Slomski, S., & Partyka, J. (2012b). The dark triad at work: How toxic employees get their way. *Personality and Individual Differences, 52*(3), 449–453.

Kets de Vries, M. F. K. (1989). *Prisoners of Leadership*. New York: Wiley.

Lee, R. T., & Brotheridge, C. M. (2006). When prey turns predatory: Workplace bullying as a predictor of counter aggression/bullying, coping, and well-being. *European Journal of Work and Organizational Psychology, 15*(3), 352–377.

Linton, D. K., & Power, J. L. (2013). The personality traits of workplace bullies are often shared by their victims: Is there a dark side to victims? *Personality and Individual Differences, 54*(6), 738–743.

Lutgen-Sandvik, P., Tracy, S. J., & Alberts, J. K. (2007). Burned by bullying in the American workplace: Prevalence, perception, degree and impact. *Journal of Management Studies, 44*(6), 837–862.

Mikkelsen, E. G. E., & Einarsen, S. (2002). Basic assumptions and symptoms of post-traumatic stress among victims of bullying at work. *European Journal of Work and Organizational Psychology, 11*(1), 87–111.

Niedl, K. (1995). Mobbing/Bullying am Arbeitsplatz. Eine empirische Analyse zum Phänomen sowie zu personalwirtschaftlich relevanten Effekten von systematischen Feindseligkeiten. *Zeitschrift für Personalforschung/German Journal of Research in Human Resource Management, 9*(H. 3), 297–300.

Padilla, A., Hogan, R., & Kaiser, R. B. (2007). The toxic triangle: Destructive leaders, susceptible followers, and conducive environments. *The Leadership Quarterly, 18*(3), 176–194.

Sankowsky, D. (1995). The charismatic leader as narcissist: Understanding the abuse of power. *Organizational Dynamics, 23*, 57–71.

Solas, J. (2015). Pathological work victimization in public sector organizations. *Public Organization Review, 15*(2), 255–265.

Vega, G., & Comer, D. R. (2005). Bullying and harassment in the workplace. In R. E. Kidwell & C. L. Martin (Eds.), *Managing Organizational Deviance* (pp. 183–204). Thousand Oaks, CA: Sage Publications, Inc.

Volmer, J., Koch, I. K., & Göritz, A. S. (2016). The bright and dark sides of leaders' dark triad traits: Effects on subordinates' career success and well-being. *Personality and Individual Differences, 101*, 413–418.

Zapf, D., & Einarsen, S. (2003). Individual antecedents of bullying. In S. Einarsen, H. Hoel, D. Zapf, & C. L. Cooper (Eds.), *Bullying and Emotional Abuse in the Workplace: International Perspectives in Research and Practice* (pp. 165–184). London: Taylor & Francis.

Zapf, D., & Einarsen, S. (2011). Individual antecedents of bullying: Victims and perpetrators. In S. Einarsen, H. Hoel, D. Zapf, & C. L. Cooper (Eds.), *Bullying and Harassment in the Workplace* (pp. 177–200). Boca Raton, FL: CRC Press.

10 Cultural Aspects of the Dark Triad

Most of the studies on the dark triad personalities in the workplace were conducted in the North American culture. However, to understand these personalities better, it is necessary to know more about their mode of operation in different cultures and settings. As globalization continues to increase, companies are increasingly likely to manage individuals in different countries with different cultural values; therefore, scholars and practitioners should focus on identifying how cultural differences may interact with these personalities (Grijalva & Newman, 2015). Indeed, research examining personality differences across cultures suggests that country or culture may serve as potential moderators (Gaddis & Foster, 2015). Certain dark traits are more likely to be viewed as destructive in particular cultural settings, depending on the prevailing cultural norms (Harms & Spain, 2015).

There is little reason to believe that psychopathy is a geographically localized phenomenon, although there is evidence that its manifestations in behavior are regulated by the type of culture in which the psychopath lives. Psychopaths need to appear to conform to their society to be able to operate successfully and undetected, and this means adapting their overt behavior to conform to group norms and expectations (Boddy, 2011a). Culture defines the range, depth, and breadth of external mechanisms, which may limit the extent to which psychopaths (as well as narcissists and Machiavellians) can express their personality. Cross-cultural studies can indicate whether some psychopathic traits are favored in particular environments (Glenn, Kurzban, & Raine, 2011). For example, in some environments, the expected value of the benefits from psychopathic traits may outweigh the costs. However, in other environments, the reverse may be true. Evidence suggesting that psychopathic traits are more prevalent in specific environments would provide some support for the idea that psychopathy, narcissism, and Machiavellianism are adaptive strategies that may be beneficial in some environments.

Unfortunately, cross-cultural research that focuses on psychopathy (i.e., examines psychopathic traits in different environments), as well as on narcissism and Machiavellianism, is still in its infancy and has primarily been conducted in Western, developed cultures. Observed differences across cultures may indicate that environmental cues influence the expression of traits. For example, it is possible that features of contemporary modern environments, such as relative anonymity, evoke psychopathic traits. In modern large-scale societies, many interactions may be one-time encounters, in which individuals may use strategies of deceit and manipulation with little risk of developing a reputation as a cheater; it is also considerably easier for individuals to move to other locations and start anew. Further ethnographic research on psychopathy may discover whether psychopathic traits are less beneficial in small-scale societies where the interactions between individuals are more continuous (Glenn et al., 2011). This chapter discusses cultural differences among the dark triad personalities and the effect of culture on their behaviors. In addition, the possible differences in the behavior of dark triad personalities in different settings, each assumed to represent a different culture, such as the private versus the public sector, are elaborated.

The Definition of Culture

Culture plays an important role in understanding dark triad personalities. Culture can be viewed as a lens through which one interprets events (Steiner, 2001). As mentioned in previous chapters, dark triad personalities assess their environment very carefully before taking action. This assessment might differ in different cultures, depending on the norms and rules governing the specific culture. What exactly is meant by culture? According to Thomas et al. (2003, 2010), culture, a group-level construct, is neither generic nor about individual behavior. Rather, it exists within the knowledge systems of individuals, formed during childhood and reinforced throughout life. Much of our understanding of cultural variation has developed through the study of values. Value orientations are the shared assumptions about how things ought to be or how one should behave. They result from the solutions that social groups have devised for dealing with a finite number of problems that all people confront. Given the limited number of ways in which different societies can deal with these problems, a system can be developed that categorizes and compares societies on the basis of their values. Thus, while national culture influences the cultural profile of individuals raised within it, individual sources of variation, such as idiosyncratic experiences and personality, also affect value orientations, creating variation within sociocultural groups. Individual-level variation in cultural profiles is most closely tied to individual perceptions of exchange relationships, and individual-cultural profiles serve as a conduit of influence of that part of the mental programming of individuals that is shared by society (Thomas et al., 2003, 2010).

As mentioned by Cohen (2015) and explained by Thomas et al. (2003, 2010), the cultural profiles of individuals act as both processors of information and sources of influence on preferences and behavior. In other words, while cultural values operate at the cognitive level, their influence runs through cognitive and motivational channels. Thomas and colleagues (2003, 2010) defined cognitive mechanisms as those operating through a neuropsychological information processing channel and motivational mechanisms as those operating through preferable end states or modes of behavior. While these pathways are related, they suggested that distinct effects based on each process can be identified. The cognitive domain involves cultural variations in the perception and interpretation of signals from the organization and in the behavioral scripts associated with an individual's relationship to the organization, while the motivational domain involves the effect of culturally different self-concepts on what is desirable, resulting in variations in preferred outcomes and behavior.

Shao, Rupp, Skarlicki, and Jones (2013) contended that because cultural values can influence how people understand their world and their emotional, attitudinal, and behavioral responses to events in their world, it is reasonable to assume that cultural values play a role in the reactions and behaviors of individuals, including dark triad personalities, who are relatively very sensitive to such clues. According to Hofstede (1980, 1991, 1993, 2001) four cultural dimensions constitute the best conceptualization through which the effect of culture on individuals can be understood. Accepting this view, the four cultural dimensions, as cited by Shao et al. (2013), are presented next.

Individualism/collectivism refers to whether the identity of individuals is formed through individual accomplishments or group identification. According to Hofstede, people in highly individualistic societies emphasize individual rights more than their duties, focusing on self-autonomy and self-fulfillment. Individualists are typically independent of their social groups and prioritize their personal interests and goals over those of the group. Their behaviors are largely determined by their attitudes rather than by the norms of their affiliated social collective. In contrast, collectivists see themselves as interdependent with their social groups and prioritize group over self-interests.

Uncertainty avoidance reflects the extent to which individuals are comfortable with ambiguity. Whereas people from countries or societies that score high on uncertainty avoidance are active, aggressive, emotional, security seeking, and intolerant, people with lower needs to avoid uncertainty are contemplative, less aggressive, unemotional, willing to accept personal risk, and relatively tolerant. People in societies that score high on uncertainty avoidance prefer clearly defined, structured situations to ambiguous, unstructured situations. In countries that score high on uncertainty avoidance, people are comfortable with clear rules, procedures, and strict codes of behavior and tend to feel anxious when things are different, unexpected, or unpredictable.

Power distance concerns the degree to which individuals are accepting an unequal distribution of power. Although inequality exists across all countries, societies differ in the degree to which less powerful individuals are tolerant of inequality in the distribution of power across different social hierarchies. People in countries that score high on power distance accept that those higher in the social hierarchy should have more power than those who are lower. In such cultures, people often tend to be submissive and are unlikely to disobey the demands made by authorities. In contrast, in cultures that score low on power distance, people often desire equality in power and demand justification for inequalities. In such cultures, superiors are often expected to consult subordinates when making important decisions.

Masculinity/femininity concerns the values that emphasize competition versus quality of life. In masculine cultures, men (as opposed to women) are expected to be assertive, ambitious, and competitive and strive for material success. In such cultures, women are expected to promote quality of life and care for children and the weak. Whereas people in highly masculine societies emphasize material gains and personal assertiveness, people in highly feminine societies emphasize interpersonal relationships and concern for others.

Hofstede's conceptualization of culture seems to be suitable when exploring the relationships between culture and dark triad personalities. It is not surprising that most studies that examined the effect of cultural differences on dark triad personalities applied this conceptualization.

Dark Triad in Collectivist versus Individualistic Cultures

It seems that the main value dominating current research on the effect of culture on the dark triad is the comparison between collectivist and individualistic cultures. The effect of this value is reviewed for each element of the dark triad separately.

Narcissism and Culture

Culture has an impact on narcissistic personality traits. More individualistic nations produce more narcissistic culture and more individuals who self-report high levels of narcissism (Twenge, 2011). The relationship between culture and individual traits is likely to be reciprocal, that is, a higher narcissistic culture produces more narcissistic individuals, and narcissistic individuals are pushing cultures toward greater narcissism. According to Twenge, even a small number of individuals may have an influence. Because they seek to influence others, narcissistic individuals may be one of the primary drivers of social change. Unless larger forces are at work to curtail that influence, most cultures gradually become more narcissistic over time.

Twenge contended that individualistic cultures have enormous upsides, among them less prejudice and greater opportunities for people, regardless of their backgrounds. However, when a culture becomes so individualistic that it is narcissistic, negative outcomes are likely to follow. A society of narcissistic individuals might seem attractive and fun in the short term, but in the long term, society breaks down as people focus only on themselves and have little empathy for others. Similarly, cultures can fall victim to the belief that they are inherently superior, leading to aggression toward out-groups. Most cultural characteristics (e.g., uncertainty avoidance and individualism versus collectivism) have both advantages and disadvantages, but a culture built on narcissism is likely to have significant problems. Understanding the relationship between narcissism and culture is a first step toward viewing cultural narcissism as potentially dangerous (Twenge, 2011).

O'Boyle, Forsyth, Banks, and McDaniel (2012) raised the possibility that in-group collectivism moderates the relationship between narcissism and counterproductive work behavior (CWB). According to them, cultures high in in-group collectivism emphasize duty and loyalty to the organization and its members, cohesiveness among coworkers, and relatedness among peers. Collectivist cultures place great emphasis on norms of reciprocity and are less likely to tolerate the social exchange violations perpetrated by the dark triad. Manipulation of coworkers, self-promotion, and antisocial behavior are interpreted as betrayal of the in-group and are sanctioned accordingly. As a result, the relationship between narcissism and CWB is expected to be weak because of the effect of collectivism.

Grijalva and Newman (2015) followed the reasoning of O'Boyle et al. (2012) and contended that in-group collectivist cultures are less likely to tolerate the CWB perpetrated by narcissists. Cultures with high in-group collectivism create a situation that suppresses the expression of narcissistic personality in the form of CWB (i.e., a moderator effect). Their study also found that when cultures were high in in-group collectivism, narcissism had a weaker relationship with CWB. They concluded that narcissists seem to perform fewer CWBs in high in-group collectivist countries than in low in-group collectivist countries. This interaction effect (narcissism × in-group collectivism) is an example of a situation in which an in-group collectivist culture constrains the narcissist's options to engage in CWB, thereby buffering the narcissism–CWB relationship. That is, collectivist cultural cues suggest to narcissists that there will be harsher sanctions for individuals who violate group norms and harm the group or organization.

In another interesting study, Jonason, Li, and Czarna (2013a) found that the rates of narcissism were higher in Poland and the US than in Singapore. The researchers noted that it is unclear why these effects were found, suggesting that collectivist sentiments in Asian societies might be responsible for decreasing the rates of narcissism overall and equalizing them across genders. Narcissism might be diametrically opposed to the collectivist ethos of East Asians. In short, this theory and these findings strongly suggest that collectivist cultures reduce the relationship between narcissism and CWBs.

Psychopathy and Culture

A similar logic as for narcissism is advanced for psychopaths. Differences in the rate of psychopathy in different countries stem from cultural differences. Whereas the individualistic culture of North America, and especially of the

US, enables the free expression of psychopathic behavior, more collectivist cultures are said to suppress the overt expression of antisocial behavior. Individualistic cultures are said to encourage competitiveness and a tendency to shallowness and selfishness (Boddy, 2011a). Boddy cited Stout (2005a, 2005b), who contended that societies such as the US that promote and idealize individualism allow the development of antisocial behavior patterns and a "me first" attitude. These societies also facilitate the camouflage of such behavior because it blends in more readily with accepted societal norms in which personal advancement and self-fulfillment are seen as noble and desirable aims. Western societies allow and encourage the pursuit of domination of others.

According to Boddy (2011a), it is possible that Western society is permissive toward the manifestation of psychopathic behaviors, probably because it is much more materialistic and competitive than other societies, thus promoting psychopathic traits. Boddy cited Hare's (1999) argument that modern society values some of the traits associated with psychopathy, such as egocentricity, lack of concern for others, a manipulative approach, and superficiality, making it easy for psychopaths to blend in with the rest of society and facilitating their entry into business organizations, politics, government, and other social structures (Boddy, 2011a).

Boddy also cited Stout's (2005a, 2005b) argument that cultures that promote the advancement of the group as a whole (e.g., more collectivist cultures), rather than the individuals in it, and that teach that all living things are interconnected may provide stronger environmental constraints against psychopaths than more individualistic Western cultures. Stout presented the example of Tainan, a Confucian and Buddhist culture, where the levels of antisocial personality disorder are far lower than in Western cultures. Psychopaths appear to exist everywhere, but they may well be limited in their possible actions in more collectivist societies. The global spread of Western individualistically oriented corporations, which may contain corporate psychopaths who operate without such collectivist limitations, may therefore pose a threat to the countries in which these companies operate (Boddy, 2011a).

Some support for the above contention was found by Robertson, Datu, Brawley, Pury, & Mateo (2016), who compared employees from the US (individualistic culture) and the Philippines (a more collectivist culture). They found that psychopathy was related to interpersonal CWB in both countries. They also found differential relationships between the US and the Philippines regarding the manner in which the dark triad traits are expressed in an individualist vs. a collectivist context. According to them, the behaviors that constitute a dark personality trait may have been shaped by the individualist context in which they were developed. Therefore, these same behaviors might not be socially undesirable in non-Western societies. In collectivist cultures, individuals have a strong sense of duty to the family and others that form their societal in-group.

In short, the research strongly suggests that dark triad personalities adjust better to individualistic cultures. As a result, the negative consequences of their actions are more pronounced in individualistic cultures than in collectivist ones. Naturally, much more research is needed to validate these explanations. In addition, research is needed to examine the effect of culture on Machiavellianism, an issue that has rarely been examined, as well as on the two other dark triad dimensions on which some research exists but is far from being sufficient to establish any affirmation regarding the effect of culture on dark triad personalities.

Other Values

Schwartz's definition of values (Schwartz, 1992, 2005; Schwartz & Sagiv, 1995) has also been applied in research on cultural values, although not as frequently as Hofstede's conceptualization. Schwartz and Sagiv (1995) defined human values as desirable, trans-situational goals, varying in importance, that serve as guiding principles in people's lives. They identified 10 distinct value types structured in patterns of conflict and compatibility. The values fall into higher order dimensions. These dimensions are composed of higher order value types that combine the standard types. The first dimension—openness to change versus conservation—juxtaposes values emphasizing independent thought and action and favoring change (self-direction and stimulation) with those emphasizing submissive self-restriction, preservation of traditional practices, and protection of stability (security, conformity, and tradition). The second dimension—self-enhancement versus self-transcendence—juxtaposes values emphasizing the acceptance of others as equals and concern for their welfare (universalism and benevolence) with those emphasizing the pursuit of one's own relative success and dominance over others (power and achievement). Hedonism is related both to openness to change and to self-enhancement.

Kajonius, Persson, and Jonason (2015) examined individual values in their relation to the dark triad, using Schwartz's conceptualization, and found that hedonism, stimulation, achievement, and power appear to be the primary values held by those high in the dark triad traits. They also found that the dark triad traits account for a unique variance in social values that is not accounted for by the Five-Factor Model (FFM), indicating that meaningful personality traits are located outside the FFM model. Kajonius et al. (2015) concluded that the relationship between the dark triad traits and the values examined reveal a value system that they call "dark values," which is primarily characterized by self-enhancing values but also by the opposing self-transcending values. The dark values are associated with manipulating people and viewing other people as a means for achieving selfish gains.

Jonason, Strosser, Kroll, Duineveld, and Baruffi (2015) also documented the value systems associated with each of the dark triad traits using some of Schwartz's conceptualization of individual values. They found that Machiavellianism was associated with moral flexibility. Psychopathy revealed the most consistent evidence across their studies, in that it places little value on the systems of moral foundations, collective interests, conservation, and self-transcendence. Finally, narcissism is associated with a socially desirable moral value system. Narcissism was also associated with more of an individualistic value system through self-enhancement, unlike the other traits. While the existing findings on the relationship between dark triad personalities and values are interesting and stimulating, much more research is needed on the effect of values system on the attitudes and behaviors of the dark triad personalities. Yet it seems based on the existing theory and findings that dark triad traits will have more difficulties in performing CWBs in collectivist traditional cultures compared with individualistic modern cultures.

Public versus Private Sector

A more specific type of cultural influence is found in the differences between the public and private sectors. Boddy (2015) argued that the issue of the types of organization that encourage the congregation of corporate psychopaths has not properly been researched. If, as theoretically expected, they tend to gravitate toward organizations that can provide them with the control, power, and prestige that they desire, this means that corporate psychopaths will be found in some environments more than in others. Psychopaths in politics, for example, could theoretically amass enormous power toward selfish ends and divert resources from more deserving members of society.

There is no doubt that the two types of organizations (public and private) represent different values. Van der Wal, De Graaf, and Lasthuizen (2008) compared 382 managers from a variety of public and private sector organizations in The Netherlands. They found a traditional and consistent value pattern in both the public and private sectors. The most important values of the public sector—for example, "accountability," "lawfulness," "incorruptibility," "expertise," "reliability," "effectiveness," "impartiality," and "efficiency"—are consistent with those often mentioned in the administrative and business ethics literature as the crucial values of the public sector. The values ranking highest in the private sector—"profitability," "accountability," "reliability," "effectiveness," "expertise," "efficiency," "honesty,' and "innovativeness"—also approximate to the crucial values of the private sector that are mentioned in the administrative and business ethics literature. The researchers concluded, based on their findings, that the organizational values of the traditional public sector, such as "impartiality," are not among the most important organizational values of the private sector, and the values of the traditional private sector, such as "profitability" and "innovativeness," are not among the most important values in the public sector.

Based on these findings, would it be possible to argue that the value system of the public sector represents a friendlier environment to the dark triad than that of the private sector? Dark triad personalities prefer a more ambiguous environment, where they can better hide their own performance and manipulate the performance of others, particularly their victims. Therefore, despite some overlap found in the study, values such as "profitability," "accountability," "reliability," and "effectiveness," found to be ranked among the highest values of the private sector, do not represent a friendly environment for dark triad personalities.

The literature is quite supportive of the fit between dark triad personalities and the values and culture of the public sector. According to Fennimore and Sementelli (2016), in terms of the person–organization fit theory, the public sector may attract more subclinical psychopaths because of the ambiguity of its goals, higher organizational politics, and an indirect relationship between employee performance and the organization's success. Such circumstances create a more conducive environment for psychopaths, as well as one in which it is difficult to detect counterproductive activities. The presence of corporate psychopaths in greater numbers in public and financial services should be of considerable interest to those organizations and their stakeholders. This finding is especially relevant in the current global financial crisis, which was partly caused by corporate psychopaths in senior positions in financial companies (Boddy, 2010a, 2010b, 2011a).

This contention about the global financial crisis was supported by the results of Boddy's (2011a) study, which found that the government and financial sectors have the highest percentages of corporate psychopaths. Boddy (2011a) explained the high prevalence of psychopaths in public sector organizations by the fact that organizations in the public sector are more political in terms of their internal behavior than commercial organizations. Such political environments would seem ideal for the smooth, conning, and manipulative talents of corporate psychopaths. It is also probably easier for corporate psychopaths to cover their lack of effort in the public sector, as performance appraisals in such organizations are less objective, because they are not directly linked to the external and objective performance indicators, such as profits, employed by commercial organizations. This means that organizational politics can potentially play a larger part in performance appraisals and promotions, giving an advantage to those who are able to influence and manipulate others, as corporate psychopaths do. However, Boddy (2011a) noted that ministerial control and public scrutiny may serve as barriers to corporate psychopaths' gaining the promotions and power they crave and seek in the public sector organizations.

Another advantage for psychopaths in the public sector is that these organizations are commonly large and complex, offering subclinical psychopaths great opportunities to attain rewards and power, because competitive self-interest and accountability are more difficult to monitor (Fennimore & Sementelli, 2016). Moreover, self-interested behavior is more likely to go undetected for longer periods of time. Both subclinical psychopaths and public entrepreneurs appear to be drawn to organizations having conditions that are similar to those that encourage opportunistic behavior in relation to the transactional costs (i.e., large, complex, and decentralized organizations). It is considerably more difficult to monitor public managers in large organizations than in small, centralized organizations with clear supervision. Subclinical psychopaths navigate in complex organizations for personal gain by using their intelligence, charm, ingenuity, and charisma. According to Fennimore and Sementelli (2016), subclinical psychopathic public managers who engage in entrepreneurial activities may potentially compromise institutionalized public values such as democracy, accountability, representativeness, and serving public needs. Self-interested public managers seeking to benefit themselves are often called "climbers." Climbers seek promotion to increase their status by overvaluing their input. Subclinical psychopaths, too, are motivated by power, income, and prestige. Both are attracted to rapidly growing and large organizations because of the greater likelihood of fast promotion.

Hanson and Baker (2017) mentioned several reasons for the concern that dark triad personalities raise for public agencies. First, if more subclinical psychopathic personalities are actually becoming high-level leaders through selection and promotion processes that advance them more smoothly now than in the past, it follows that other dark types could be doing so as well through a similar agentic disposition to manipulate patrons and discredit opposition. In turn, if more psychopaths are, in fact, in the public sector than in business as a result of human resources and promotion processes that are more susceptible to manipulation and self-concealment than those in private industry, higher proportions of the other dark triad types could be in public agencies as well.

Second, while a trained clinician may be able to identify disordered personality types, the typical public agency today lacks this capability. In practice, if or when lay coworkers (including public employees) call a manipulative or abusive leader a "corporate psychopath," they often are likely to be using it as a catchall for what could be any of the dark triad personalities. The practical organizational need is less to confirm a dark leader clinically and more for decision makers to respond effectively to a potentially malevolent personality of whatever kind. Finally, regarding the concern that subclinical psychopaths could lead in ways that endanger the traditional values of public service, Hanson and Baker (2017) responded that such a threat is posed by all dark types, ultimately because of similar agentic behavior.

Mathieu, Neumann, Hare, and Babiak (2014) found that perceived psychopathic features in supervisors had a less direct impact on employee psychological distress in a sample of the private sector than in one of the public sector. Additionally, Mathieu et al. (2014) found that perceived psychopathic features in supervisors had a greater direct influence on employee psychological distress in the public sector. The possibility of hiding risk-taking behavior may account for psychopathic entrepreneurs' attraction to the public sector. Higher risk-taking behavior has also been linked to dysfunction in key brain regions, justifying clinical investigation as well.

The public sector is an ideal setting not only for psychopaths but also for Machiavellians mainly because of the strong political culture in the public sector. Dahling, Whitaker, and Levy (2009) cited Ferris, Fedor, and King (1994) who developed a theoretical model of politics in which they placed Machiavellianism as a dispositional antecedent of political behaviors. They reasoned that high Machiavellians have a talent for using tactics of influence, which allows them to forge important connections and secure their positions. Dahling et al. (2009) contended that high Machiavellians may also be more likely to perceive politics in organizations, as well as to engage in political behaviors. High Machiavellians are unlikely to respond negatively to perceptions of politics; the ambiguity and unfairness inherent in political environments are advantageous to high Machiavellians.

According to Boddy (2011a), a political environment, a strong characteristic of the public sector, is ideal for Machiavellians who have commonalities with corporate psychopaths in that they have no regard for any moral standards; promote the idea that the end justifies the means; advocate a political and manipulative approach to management, including the use of a fraudulent persona when necessary (entailing the use of apparent honesty, charm, and tact to gain an advantage); and advocate the use of force if it is deemed necessary to achieve desired ends. Similar to psychopathy, Machiavellianism reportedly entails the manifestation of high levels of manipulative behavior. Given that the Machiavellian trait was derived from Machiavelli's writings on governance, it is not surprising that Machiavellianism has been theoretically tied to the emerging literature on organizational politics. Political environments are inherently risky, suggesting that those who accrue power and influence will remain most successful. High Machiavellians are therefore likely to embrace political environments for the opportunities they provide to secure personal rewards.

Organizational Type and Culture

Additional characteristics of organizations impact the behavior of dark triad personalities. Engelen, Neumann, and Schmidt (2016) asked whether entrepreneurially oriented firms should employ narcissistic CEOs. While the general assumption is that firms with high levels of entrepreneurial orientation outperform their competitors, their specific study, which included a sample of publicly listed high-tech firms, examined whether the strength of this relationship depends on the CEO's narcissism. Their study introduced the CEO's narcissism as a moderator in the entrepreneurial orientation–performance relationship, and its findings indicate that the positive relationship between entrepreneurial orientation and shareholder value is in general weakened when CEO narcissism is strong. They concluded that narcissistic CEOs should usually not be hired to lead entrepreneurially oriented firms because the negative effects of these CEOs on performance usually outweigh their positive effects.

Pilch and Turska (2015) found that being bullied is related to perceptions of the cultures of clan, adhocracy, and hierarchy. The relationships between the clan and adhocracy cultures and being bullied are negative. Lack of excessive rules limiting freedom of action may be advantageous for minimizing the phenomenon of bullying. The clan culture does not favor bullying because of the high appreciation of interpersonal contacts, cooperation, and teamwork; a friendly atmosphere; and a sense of community among the clan members. Adhocracy may limit the bullying of employees by managers because of the fluent structure and lack of strict hierarchy that distinguish this culture from that of hierarchy. The culture of hierarchy seems to be in favor of bullying behaviors. In large bureaucratic structures, employees' problems may not be noticed and authority may be abused (Pilch & Turska, 2015).

In their study among employees in Poland, Pilch and Turska (2015) found that Machiavellianism was a moderator of the relations between perceptions of the hierarchy and adhocracy culture and being a victim of workplace bullying. If the culture is in favor of bullying behaviors (as in the case of hierarchy), non-aggressive and prosocial non-Machiavellians may experience violence more often than manipulative and cynical Machiavellians. Conversely, when the culture consists of features discouraging the abuse of others (adhocracy), employees low in Machiavellianism benefit more. The study also showed that the favorable working environment seems to have a protective function also against high-Machiavellian employees.

Penney and Spector (2002) found an effect of job constraint on the relationship between narcissists and CWB. First, a small but significant positive correlation was found between narcissism and job constraints, suggesting that narcissistic individuals were more likely to perceive constraints. In addition, job constraints and CWB were strongly and positively correlated. The more interesting finding, however, was the moderating effect of narcissism on the relationship between job constraints and CWB. Specifically, their results indicated that when narcissism was low, the incidence of CWB remained low across several levels of constraints. However, when narcissism was high, the slope of the line changed, so that CWB increased as the constraints increased. These findings suggest that job constraints, or circumstances that prevent successful job performance, do not affect everyone in the same manner. That is, there are individual differences in the way people respond to constraining circumstances. Taken together, these findings suggest that personality traits may be effective predictors of CWB under difficult or trying conditions.

Boddy (2011a) cited Wakefield's (2008) study that found an effect of the profession on the relative Machiavellianism scores. According to the study, accountancy is among the least Machiavellian and purchasing management among the most Machiavellian professions. Similarly, the Machiavellianism scores of students majoring in social work were significantly lower than those of students majoring in law and business. Boddy suggested, based on Wakefield's (2008) findings, that perhaps the "caring professions" attract lower numbers of those selfishly attracted to power and money, including Machiavellians and corporate psychopaths, than do other professions. Support for the above contention was found by Bucknall, Burwaiss, MacDonald, Charles, and Clement (2015). Their study on a sample of UK health care professionals showed that the respondents expressed lower levels of dark triad personality traits than the general population. According to the authors, their results demonstrate that the integrity of the health care profession remains steadfast. The low levels of Machiavellianism in this cohort show that they are able to put their patients' concerns above their own. They also found that as a group, health care workers are less narcissistic than the general public, with a mean score in the general population cohort similar to that reported by other studies.

Finally, an interesting issue regarding a highly relevant setting was noted by Perry (2015), who asked whether a leader of a university department with high levels of the dark triad traits could derail his or her unit. The term "leader" refers to any academic who is given responsibility for major outcomes in a university, such as a department or program head. The term "derail" refers to a unit going "off the rails" because it does not produce the required outcomes. In contrast to businesses, universities are usually heavily regulated, government subsidized organizations. Leadership in university is different from leadership in other types of organizations. The concept of academic freedom within a classroom or laboratory limits most of the "executive" power. Paradoxically, it may also foster the development of dark triad personalities among academics who are non-leaders and who may become leaders in the medium to long term. Their freedom could mean there are few constraints on the rise of narcissism among them, so the emergence of dark triad traits among academic leaders may actually be more pronounced than in business settings (Perry, 2015).

According to Perry, dark triad leaders foster less collaboration in the university unit, leaving the unit at a mediocre rather than an excellent level. There are managerialism forces operating in universities that may enhance sociopathy, but the unusual characteristics of the structure of universities suggest that leaders with dark triad traits cannot derail them. That is, a dark triad leader could degrade the collaborative nature of the academic work, as well as affect students and society enough to create mediocrity in the department but not enough to derail it. Dark triad leaders can probably create mediocrity but not much else. Yet there has been little examination of the effect of the dark triad leaders in universities (Perry, 2015). Perry and Miller (2017) demonstrated, drawing on case research, that sociopathic leaders exist in universities and that their actions can cause a toxic environment, leading to dysfunctional outcomes for the institutions. The case studies presented by Perry and Miller (2017) demonstrated that sociopathic leadership might produce an outcome of mediocrity or one of derailment of the organizational unit. Perry and Miller (2017) concluded the examination of dark triad personalities in university settings presents a very challenging and fascinating research area. More research on it can only enrich our understanding of the dark triad in general and in university settings in particular. We all should remember that they are among academics, too.

In sum, the issue of the cultural effects of dark triad personalities in the workplace is both stimulating and important. Yet the research in this area is quite sparse (Cohen, 2016). Most of the studies on the cultural effects on dark triad personalities have applied only to the dimension of individualism/collectivism. Future research should look at the relationship between other cultural values and dark triad personalities because it is reasonable to assume that the other three individual values might also affect the dark triad traits across cultures. More research is needed on almost every aspect reviewed here. The comparison of the public and the private sectors is important both conceptually and practically. We need more evidence to be certain that the public sectors attract more dark triad personalities. Is it possible that the higher prevalence of dark triad personalities in the public sector causes the assumed lower effectivity of the public sector in comparison with the private sector? This is a very important question that can be answered only by future research.

References

Boddy, C. R. (2010a). Corporate psychopaths and organizational type. *Journal of Public Affairs*, 10(4), 300–312.

Boddy, C. R. (2010b). *Corporate Psychopaths in Australian Workforce: Their Influence on Organizational Outcomes*. Perth: Curtin University of Technology.

Boddy, C. R. (2011a). *Corporate Psychopaths: Organizational Destroyers*. London: Palgrave MacMillan.

Boddy, C. R. (2015). Organizational psychopaths: A ten-year update. *Management Decision*, 53(10), 2407–2432.

Bucknall, V., Burwaiss, S., MacDonald, D., Charles, K., & Clement, R. (2015). Mirror mirror on the ward, who's the most narcissistic of them all? Pathologic personality traits in health care. *Canadian Medical Association Journal*, 187(18), 1359–1363.

Cohen, A. (2015). *Fairness in the Workplace: A Global Perspective*. New York, NY: Palgrave McMillan.

Cohen, A. (2016). Are they among us? A conceptual framework of the relationship between the dark triad personality and counterproductive work behaviors (CWBs). *Human Resource Management Review*, 26(1), 69–85.

Dahling, J. J., Whitaker, B. G., & Levy, P. E. (2009). The development and validation of a new Machiavellianism scale. *Journal of Management*, 35(2), 219–257.

Engelen, A., Neumann, C., & Schmidt, S. (2016). Should entrepreneurially oriented firms have narcissistic CEOs? *Journal of Management*, 42(3), 698–721.

Fennimore, A., & Sementelli, A. (2016). Public entrepreneurship and sub-clinical psychopaths: A conceptual frame and implications. *International Journal of Public Sector Management*, 29(6), 612–634.

Ferris, G. R., Fedor, D. B., & King, T. R. (1994). A political conceptualization of managerial behavior. *Human Resource Management Review, 4*, 1–34.

Gaddis, B. H., & Foster, J. L. (2015). Meta-analysis of dark side personality characteristics and critical work behaviors among leaders across the globe: Findings and implications for leadership development and executive coaching. *Applied Psychology: An International Review, 64*(1), 25–54.

Glenn, A. L., Kurzban, R., & Raine, A. (2011). Evolutionary theory and psychopathy. *Aggression and Violent Behavior, 16*(5), 371–380.

Grijalva, E., & Newman, D. A. (2015). Narcissism and counterproductive work behavior (CWB): Meta-analysis and consideration of collectivist culture, Big Five personality, and narcissism's facet structure. *Applied Psychology: An International Review, 64*(1), 93–126.

Hanson, L., & Baker, D. L. (2017). "Corporate psychopaths" in public agencies? *Journal of Public Management & Social Policy, 24*(1), 21–41.

Hare, R. D. (1999). *Without Conscience: The Disturbing World of the Psychopaths among Us*. New York, NY: Guilford Press.

Harms, P. D., & Spain, M. S. (2015). Beyond the bright side: Dark personality at work. *Applied Psychology: An International Review, 64*(1), 15–24.

Hofstede, G. (1980). *Culture's Consequences: International Differences in Work-Related Values*. Beverly Hills, CA: Sage Publications, Inc.

Hofstede, G. (1991). *Cultures and Organizations: Software of the Mind*. New York, NY: McGraw-Hill.

Hofstede, G. (1993). Cultural constraints in management theories. *Academy of Management Executive, 7*(1), 81–94.

Hofstede, G. (2001). *Culture's Consequences: Comparing Values, Behaviors, Institutions and Organizations across Nations*. Thousand Oaks, CA: Sage Publications, Inc.

Jonason, P. K., Li, N. P., & Czarna, A. Z. (2013a). Quick and dirty: Some psychosocial costs associated with the dark triad in three countries. *Evolutionary Psychology, 11*(1), 172–185.

Jonason, P. K., Strosser, G. L., Kroll, C. H., Duineveld, J. J., & Baruffi, S. A. (2015). Valuing myself over others: The dark triad traits and moral and social values. *Personality and Individual Differences, 81*, 102–106.

Kajonius, P. J., Persson, B. N., & Jonason, P. K. (2015). Hedonism, achievement, and power: Universal values that characterize the dark triad. *Personality and Individual Differences, 77*, 173–178.

Mathieu, C., Neumann, C. S., Hare, R. D., & Babiak, P. (2014). A dark side of leadership: Corporate psychopathy and its influence on employee well-being and job satisfaction. *Personality and Individual Differences, 59*, 83–88.

O'Boyle Jr., E. H., Forsyth, D. R., Banks, G. C., & McDaniel, M. A. (2012). A meta-analysis of the dark triad and work behavior: A social exchange perspective. *Journal of Applied Psychology, 97*(3), 557–579.

Penney, L. M., & Spector, P. E. (2002). Narcissism and counterproductive work behavior: Do bigger egos mean bigger problems? *International Journal of Selection and Assessment, 10*(1–2), 126–134.

Perry, C. (2015). The "dark traits" of sociopathic leaders: Could they be a threat to universities? *Australian Universities' Review, 57*(1), 17–24.

Perry, C., & Miller, P. (2017). Dysfunctional leadership in universities: Identifying and dealing with sociopaths. *Management, Leadership and Marketing of Universities and Colleges of Higher Education*, Forthcoming.

Pilch, I., & Turska, E. (2015). Relationships between Machiavellianism, organizational culture, and workplace bullying: Emotional abuse from the target's and the perpetrator's perspective. *Journal of Business Ethics, 128*(1), 83–93.

Robertson, S. A., Datu, J. A. D., Brawley, A. M., Pury, C. L., & Mateo, N. J. (2016). The dark triad and social behavior: The influence of self-construal and power distance. *Personality and Individual Differences*, 98, 69–74.

Schwartz, S. H. (1992). Universals in the content and structure of values: Theory and empirical tests in 20 countries. In M. Zanna (Ed.), *Advances in Experimental Social Psychology* (Vol. 25, pp. 1–65). New York: Academic Press.

Schwartz, S. H. (2005). Robustness and fruitfulness of a theory on universals in individual human values. In A. Tamayo & J. B. Porto (Eds.), *Valores e trabalho* [*Values and Work*] (pp. 56–95). Brasilia: Editora Universidade de Brasilia.

Schwartz, S. H., & Sagiv, L. (1995). Identifying culture-specifics in the content and structure of values. *Journal of Cross-Cultural Psychology*, 26, 92–116.

Shao, R., Rupp, D. E., Skarlicki, D. P., & Jones, K. S. (2013). Employee justice across cultures: A meta-analytic review. *Journal of Management*, 39, 263–301.

Steiner, D. D. (2001). Cultural influences on perceptions of distributive and procedural justice. In S. W. Gilliland, D. D. Steiner, & D. Skarlicki (Eds.), *Theoretical and Cultural Perspectives on Organizational Justice: Research in Social Issues in Management* (pp. 111–137). Greenwich, CT: Information Age Publishing.

Stout, M. (2005a). The ice people: Living among us are people with no conscience, no emotions and no conception of love: Welcome to the chilling world of the sociopath. *Psychology Today*, 38(1), 72–76.

Stout, M. (2005b). *The Sociopath Next Door: The Ruthless vs. the Rest of Us*. New York: Broadway Books.

Thomas, D. C., Au, K., & Ravlin, E. C. (2003). Cultural variation and the psychological contract. *Journal of Organizational Behavior*, 24(5), 451–471.

Thomas, D. C., Fitzsimmons, S. R., Ravlin, E. C., Au, K., Ekelund, B., & Barzantny, C. (2010). Psychological contracts across cultures. *Organization Studies*, 31(11), 1437–1458.

Twenge, J. M. (2011). Narcissism and culture. In W. K. Campbell & J. D. Miller (Eds.), *The Handbook of Narcissism and Narcissistic Personality Disorder: Theoretical Approaches, Empirical Findings, and Treatments* (pp. 202–209). New York: Wiley.

Van der Wal, Z., De Graaf, G., & Lasthuizen, K. (2008). What's valued most? Similarities and differences between the organizational values of the public and private sector. *Public Administration*, 86(2), 465–482.

Wakefield, R. L. (2008). Accounting and Machiavellianism. *Behavioral Research in Accounting*, 20(1), 115–129.

11 Conceptual and Practical Implications

"Why does evil exist?" is a classic question about the nature of the universe and humankind (Jonason, Icho, & Ireland, 2016). Despite considerable efforts to eliminate antisocial personality traits from the population through religion (e.g., by the threat of damnation), laws (e.g., by the threat of imprisonment), social movements (e.g., by encouraging self-esteem), and institutional sanctions (e.g., by the threat of being fired), these traits continue and, by all accounts, may have always been present. It may be impossible to eliminate them because they are present in everyone to some extent. All people may have the potential to be high or low in the dark triad traits, which are inherent in the human genotype. Over the course of life, events narrow that potential and shape individuals' personalities and attitudes to create their affective phenotypes. This means that exposure to specific conditions is the precipitating factor that determines people's trait activation and positions on the dark triad continuum. Childhood experiences, which are unpredictable, may be some of the prerequisite conditions to activate the dormant selfishness, competiveness, and antisociality found in the dark triad traits (Jonason et al., 2016).

Although the dark triad traits are part of the encoded genotype at least of humans, if not of most species that could benefit from opportunism, selfishness, and exploitiveness at times given certain contextual factors, they become the affective phenotype only in a few. As discussed in Chapter 3, the dark triad traits may be condition-dependent adaptations to solve life's adaptive problems in the face of an unpredictable and harsh world. From this perspective, the dark triad traits could be phenotypic responses to predetermined and evolutionary relevant information, responses (Jonason et al., 2016). The dark personalities are among us everywhere and in every setting (Cohen, 2016). They will always be there. The best way to cope with them is to know them better.

The present book covers the characteristics and the behavioral and organizational implications of dark personalities in the work setting, an area that was rather neglected in managerial research for many years. However, in recent years, probably also because of specific financial and organizational crises, there has been a greater awareness of the dark triad personalities and as a result, increasing academic research on the issue. Further research is badly needed in this area to contribute to the building of a body of knowledge that will explain the impact of dark triad personalities on organizations (Boddy, 2006). This book is a result of the evident revitalized interest in the subject. It is based on the more updated, although somewhat limited, amount of research on the topic. As mentioned in the introduction, the book takes a strong managerial rather than a clinical approach; it is academic and managerial orientated but not clinical or psychological oriented. It is intended for researchers and practitioners in management because, evidently, dark triad personalities exist and negatively influence organizations and employees. Therefore, there is a growing need to familiarize scholars and managers with these dark personalities to enable them to better understand and cope with them.

The previous chapters covered many of the relevant managerial aspects of this phenomenon. The present chapter presents issues that according to leading scholars need further clarification. The present chapter also suggests directions for future research. Such research would stimulate debate on this issue in academic circles outside the disciplines of psychology and criminology and in particular bring it to the attention of business strategists and other academics involved in conducting research in the field of business (Boddy, 2006). In addition, this chapter also presents practical guidelines for optimally managing the dark triad personalities. These guidelines are based on the knowledge accumulated so far and might assist in managing destructive employees and managers.

Conceptual Issues

More darkness or less? (Do we need more or fewer dark traits?) One of the more important issues for future research is whether knowledge of dark triad traits provides the optimal approach for understanding the malevolent side of human nature. While some scholars strongly believe in the explanatory power of these three traits operating in concert, some scholars suggest expanding the dark triad into the "dark tetrad" by adding a fourth trait, sadism (Muris, Merckelbach, Otgaar, & Meijer, 2017). Sadism represents a combination of different behavioral, cognitive, and interpersonal characteristics related to pleasure in connection with inflicting physical or emotional pain on other persons, with the aim to control, punish, and humiliate them (Mededović & Petrović, 2015). According to Mededović and Petrović (2015), studies have shown that sadism and the dark triad traits, primarily psychopathy, have many characteristics in common, such as a lack of empathy and readiness for emotional involvement (Kirsch & Becker, 2007), a willingness to inflict suffering on others, and a connection with antisocial behavior (Chabrol, Van Leeuwen, Rodgers, & Séjourné, 2009). They also noted that, at the same time, findings indicate that these are connected but distinct traits (Mokros, Osterheider, Hucker, & Nitschke, 2011).

Based on their study, Mededović and Petrović (2015) concluded that it is plausible to broaden the dark triad model to include sadistic traits. They mentioned that such a model was already proposed by some researchers (Buckels, Jones, & Paulhus, 2013; Chabrol et al., 2009; Paulhus, 2014). According to them, the expanded model of the dark traits would deepen our understanding of amoral and antisocial personality dispositions, which could result in practical implementations. However, considerably more research is needed in order to establish a conclusion as to whether it would be effective to broaden the dark triad to the dark tetrad.

Harms and Spain (2015) also contended that there is more to dark personality than just the dark triad. Despite the current situation, in which the use of the dark triad as a framework continues to dominate the organizational sciences, we are seeing the beginnings of efforts, such as the *Diagnostic and Statistical Manual of Mental Disorders,* fifth edition (*DSM-5*), to focus on other dark characteristics, in addition to sadism, that may be particularly important in the workplace. According to Harms and Spain, the new *DSM-5* model is revolutionary in that it divides the widely used dimensions of personality disorders into subdimensions in order to better understand the comorbidity of different disorders and allow effective treatment. For example, Machiavellianism might be reconsidered as a combination of the hostility, suspiciousness, callousness, deceitfulness, and manipulativeness dimensions. Harms and Spain (2015) mentioned that, beyond the new models of dark personality, a literature is emerging concerning specific traits, such as paranoia, that did not receive much attention in prior organizational research. In addition, psychodynamic frameworks may provide particularly rich theoretical models for understanding dark personalities in the workplace.

However, by the same token, there are scholars who suggest that there is a need to reduce the number of the dimensions making up the dark triad. Kowalski, Vernon, and Schermer (2016) found in a sample of Canadian employees that the General Factor of Personality, extracted from the Five-Factor Model (FFM), was significantly and negatively correlated with Machiavellianism and psychopathy and had a non-significant correlation with narcissism. Based on this finding, they suggested that perhaps it would be justified to view narcissism as not belonging in the dark triad. Unlike Machiavellianism and psychopathy, narcissism is associated with some positive outcomes. Instead, a dark dyad of Machiavellianism and psychopathy, with a related but separate narcissism model, should be proposed. Kowalsk et al. maintain that their findings are in line with previous studies, suggesting that narcissism is less malevolent than Machiavellianism and psychopathy. Similarly, Klotz and Neubaum (2016) cited DiNisi (2015), who noted that, while narcissists want to be praised and recognized for their work, this does not necessarily mean that they will engage in deviance to achieve these ends. Narcissism is the lighter dimension of the dark triad and has also positive outcomes for organizations and individuals. Future research should explore whether narcissism should be included among the dark traits.

Clearly, much more research is needed to explore these important issues regarding the dimensionality of the dark triad, in light of some of the findings presented in this book. For example, the findings showing that psychopathy is the core dimension of the dark triad and the two other dimensions do not add much to the explanatory power of the dark triad traits. Another issue mentioned earlier is whether narcissism is dark enough to be considered a dark personality construct. Or perhaps sadism should replace it? Furthermore, research suggests that the similarity between the dimensions is stronger than their differences and therefore research should consider the dark triad as one dimension. Should we use a combined measure of the dark triad instead of separate dimensions? All these issues are important and need further research in order to develop a more valid conceptualization of the dark traits.

Measurement Issues

Measurement of counterproductive work behavior (CWB): CWB is the reason for the growing interest in the dark triad personalities. Therefore, valid information and measurement of this behavior is needed. One important issue is the source of the data on CWB. According to Kim and Cohen (2015), information obtained through self-reports on organizational deviance, including CWB, is in many cases preferable to other reports, including the supervisor's report. In support of self-reports over other-reports when investigating workplace deviance, they argued that employees' self-ratings revealed more instances of CWB than the ratings of coworkers. Furthermore, other-reported CWB did not provide incremental predictive power beyond the self-reported CWB. Presumably, this is because employees keep many of their deviant behaviors private, hiding them from colleagues and supervisors. Thus, while acquaintance ratings of moral character add information beyond self-reports, the same is not necessarily true of ratings of workplace deviance. This information should be taken into account in future research on the relationship between the dark triad and any form of organizational deviant behavior. Future research should further examine the differences between self-reported CWB and supervisors' reports so that researchers will have more information regarding the preferred measure of CWB. In addition, more research is needed on the dimensionality of CWB.

Measurement of the dark triad traits: More precise measurement of dark personality traits is needed. Efforts should be invested in ensuring that both construct breadth and construct specificity are maintained. That is, measures that are so short that they lose construct validity should be avoided. Moreover, measures should be developed with the goal of ensuring that the characteristics under investigation are unique and well defined. For this reason, it is preferable to develop measures that assess more comprehensive models of dark personalities than those of the traits in isolation. This would allow researchers to avoid problems related to overlapping content (Harms & Spain, 2015).

Because most dark triad research relies exclusively on self-report measures, it suffers from the same shortcomings that limit all self-report findings (e.g., socially desirable responding). Therefore, there is a real need for alternative measurement techniques. Some interesting alternative techniques mentioned by Harms and Spain (2015) are peer nominations, projective measures, and conditional reasoning tests. Another technique for assessing dark characteristics concerns content coding of written statements and interviews and using behavioral markers to indicate the presence of dark characteristics. A related technique, using personal appearance as an indicator of dark personality, has shown promise as well. Most of these approaches are in their infancy, and only time will tell whether or not they will prove effective for research and practice.

Finally, future research should also examine the effect of the magnitudes of the dark triads. According to Herbst (2014), personality disorders are not taxonomic but rather dimensional. This means that there are not differences in the kind of psychopathology per se but rather differences in degree. Someone can therefore have a low or a high level of a dark triad trait or somewhere in between. This book argues that all managers, as well as all politicians, need a certain level of the dark triad traits to function effectively. They need to have confidence in themselves, which is a certain level of narcissism; they need to have political qualifications, which involves a certain level of Machiavellianism; and they need to have a degree of insensitivity to the feelings of others when, for example, they terminate the employment of unqualified employees or promote one person instead of another. But what is the level of the dark triad traits that turns managers from effective managers into managers that only damage the organization? Can we develop a diagram that will show us from which level of the dark triad traits a manager becomes ineffective for the organization and his or her colleagues (Herbst, 2014)? Future research should examine and determine the effect of different levels of the dark triad traits on the effectiveness of managers and employees.

Conceptual recommendations: Despite the promising conceptual work on dark triad personalities, well-developed theoretical models to guide research and practice as to when dark personality characteristics should matter most and the potential mediators and moderators of their effects are still scarce (Harms & Spain, 2015; Cohen, 2016). Little is known about the processes or mechanisms that link the dark triad traits with behavior (Jonason, Webster, Schmitt, Li, & Crysel, 2012a). Boddy (2015), for example, mentioned that the issue of the reasons why psychopaths bully has not been adequately explored in research and remains an unresolved area. However, it is clear that psychopaths and bullying go together. Future research should continue the search for additional moderators and mediators in the relationship between the dark triad traits and different forms of CWB. A promising step toward such a comprehensive model was advanced by Cohen (2016) and presented earlier. However, this model is only a preliminary step, and future research that examines Cohen's model or others should consider some of the following suggestions.

For instance, it would be interesting to examine the manner in which exchange and justice processes affect CWBs committed by dark triad personalities. How would the psychological contract breach affect dark triad CWB? O'Boyle, Forsyth, Banks, and McDaniel (2012) suggested such a perspective in their meta-analysis, but there is a need for a direct empirical examination of exchange variables as mediators or moderators. Future research should also consider demographic variables as possible moderators. For example, it would be important to examine whether the model advanced by Cohen (2016) would predict CWB more strongly for men than for women. Some evidence exists that gender affects the CWB of men more strongly than that of women (Bowling & Burns, 2015; Baughman, Dearing, Giammarco, & Vernon, 2012). While the direct relationship of demographic variables with CWB was not strong, as reported by several meta-analyses (Berry, Ones, & Sackett, 2007; Berry, Carpenter, & Barratt, 2012), these variables may operate better as possible moderators in the relationship between dark triad personalities and CWB.

Future research should examine the possible moderation of individual differences in levels of cynicism and trust because these relate, through the mediated relationship of abusive supervision, to workplace deviance through work-related negative affect (Michel, Newness, & Duniewicz, 2016). Other potential moderators that need further examination might be in-group status (in that the dark personality might only translate into toxic behaviors toward the out-group) or type of profession (in that dark personality in some contexts can be expressed in less toxic behaviors) (Schyns, 2015).

A very promising future research direction is the effect of the dark triad personalities from a collectivistic viewpoint, that is, studies that examine how the dark triad personalities of managers affect other people in the workplace. For example, Boddy (2014) found that unethical leadership in the form of corporate psychopaths involves not only behaving incorrectly but also setting a bad example and motivating others to behave badly. Future research should, therefore, examine how the unethical behavior of dark triad personalities can contaminate others in the workplace if left unchecked (Grijalva & Harms, 2014). Unethical employees can create an organizational culture in which unethical behavior becomes the norm, especially when leaders or authority figures are misbehaving. Future research should investigate whether narcissists, as well as psychopaths and Machiavellians, will take advantage of their more submissive coworkers.

Mathieu, Neumann, Hare, and Babiak (2014) found a significant positive relationship between employees' ratings of psychopathy traits in their supervisors and employee's self-reported psychological distress and low job satisfaction. They also found that the psychopathy trait in supervisors increases the work–family conflict among their subordinates. The possibility that dark triad managers cause higher absenteeism among their employees should also be examined in future research. Belschak, Den Hartog, and Kalshoven (2015) similarly contended that only limited research has been conducted on Machiavellianism and leadership to date. Whether and how leader behavior affects Machiavellian followers has not yet received research attention.

An interesting and stimulating direction based on the distinction between the three toxic personalities is to explore whether corporate psychopaths reach corporate leadership positions first. They may be surrounded by lieutenants who are Machiavellians and too ruthless and wedded to power to want to challenge the unconscionable decisions of the corporate psychopaths. Under the Machiavellians may be narcissistic managers who also do not challenge unethical decisions because they want their bosses to like them and they want power. Thus, the entire corporation might go bad from the top down (Boddy, 2011a). This is definitely a dark scenario that is worthwhile exploring in future research.

Another interesting question for future research is whether dark triad personalities are more prevalent in the public than in the private sector (Cohen, 2016). From the point of view of the person–organization fit theory (Kristof, 1996; Yu, 2014), it can be argued that the public sector may attract more such personalities than the private one. As aforementioned, in the public sector, the organization's goals are more ambiguous, the level of organizational politics is known to be higher, and the individual performance of employees is usually not related to the organizations' profits or even to the employees' income. Such circumstances create a friendlier surrounding for psychopaths because in such an environment, they and their activities are more difficult to detect. Future research should determine the incidence of psychopaths, as well as narcissists and Machiavellians, across sectors, including public and non-profit, to uncover whether dark triad personalities are more prevalent in the public, non-profit, and private sectors. Further examination of psychopaths in public organizations is necessary to build a behavioral theory for the public sector (Fennimore & Sementelli, 2016).

Mikkelsen and Einarsen (2002) noted the importance of conducting research on the cognitive coping strategies of victims. According to them, future research endeavors should focus on individuals' perception of both the bullying and its sequelae because these factors may play an important role in explaining individual differences in reported stress symptoms among victims of bullying at work. Furthermore, because their results indicate that many victims suffer from post-traumatic syndrome disorder, the need to develop therapeutic guidelines similar to those directed at other trauma groups is stressed. On the basis of their findings, the researchers suggested that an important therapeutic goal would be to assist victims in rebuilding a new set of viable and mature basic assumptions about themselves, other people, and the world.

According to Harms and Spain (2015), if we want to understand the dark personality in the workplace, we need to understand how the effects of various traits play out at different levels of analysis. To date, there has been very little research on or theory developed about the issues of the interactions of individuals using similar or different pairings of dark personality traits. There have been few systematic attempts to study the interactions between different dark traits displayed by different individuals in the workplace. There is almost no information on how different mean levels and distributions of dark personality characteristics among team members might impact team performance. At the strategic or firm level, little research has been conducted to document the role of the personality characteristics of corporate leaders and how it influences firm performance and even less research on dark personality characteristics. Harms and Spain (2015) concluded that research investigating dark personality at the dyadic, group, and firm levels would greatly enhance our understanding of these constructs and reinforce the importance of dark personality in organizational life.

As the main dimension of the dark triad traits, several specific suggestions for future research on psychopathy have been advanced by scholars. First, there is a need to resolve the conceptual definition of this construct as being unidimensional or multidimensional. How should psychopathy be best defined? In addition, according to Fennimore and Sementelli (2016), psychopathy has been related to dysfunction of the amygdala (i.e., the part of the brain that regulates emotions). Therefore, future research could adapt some of the experimental designs in the form of questionnaires that consider dysfunction of the amygdala. Future research may pursue questions of gender differences in psychopathic entrepreneurs and leaders. Psychopathy has largely been identified as existing in the male population. As a clinical personality disorder, psychopathy is estimated to occur in 1% to 3% of men and 0.5% to 1% of women. Fennimore and Sementelli contended that more gender research is needed to distinguish subclinical psychopathy in management and leadership studies. Measurement scales may need to be reassessed further to determine whether gender differences do exist.

Boddy (2006) raised an interesting issue that would contribute to a better understanding of the dark side of organizations, namely, corporations as psychopathic entities. According to Boddy, it has been suggested that corporations themselves could be psychopathic because of their lack of conscience.

Boddy cited Hare (1994, 1999), suggesting that corporations do have the characteristics of psychopathy according to the definition of the World Health Organization, which states that psychopaths display the characteristics of being callous to the feelings of others, incapable of maintaining enduring relationships, reckless regarding the safety of others, deceitful, and incapable of experiencing guilt and that they display a failure to conform to social norms and laws. Corporations that have become psychopathic engage in activities such as seeking out loopholes in the law to avoid taxes and regulations, manipulating their stock prices when possible to the benefit of executives with shares and share option schemes and the detriment of investors, pension fund holders, and workers. Corporations engage in illegal accounting practices to conceal these activities, regardless of the long-term implications of doing so. If corporations themselves display psychopathic characteristics, then the effect must be amplified or even multiplied when some or all the managers running those corporations are organizational psychopaths as well. Here, the lack of any conscience or guiding sense of morality in the corporation can be a recipe for financial, environmental, and social disaster. Future research should further examine this stimulating research agenda.

Cross-Cultural Research Recommendations

Cultural research on the dark triad personalities and their relationship to CWB is very rare. In addition to the cross-cultural perspective, which is based in many cases on nationality or ethnicity, future research should also examine organizational and occupational/professional cultures. Concerning cross-cultural/national cultures, it is clearly important to examine the relevance of the dark triad in non-Western societies because the constructs and measures have been developed primarily in the US. Robertson, Datu, Brawley, Pury, and Mateo (2016) mentioned in a recent meta-analysis of the dark triad and employee performance (O'Boyle et al., 2012) that only 4 of 186 studies drew samples from predominantly collectivistic societies. According to Jonason et al. (2012a), because samples for examining dark triad personalities tend to be drawn exclusively from countries with some Western European or American ties, these findings are difficult to generalize. As compared with the FFM personality traits, the dark triad has attracted relatively little cross-cultural research, and the subject is traditionally approached from either an etic or an emic perspective. Lacking significant empirical evidence, there is a need for further research using both etic and emic approaches, preferably a combination of the two.

Therefore, scholars strongly recommended more cross-cultural research on dark personalities. For example, further research should investigate the impacts of corporate psychopaths on employees in different countries and cultures and examine potential strategies for dealing with them in the workplace (Boddy, 2011a). Much more research on Machiavellianism from a cross-cultural perspective is also needed. In addition, most cross-cultural studies have examined one main cultural value, namely, collectivism versus individualism. Future research should examine the effect of the other values advanced by Hofstede (2001) on dark triad behaviors and also apply other cross-cultural theories, such as that of Schwartz (1992).

Another interesting cross-cultural question that requires further research is what will happen when successful narcissists (or psychopaths or Machiavellians) are sent to work abroad, especially from individualistic to collectivistic countries (Grijalva & Harms, 2014). Narcissists' sense of entitlement could blind them to the need to adapt to cultural norms, leading to them alienating coworkers, and this may harm the company's international relations. If it were known that narcissists make unsuccessful expatriates because they do not adapt their interpersonal style to that which is prevalent abroad, organizations could take this information into consideration when deciding which employees to send abroad. This kind of knowledge is directly relevant to international human resources (HR) management.

In short, although recent studies demonstrated differences in the dark triad between culturally distinct societies, this line of inquiry should still be continued, not only regarding measurement issues but also regarding the possible different patterns of dark triad personalities as predictors of CWB in different cultures. Dark triad personalities in the workplace may have different expressions in various cultures, especially in those with more collectivist versus individualistic attitudes. Research across cultures is therefore needed to provide a comprehensive understanding of the implications of dark triad personalities for the workplace. The culture of the organization itself is also important with regard to dark triad personalities and their tendencies to perpetrate CWB. As discussed in the book, dark triads are looking for clues to sense the organizational environment and to diagnose how friendly it is for them before they operate. In addition to that involving more research on the moderators and mediators presented here, scholars have advanced some other interesting research agendas. Boddy (2015), for example, suggested that it would also be useful to answer the research question of what percent of organizational leaders across different economic sectors are psychopathic. The already identified 1% to 4% distribution in an organization (Babiak, Neumann, & Hare, 2010) may not be true of some industries. In addition, the extent of the concentration of psychopathic leaders that can influence the entire culture of the organization would be a worthwhile research area. The related question of whether some industries have high concentrations of psychopaths in one group together with low average psychopathy scores among another group would also be worth investigating. For example, in a hospital, surgeons might belong to the former group and nurses to the latter. Such a setting would theoretically provide a unique combination of predator and prey in the same locale. This combination may facilitate organizational behavior such as bullying.

Boddy (2015) raised another interesting issue for a future research agenda, namely, the speed with which the culture of an organization changes after the appointment of a psychopathic manager. Qualitative research indicates that such a change is more rapid than may be expected and that the work ethic and culture of an organization changes within weeks or months of appointing a psychopath to a leadership position. Any such finding would reinforce the need for screening for psychopaths in leadership positions. According to Boddy (2015), the speculated links between corporate psychopaths and corporate failure, such as that which is evident in the corporate banks involved in the global financial crisis, is under-explored. Also in need of exploration is the possible connection between corporate psychopaths, their recruitment by corporate banks, the global financial crisis, and the recurring ethical (and legal) lapses of corporate banks. It would be very interesting in that regard to examine the effects of psychopaths in the academia. Perry (2015) suggested that perhaps the nature of the university culture and its relatively autonomous system of governance may mitigate the effects of a single psychopath in that workplace. An empirical investigation of dark triads in the academic setting would be both challenging and useful.

Finally, Boddy (2011a) suggested that it would be interesting to investigate whether certain professional groups contain more corporate psychopaths than others. Do social workers, for example, exhibit lower corporate psychopathy scores than corporate bankers or accountants or purchasing managers? Research examining occupations and avocations that may attract psychopathic individuals is also sorely needed. For example, individuals who are fearless and enjoy risk taking may find high-risk professions, such as the military, law enforcement, and extreme sports, particularly desirable. Research targeting these and other professions may help us to better understand the controversial and often elusive successful psychopath (Smith, Watts, & Lilienfeld, 2014).

Practical Implications

This section discusses practical recommendations for managers and practitioners. Despite the complexity of detecting and avoiding dark triad personalities, organizations can limit their destructive conduct (Cohen, 2016). The best option for organizations wishing to forestall the destructive activities of dark triad personalities is to create an environment that discourages such activities. The literature offers some interesting practical suggestions on how to deal with and minimize the destructive behavior and outcomes of dark triad personalities. These are presented next, first in more general terms and then specifically for each of the dark triad personalities.

How to Manage Dark Triad Personalities

An important issue is the detection of dark personalities during the selection process, which can be complicated because of the often covert nature of their traits. As discussed in previous chapters, organizations find it difficult to prevent the infiltration of psychopaths by means of the usual selection tools. In terms of relationships with others, narcissists seem often to come across as positive in the beginning but not in the longer run. This means that some dark personality traits might be difficult to detect in job interviews; in fact, the characteristics of psychopathy typically come across as positive attributes in the short term (Kaiser & Hogan, 2006). It should be noted that, while currently very limited attempts are made to detect psychopathy in the workplace for selection purposes, some studies employed scales developed for the evaluation by employees of their supervisors' level of psychopathy (Mathieu et al., 2014). Continued effort is needed in this direction to provide HR management with some tools that would enable them to screen job candidates for potential psychopaths.

In addition to improved screening procedures, dark triad personalities should be properly managed because preventing them from entering the organization is almost impossible. Delbecq (2001) mentioned several steps managers can take to prevent dark personalities from damaging the organization. The first step is to establish very clear group norms regarding collegial behavior, decision processes, and cultural values in the organization. According to Delbecq, culture does matter, and behavior that is normatively deviant will be identified much earlier when a strong organizational culture is in place. It is important that an organization does not leave managers and employees to rely on their moral intuition and good judgement alone but rather creates a culture in which the distinction between ethical and unethical behavior is clear (Kaptein, 2011). Taking time to establish the cultural norms, providing reminders of the norms, providing clear verbal reprimands when norms are violated, and keeping written records of deviation all help to bring destructive behavior to the surface (Hegarty & Sims, 1979; Padilla, Hogan, & Kaiser, 2007; Marshall, Ashleigh, Baden, Ojiako, & Guidi, 2015).

Another step is to take early warning signals seriously. Pausing to actually find out what is going on when morale signals are troubling is critical (Delbecq, 2001). When an evil behavior is discovered, it is important to persuade the management group and the work unit involved to stand shoulder to shoulder in confronting the problem. If it is deemed necessary to remove the destructive individual from the organization, it is important to seek counsel from experts who are experienced in dealing with this special category of behavior, given the modern legal climate.

Padilla et al. (2007) also suggested appropriate human resource management (HRM) development tools as an important tool for managing dark triad personalities. According to them, feedback and assessment tools are typically based on competency models, which focus on positive attributes associated with effective leaders and desirable leader qualities. Expanding this domain to include undesirable leader behaviors and attributes might lead to remedial activities to stave off destructive tendencies in leaders. The development of stronger followers by promoting a culture of empowerment is important in managing potential destructiveness. Destructive leaders exert their influence through unilateral power. Cultures that reinforce collaboration and employee initiative and involvement maintain balance and control over authoritarian power.

A related strategy is to reward leaders who develop leadership potential in their subordinates. Destructive leaders, particularly those who are unethical charismatics, neglect staff development. Making follower development an explicit criterion for promotion could reduce the likelihood that destructive individuals will emerge. In addition, by encouraging managers to develop subordinates, organizations might make their employees less likely to conform to destructive influences. Perhaps the most important environmental factor for preventing destructive leadership is the presence of checks and balances. Hierarchy, accountability, and a chain of command often provide the controls required at the lower organizational levels (Padilla et al., 2007).

Solas (2015) contended that it would be advisable to take seriously the results of behavioral audits of those at the top and bottom of an organization, published in annual reports. Comparisons, such as those included in the *State of the Service* reports, reveal the extent to which adherence to the moral tone, rather than code, of the organization, is shared. Organizations with a genuine interest in deterring psychopathic behavior may benefit from promoting the "mavericks" who resist enculturation rather than those credited with delivering "outstanding" corporate performances. Unsullied interpersonal processes are as important as exceeding key performance indicators and productivity levels. Developing valid and reliable performance evaluation systems is also a valuable tool for minimizing the destructive behaviors of dark triad personalities. For example, when evaluation criteria are unclear, greater reliance on factors unrelated to work behaviors are likely to influence job performance evaluations; workers can avoid being held accountable and blame others for negative outcomes (or take credit for positive ones). Thus, the importance of conducting quality performance evaluations cannot be overstated and in fact may be the only way to deal with dark triad personalities (Chiaburu, Muñoz, & Gardner, 2013).

How to Manage Psychopaths

There is little progress in research regarding the treatment of psychopaths because this disorder is mostly regarded as untreatable (Herbst, 2014). Herbst cited Hare (1999), who argued that most therapists are reluctant to work with sociopaths or psychopaths because they often end up damaged in the process. According to Hare, counseling would be wasted on psychopaths. Some of the psychopaths reflect the wishes of the therapist and pretend to be getting better. As stated by Herbst, the core elements of psychopathy make it particularly unapproachable and one of the most difficult disorders to treat. Herbst also mentioned Harris and Rice's (2006) conclusion that, for psychopaths, no clinical intervention would ever be helpful, and no effective interventions yet exist for them. In a more optimistic vein, some hope can be found in Fennimore and Sementel's (2016) contention that the prospect of rehabilitating the subclinical psychopath warrants further investigation. For instance, is there a threshold psychopathy score that would hinder or facilitate the likelihood of rehabilitation? Can positive aspects, such as tenacity and ambition, be channeled to benefit the organization and its subordinates?

Following this contention, it is not surprising that Boddy (2006), in a very pessimistic tone, cited Hare (1994, 1999), who argued that if we cannot identify psychopaths, we are forever doomed, both as individuals and as a society, to be their victims. Psychopaths are able to succeed in society and in corporations largely because their colleagues are unaware that people like them actually exist. Moreover, although more research has been conducted on psychopathy in men than women, inside and outside institutional settings, evidence suggests little gender differentiation between the syndrome's main personality factors and facets (Solas, 2015). Gender studies also indicate greater behavioral similarity between primary (negative affect) and secondary (antisociality) female than male psychopaths. Thus, policies promoting affirmative action and positive discrimination toward women are unlikely to attenuate the prevalence or impact of corporate psychopathy. The same may be said about succession planning designed to groom younger recruits for executive positions. Enterprising young employees with psychopathic tendencies have what it takes to excel as future corporate leaders. Organizations that intend to safeguard the health and welfare of their employees could do no worse than to cultivate the killer instinct.

However, the literature does provide some important recommendations for managing psychopaths better. Boddy (2011a) complained that organizations encourage the recruitment of corporate psychopaths. They do so by looking for aggressive, impartial, cunning, ruthless, go-getting, determined, dynamic, and highly ambitious employees. By following this strategy, corporations run a real risk of attracting people who will "go get" for themselves rather than for the company. Boddy suggested that organizations should be more measured and careful about how they advertise positions and about whom they recruit to avoid hiring corporate psychopaths who will go on to destroy the corporation from within. Next, according to Boddy (2011a), organizations should create an awareness among managers that psychopaths do exist, as a good first step in attempting to stem the havoc that these people cause in organizations.

Solas (2015) contended, similar to Boddy (2011a), that screening methods cannot be relied on to prevent psychopathy from infiltrating an organization. However, this is not the only bad news. It is no less difficult to "spot" psychopathy in workplaces where the behavior that typifies it has become institutionalized. Under such circumstances, the work of deterring psychopathy begins by acknowledging its existence, counting it among the probable causes of serious organizational dysfunction, and being determined to address it. According to Solas, it would be more efficacious to examine normative, rather than deviant, behavior, especially because only "unsuccessful" or secondary (i.e., antisocial) psychopaths tend to get caught. If organizations develop and maintain a strong culture of social responsibility, it will be difficult for psychopaths in the workplace to apply CWB to achieve their goals. Higher levels of transparency and accountability are the best tools organizations can use to limit the activities of psychopaths (Cohen, 2016; Frink & Klimoski, 2004). It may be more profitable for organizations to invest in intensive and ongoing training programs in servant leadership as a way of turning the tide against flagrant institutionalized psychopathy (Solas, 2015).

How to Manage Narcissists

Organizations need to develop effective tools to manage narcissists so that their destructive nature will be minimized. Given the large number of narcissists at the helm of corporations today, the challenge facing organizations is to ensure that such leaders do not self-destruct or lead the company to disaster (Maccoby, 2000). This can take some doing because it is very hard for narcissists to work through their issues—and virtually impossible for them to do it alone. Narcissists need colleagues and even therapists if they hope to break free from their limitations. But because of their extreme independence and self-protectiveness, it is very difficult to get near them. A therapist would have to demonstrate an extraordinarily profound empathic understanding and sympathy for the narcissist's feelings to gain his or her trust. On top of this, narcissists must recognize that they can benefit from such help. For their part, employees must learn how to recognize—and work around—narcissistic bosses (Maccoby, 2000).

Judge, LePine, and Rich (2006) mentioned three categories of jobs in which narcissism may be undesirable. The practical implication is that organizations should do all in their power to prevent narcissists from working in these jobs. First, narcissism may be a significant liability in jobs in which a realistic conception of one's talents and abilities is critical. If narcissism leads to an inflated self-concept (an issue our results do not specifically address) and an exaggerated sense of control in this regard, it could be damaging in jobs in which accurate self-assessments are required. Second, narcissism may be detrimental in team contexts that require cooperation and a positive social-psychological climate. Narcissists have a grandiose sense of self-importance and believe they are extraordinary performers; this may translate into a climate of competitiveness and distrust. Narcissism may even be problematic in situations when the narcissist admits he or she has not performed well, given that narcissists derogate those close to them who outperform them. Finally, narcissists derogate unfavorable evaluators and tend to act aggressively against those whom they believe threaten them. Thus, narcissism may be particularly problematic in a 360-degree ratings context, given that the narcissists will tend to enhance their ratings and act aggressively against those who may rate them less favorably. In fact, the situation may be especially problematic when the narcissist being rated is in a position of power and is able to adversely affect the raters' jobs and careers.

Grijalva and Harms (2014) recommended several ways to counteract narcissists. First, because narcissists often perceive their capabilities inaccurately and distort recollections of past events, in case of negative behavior, supervisors should confront them with specific, behavior-based feedback and carefully explain the decision-making processes that led to disciplinary actions. Regardless, narcissists are likely to believe they are being treated unfairly, so supervisors should comprehensively document cases of inappropriate or forbidden behavior and consider including objective observers such as HR or union representatives at performance evaluation meetings. It is reasonable to assume that narcissists will continue to have excuses for their behavior, so it is in the supervisors and organization's best interest to have documentation on hand in case narcissistic employees challenge disciplinary decisions.

Second, supervisors and organizations should be aware that narcissistic individuals handle negative feedback poorly and are likely to react to self-esteem threats with explicit or covert destructive behaviors. Increased organizational awareness may enable them to monitor individuals during vulnerable periods, such as after they receive negative feedback, thus detecting and preempting CWB. Third, studies found that narcissism had a weaker relationship with CWB in organizations with in-group collectivist cultures (O'Boyle, Forsyth, Banks, Story, & White, 2015). This means that narcissists are less likely to harm their organization or coworkers when they work in environments that discourage selfish and exploitative behaviors and encourage teamwork rather than competition. Organizations concerned with increased CWB can emphasize collectivist in-group culture. For example, supervisors can structure job tasks so that there is less competition and encourage "team-building" activities to increase group cohesiveness (Grijalva & Harms, 2014).

Hogan and Fico (2011) provided some guidelines for coaching narcissistic leaders. They mentioned that coaching narcissists requires focusing on their need for self-enhancement. Narcissists ignore or reject as naïve appeals to their sense of loyalty to the team or to the value of participating in something greater than themselves. According to Hogan and Fico, when coaching narcissists, one must appeal only to their self-interest. They suggested that it would be useful to tell narcissists that certain behaviors will harm their career and that certain others will enhance it. They mentioned Collins' work (2009) that provided substantial insights about overconfident leaders. Based on this work, they portrayed several behaviors narcissistic leaders must learn to avoid. These behaviors include a careless attitude toward accepted performance standards, restrictions, or regulations, risky decisions that yield short-term benefits but provide evidence (to more cautious team members) about their long-term negative consequences, rejecting and derogating anyone who is different or who challenges them, blaming others for poor organizational outcomes, and making secret unilateral decisions. The behaviors to be encouraged include increased frequency of *equitable* interactions with subordinates, listening to the customer, avoiding special treatment of high-performing team members, performing retrospective reviews of all major projects, embracing equitably applied regulations as an insurance against long-term risk, and identifying colleagues who are skilled at maintaining bonds among team members and turning them into allies.

Another way, and a very important one, to cope with narcissists' CWB is to create a workplace environment, such as an ethical climate, culture, and codes of conduct, that promotes ethical behavior. Given that narcissism may also be more problematic in organizations that lack formal ethical codes of conduct or fail to enforce these codes, it is recommended that organizations adopt an ethical code of conduct if they lack one. If a code exists, it should be enforced consistently to ensure employees realize that ethical behavior is important to their company (Grijalva & Harms, 2014). Finally, it has been suggested that organizations implement safeguards, such as checks and balances, as well as executive training, to keep narcissists under control. Grijalva and Harms (2014) recommend that organizations provide checks and balances for employees who display reckless or harmful behavior. This recommendation especially applies to employees in upper management who have the power to seriously damage their organizations (Grijalva & Harms, 2014).

How to Manage Machiavellians

Castille, Kuyumcu, and Bennett (2017) advanced a suggestion that is relevant to situations when Machiavellians are attempting to undermine their peers and employees to gain more resources for themselves. Castille et al. recommended that, when evaluating employees, managers might consider gathering relevant evidence to determine the added value of performance by means such as using due process performance appraisals. Due process performance appraisals, which promote judgments based on relevant evidence, should reduce the chances that Machiavellians are rewarded for counterproductive behavior. To gather evidence for substantiating these ratings, supervisors may consider using peer reports to inform their judgments, which can be valuable for substantiating performance and evaluating potential leadership success. Of course, managers should first develop a dialogue with their subordinates and agree on this practice as a fair standard of evaluating performance.

Having gained buy-in, supervisors could then obtain reports as to whether a specific employee has intentionally helped or harmed another coworker's success. By using peer reports to make judgments, due process performance appraisals might create a work environment in which workers feel safe voicing concerns, making social undermining an ineffective strategy for gaining higher relative status. It was found that employees treated by a due process performance appraisal, although receiving lower evaluations, had more favorable reactions. For example, they believed the system was fair, resulting in accurate evaluations, and wanted to stay with the organization. Due process performance appraisals should help managers curb undermining with the added benefits of promoting a work environment where employees develop a functional kind of *pronoia*, or the feeling that their coworkers conspire to promote their career success (Castille et al., 2017).

Because of the relative limited material on Machiavellians, naturally much more research is needed on ways to manage them, as well as on all other issues regarding this dark personality.

Final Comments

Over the years, researchers have acknowledged the need to examine not only the positive aspects of organizational behavior but also the disastrous effects of negative behaviors in the workplace (Schyns, 2015). CWB represents the dark side of organizational behavior (Vardi & Weitz, 2004). One issue that has not received sufficient attention in the context of the dark side in organizations is that of dark triad personalities, a concept that only recently has gained adequate academic attention (Harms & Spain, 2015). As was clearly demonstrated in this book, the construct of the dark triad potentially bears important implications for the workplace. A better understanding of how dark triad personalities manifest themselves in the workplace is critical for both practical and theoretical reasons (Smith & Lilienfeld, 2013).

According to Perri (2013), one way to respond to the potential financial havoc resulting from unethical decisions in an organization is through a deeper understanding of the individuals who are likely to participate in those decisions: successful psychopaths. Although current evidence that ties psychopathy, as well as narcissism and Machiavellianism, to negative outcomes in a business environment context has not been sufficiently studied and its connection to white-collar crime requires further refinement, its importance for further empirical research cannot be overstated (Smith & Lilienfeld, 2013). Despite the growing attention to the implications of the dark triad personalities on the workplace in general and on CWB in particular, still little is known about the processes that determine this relationship. One of the goals of this book is to increase our knowledge and understanding on this important topic.

This book applied a managerial approach to the dark triad to assist both researchers and practitioners to understand and manage dark triad personalities better. The book is based on relevant and up-to-date studies. However, there is no doubt that this book is only a preliminary work on this important issue. Much more research is needed on dark triad personalities (Cohen, 2016) with the hope that the next book on the topic will be based on more theories and research findings, leading to more established knowledge of this phenomenon. We must enrich our knowledge of the dark side of organizations in general and dark personalities in particular. A great deal of damage and destruction to many organizations and individuals has been caused by these personalities. It is the role of scholars and practitioners to find out much more about the characteristics and pattern of behaviors of these dark personalities in order to prevent them from continuing to hurt employees and damage organizations. At the very least, we must find out ways to manage them properly in order to neutralize their negative potential as destructive employees and destructive managers. This book is only one of the first steps toward this goal.

References

Babiak, P., Neumann, C. S., & Hare, R. D. (2010). Corporate psychopathy: Talking the walk. *Behavioral Sciences & the Law, 28*(2), 174–193.

Baughman, H. M., Dearing, S., Giammarco, E., & Vernon, P. A. (2012). Relationships between bullying behaviors and the dark triad: A study with adults. *Personality and Individual Differences, 52*(5), 571–575.

Belschak, F. D., Den Hartog, D. N., & Kalshoven, K. (2015). Leading Machiavellians: How to translate Machiavellians' selfishness into pro-organizational behavior. *Journal of Management, 41*(7), 1934–1956.

Berry, C. M., Carpenter, N. C., & Barratt, C. L. (2012). Do other-reports of counterproductive work behavior provide an incremental contribution over self-reports? A meta-analytic comparison. *Journal of Applied Psychology, 97*(3), 613–636.

Berry, C. M., Ones, D. S., & Sackett, P. R. (2007). Interpersonal deviance, organizational deviance, and their common correlates: A review and meta-analysis. *Journal of Applied Psychology, 92*(2), 409–423.

Boddy, C. R. (2006). The dark side of management decisions: Organizational psychopaths. *Management Decision, 44*, 1461–1475.

Boddy, C. R. (2011a). *Corporate Psychopaths: Organizational Destroyers*. London: Palgrave MacMillan.

Boddy, C. R. (2014). Corporate psychopaths, conflict, employee affective well-being and counterproductive work behavior. *Journal of Business Ethics, 121*(1), 107–121.

Boddy, C. R. (2015). Organizational psychopaths: A ten-year update. *Management Decision, 53*(10), 2407–2432.

Bowling, N. A., & Burns, G. N. (2015). Sex as a moderator of the relationships between predictor variables and counterproductive work behavior. *Journal of Business and Psychology, 30*(1), 193–205.

Buckels, E. E., Jones, D. N., & Paulhus, D. L. (2013). Behavioral confirmation of everyday sadism. *Psychological Science, 24*, 2201–2209.

Castille, C. M., Kuyumcu, D., & Bennett, R. J. (2017). Prevailing to the peers' detriment: Organizational constraints motivate Machiavellians to undermine their peers. *Personality and Individual Differences, 104*, 29–36.

Chabrol, H., Van Leeuwen, N., Rodgers, R., & Séjourné, N. (2009). Contributions of psychopathic, narcissistic, Machiavellian, and sadistic personality traits to juvenile delinquency. *Personality and Individual Differences, 47*, 734–739.

Chiaburu, D. S., Muñoz, G. J., & Gardner, R. G. (2013). How to spot a careerist early on: Psychopathy and exchange ideology as predictors of careerism? *Journal of Business Ethics, 118*(3), 473–486.

Cohen, A. (2016). Are they among us? A conceptual framework of the relationship between the dark triad personality and counterproductive work behaviors (CWBs). *Human Resource Management Review, 26*(1), 69–85.

Collins, J. (2009). *How the Mighty Fall and Why Some Companies Never Give In.* New York: Jim Collins.

Delbecq, A. L. (2001). "Evil" manifested in destructive individual behavior: A senior leadership challenge. *Journal of Management Inquiry, 10*(3), 221–226.

DiNisi, A. S. (2015). Some further thoughts on entrepreneurial personality. *Entrepreneurship Theory and Practice, 39,* 997–1003.

Fennimore, A., & Sementelli, A. (2016). Public entrepreneurship and sub-clinical psychopaths: A conceptual frame and implications. *International Journal of Public Sector Management, 29*(6), 612–634.

Frink, D. D., & Klimoski, R. J. (2004). Advancing accountability theory and practice: Introduction to the human resource management review special edition. *Human Resource Management Review, 14*(1), 1–17.

Grijalva, E., & Harms, P. D. (2014). Narcissism: An integrative synthesis and dominance complementarity model. *The Academy of Management Perspectives, 28*(2), 108–127.

Hare, R. (1994). Predators: The disturbing world of the psychopaths among us. *Psychology Today, 27*(1), 54–61.

Hare, R. D. (1999). *Without Conscience: The Disturbing World of the Psychopaths among Us.* New York, NY: Guilford Press.

Harms, P. D., & Spain, M. S. (2015). Beyond the bright side: Dark personality at work. *Applied Psychology: An International Review, 64*(1), 15–24.

Harris, G. T., & Rice, M. E. (2006). Treatment of psychopathy: A review of empirical findings. In C. J. Patrick (Ed.), *Handbook of Psychopathy* (pp. 555–572). New York: Guilford Press.

Hegarty, W. H., & Sims, H. P. (1979). Organizational philosophy, policies, and objectives related to unethical decision behavior: A laboratory experiment. *Journal of Applied Psychology, 64*(3), 331–338.

Herbst, T. (2014). *The Dark Side of Leadership: A Psycho-Spiritual Approach towards Understanding the Origins of Personality Dysfunctions: Derailment and the Restoration of Personality.* UK: Author House.

Hofstede, G. (2001). *Culture's Consequences: Comparing Values, Behaviors, Institutions and Organizations across Nations.* Thousand Oaks, CA: Sage Publications, Inc.

Hogan, R., & Fico, J. M. (2011). Leadership. In W. K. Campbell & J. D. Miller (Eds.), *The Handbook of Narcissism and Narcissistic Personality Disorder: Theoretical Approaches, Empirical Findings, and Treatments* (pp. 393–402). Wiley: New York.

Jonason, P. K., Icho, A., & Ireland, K. (2016). Resources, harshness, and unpredictability: The socioeconomic conditions associated with the dark triad traits. *Evolutionary Psychology, 14*(1), 1474704915623699.

Jonason, P. K., Webster, G. D., Schmitt, D. P., Li, N. P., & Crysel, L. (2012a). The antihero in popular culture: Life history theory and the dark triad personality traits. *Review of General Psychology, 16*(2), 192–199.

Judge, T. A., LePine, J. A., & Rich, B. L. (2006). Loving yourself abundantly: Relationship of the narcissistic personality to self-and other perceptions of workplace deviance, leadership, and task and contextual performance. *Journal of Applied Psychology, 91,* 762–776.

Kaiser, R. B., & Hogan, R. (2006). The dark side of discretion: Research report. Available at: www.hoganassessments.com/_hoganweb/documents/dark%20side%20of%20discretion.pdf (accessed 11 December 2015), Tulsa, OK: Hogan Assessment Center.

Kaptein, M. (2011). Understanding unethical behavior by unraveling ethical culture. *Human Relations, 64*(6), 843–869.

Kim, Y., & Cohen, T. R. (2015). Moral character and workplace deviance: Recent research and current trends. *Current Opinion in Psychology, 6*, 134–138.

Kirsch, L. G., & Becker, J. V. (2007). Emotional deficits in psychopathy and sexual sadism: Implications for violent and sadistic behavior. *Clinical Psychology Review, 27*(8), 904–922.

Klotz, A. C., & Neubaum, D. O. (2016). Research on the dark side of personality traits in entrepreneurship: Observations from an organizational behavior perspective. *Entrepreneurship Theory and Practice, 40*(1), 7–17.

Kowalski, C. M., Vernon, P. A., & Schermer, J. A. (2016). The general factor of personality: The relationship between the big one and the dark triad. *Personality and Individual Differences, 88*, 256–260.

Kristof, A. L. (1996). Person-organization fit: An integrative review of its conceptualizations, measurement, and implications. *Personnel Psychology, 49*(1), 1–49.

Maccoby, M. (2000). Narcissistic leaders: The incredible pros, the inevitable cons. *Harvard Business Review, 78*(1), 68–78.

Marshall, A. J., Ashleigh, M. J., Baden, D., Ojiako, U., & Guidi, M. G. (2015). Corporate psychopathy: Can "search and destroy" and "hearts and minds" military metaphors inspire HRM solutions? *Journal of Business Ethics, 128*(3), 495–504.

Mathieu, C., Neumann, C. S., Hare, R. D., & Babiak, P. (2014). A dark side of leadership: Corporate psychopathy and its influence on employee well-being and job satisfaction. *Personality and Individual Differences, 59*, 83–88.

Međedović, J., & Petrović, B. (2015). The dark tetrad: Structural properties and location in the personality space. *Journal of Individual Differences, 36*, 228–236.

Michel, J. S., Newness, K., & Duniewicz, K. (2016). How abusive supervision affects workplace deviance: A moderated-mediation examination of aggressiveness and work-related negative affect. *Journal of Business and Psychology, 31*(1), 1–22.

Mikkelsen, E. G. E., & Einarsen, S. (2002). Basic assumptions and symptoms of post-traumatic stress among victims of bullying at work. *European Journal of Work and Organizational Psychology, 11*(1), 87–111.

Mokros, A., Osterheider, M., Hucker, S. J., & Nitschke, J. (2011). Psychopathy and sexual sadism. *Law and Human Behavior, 35*, 188–199.

Muris, P., Merckelbach, H., Otgaar, H., & Meijer, E. (2017). The malevolent side of human nature: A meta-analysis and critical review of the literature on the dark triad (narcissism, Machiavellianism, and psychopathy). *Perspectives on Psychological Science, 12*(2), 183–204.

O'Boyle Jr., E. H., Forsyth, D. R., Banks, G. C., & McDaniel, M. A. (2012). A meta-analysis of the dark triad and work behavior: A social exchange perspective. *Journal of Applied Psychology, 97*(3), 557–579.

O'Boyle, E. H., Forsyth, D. R., Banks, G. C., Story, P. A., & White, C. D. (2015). A meta-analytic test of redundancy and relative importance of the dark triad and five-factor model of personality. *Journal of Personality, 83*(6), 644–664.

Padilla, A., Hogan, R., & Kaiser, R. B. (2007). The toxic triangle: Destructive leaders, susceptible followers, and conducive environments. *The Leadership Quarterly, 18*(3), 176–194.

Paulhus, D. L. (2014). Toward a taxonomy of dark personalities. *Current Directions in Psychological Science, 23*, 421–426.

Perri, F. S. (2013). Visionaries or false prophets. *Journal of Contemporary Criminal Justice, 29*(3), 331–350.

Perry, C. (2015). The "dark traits" of sociopathic leaders: Could they be a threat to universities? *Australian Universities' Review, 57*(1), 17–24.

Robertson, S. A., Datu, J. A. D., Brawley, A. M., Pury, C. L., & Mateo, N. J. (2016). The dark triad and social behavior: The influence of self-construal and power distance. *Personality and Individual Differences, 98*, 69–74.

Schwartz, S. H. (1992). Universals in the content and structure of values: Theory and empirical tests in 20 countries. In M. Zanna (Ed.), *Advances in Experimental Social Psychology* (Vol. 25, pp. 1–65). New York: Academic Press.

Schyns, B. (2015). Dark personality in the workplace: Introduction to the special issue. *Applied Psychology: An International Review, 64*(1), 1–14.

Smith, S. F., & Lilienfeld, S. O. (2013). Psychopathy in the workplace: The knowns and unknowns. *Aggression and Violent Behavior, 18*, 204–218.

Smith, S. F., Watts, A., & Lilienfeld, S. (2014). On the trail of the elusive successful psychopath. *Psychological Assessment, 15*, 340–350.

Solas, J. (2015). Pathological work victimization in public sector organizations. *Public Organization Review, 15*(2), 255–265.

Vardi, Y., & Weitz, E. (2004). *Misbehavior in Organizations: Theory: Research, and Management, Mahwah.* New Jersey & London: Lawrence Erlbaum Associates.

Yu, K. Y. T. (2014). Person—organization fit effects on organizational attraction: A test of an expectations-based model. *Organizational Behavior and Human Decision Processes, 124*(1), 75–94.

Index